LEASES: COVENANTS AND CONSENTS

AUSTRALIA
The Law Book Company
Sydney

CANADA
The Carswell Company
Toronto, Ontario

INDIA
N.M. Tripathi (Private) Ltd.
Bombay

Eastern Law House (Private) Ltd.
Calcutta

M.P.P. House
Bangalore

Universal Book Traders
Delhi

ISRAEL
Steimatzky's Agency Ltd.
Tel Aviv

PAKISTAN
Pakistan Law House
Karachi

LEASES: COVENANTS AND CONSENTS

LETITIA CRABB, LL.B., LL.M.,
Solicitor

Lecturer in Law,
University College of Wales, Aberystwyth

LONDON · SWEET & MAXWELL 1991

Published in 1991 by
Sweet & Maxwell Limited of
South Quay Plaza
183 Marsh Wall, London E14 9FT

Typeset by P.B. Computer Typesetting
Pickering, N. Yorks

Printed in Great Britain by
Butler and Tanner Ltd.

British Library Cataloguing in Publication Data

Crabb, Letitia
    Leases : covenants and consents.
    1.   England. Rented residences. Tenancy agreements.
    Law
    I.   Title
    344.206434

    ISBN 0–421–40230–X

For my mother

PREFACE

It may be thought surprising to find a book devoted to just three types of leasehold covenant: those restricting a tenant's right to dispose of the lease, to alter the demised premises and to change its use. In truth however there are many variants of each of these species of covenant and a sizeable and venerable caselaw on the manner in which they are to be construed. There is also an enormous number of cases concerned with the specific issue of whether the landlord has unreasonably withheld his consent and there is no sign that the flow of cases is likely to abate. Nor has the legislature neglected this field of the law of landlord and tenant. The impact of the Landlord and Tenant Act 1927 is well known and that of the Landlord and Tenant Act 1988 will, no doubt, gradually become apparent — though it has been referred to as "that curious little Act"! The impact of statute is however even more pervasive. Disposition rights of tenants, under the Rent Act 1977, the Housing Acts 1985 and 1988, the Landlord and Tenant Act 1954 and the Agricultural Holdings Act 1986 need separate consideration (see Chapter 7). Restrictions on alterations and changes of use are also subject to legislative intervention (see Chapters 8 and 9).

I would like to acknowledge my indebtedness to the authors of the standard reference works, *Hill and Redman's Law of Landlord and Tenant, Woodfall on the Law of Landlord and Tenant* and *Emmet on Title*. These texts have been constantly at my side. I must also acknowledge the assistance I have derived from a study of the recommendations of the Law Commission, especially Law Com. Nos. 141 and 161. I am very grateful to Christopher Rodgers for his comments on certain categories of tenant, particularly the agricultural tenant. I would like to pay tribute to Sweet and Maxwell for providing me with the opportunity to write this book and guiding me through its production. My sons, Daniel and Julian, will be relieved to know that I am particularly well disposed to them: though totally mystified by the project, they have borne the brunt of its impact on family life with a patience and fortitude rarely found in those of tender years. Finally I thank my husband, Ian, for his support and encouragement throughout.

None of the above are in any way implicated in the shortcomings which may be found in the book; these will be due to my own ignorance or lack of understanding. I have hoped to state the law as at December 31, 1990.

Letitia Crabb

Aberystwyth,
Dyfed.

ACKNOWLEDGMENTS

The author and publishers with to thank the following for permission to reprint material from the publications indicated:

The Law Society:
General Conditions of Sale

The Law Society and Oyez:
Standard Conditions of Sale

Oyez:
National Conditions of Sale

CONTENTS

TABLE OF CASES

TABLE OF STATUTES

PART 1 DISPOSITION COVENANTS

1 DISPOSITION RIGHTS OF TENANTS

Freedom of disposition The tenant has, at common law, a basic freedom to dispose of the term vested in him.[1] In *Church* v. *Brown*[2] Lord Eldon L.C. referred to it as "an incident of the estate."[3] A similar freedom of disposition exists in relation to an option to acquire a lease,[4] an option to renew a lease and an agreement for a lease[5] at least where there is no indication that the lease resulting from the agreement or option was to contain a restrictive clause. Even a tenant at will enjoys freedom of disposition, but the tenancy at will is determined as soon as the landlord has notice.[6]

The power of disposition encompasses granting a sublease or mortgage, assigning or parting with possession of the premises. It is, however, subject both to statute and to **Statutory curtailment** contract. The effect of statute is very various. It can include the imposition of a statutory incapacity, for example section 91 of the Housing Act 1985 renders the majority of secure tenancies incapable of assignment and section 54(2) of the Housing Act 1980 has a similar operation in relation to protected shorthold tenancies. It may involve the implication of terms into the lease, as in section 91(1)(*b*) of the Housing Act 1985 which implies a term into secure tenancies restricting subletting, section 15(1) of the Housing Act 1988 which implies into assured periodical tenancies restrictions on assignment and subletting and section 6 of the Agricultural Holdings Act 1986 which may result in the incorporation, after arbitration, of a covenant restricting most sorts of disposition of tenancies subject to that Act. Use has also been made of provisions which attach adverse consequences to certain types of disposition. Thus the Rent Act 1977, section 98 & Schedule 15, Pt. 1, Case 6 makes assignments and certain sublettings of tenancies subject to that Act a discretionary ground of possession. These statutory provisions are dealt with in Chapter 7.

Any contractual limitation of the common law freedom of **Contractual curtailment** alienation must be express. Restrictions on alienation are not readily implied into a legal lease and, traditionally, they do not constitute usual covenants for the purposes of inclusion into an agreement for a lease,[7] because their effect is to contradict

"the incidents of the estate belonging to a lessee, one of which is the right to have the estate without restraint

[1] *Doe d. Mitchinson* v. *Carter* (1798) 8 Term.Rep. 57 at pp. 60, 61.
[2] (1808) 15 Ves. 258.
[3] At p. 264.
[4] *Buckland* v. *Papillon* (1866) L.R. 1 Eq. 477, *per* Lord Romilly at p. 482.
[5] *Tolhurst* v. *Associated Portland Cement Manufacturers (1900) Ltd.* [1903] A.C. 414, 423.
[6] *Pinhorn* v. *Souster* (1853) 8 Ex. 763, *per* Park B., at p. 772. (Concerned an assignment).
[7] See *infra*, Chap. 10.

beyond what is imposed upon it by operation of law, unless there is an express contract for more."[8]

A contractual limitation can take the form of a condition, limitation, agreement or, more usually, covenant, restricting all or certain types of disposition. Whichever form the contractual provision takes, the limitation which it imposes may be absolute, qualified or fully qualified. Before considering these possibilities it should perhaps be noted that in certain cases, statute steps in to bolster some or all of the tenant's disposition rights. Such provisions are contained in the Law of Property Act 1925,[9] the Landlord and Tenant Act 1927,[10] and the Housing Act 1985.[11]

Conditions ("on condition that," "provided always") and limitations (term to continue "only so long as") impose no contractual obligation upon the tenant, with the result that the landlord is unable to sue for damages in the event of their contravention. He is able to terminate the lease if the condition or limitation is not complied with, but this is subject, in both cases, to his giving notice to the tenant in accordance with section 146 of the Law of Property Act 1925 and to the tenant's right to seek relief thereunder.[12] Covenants and agreements do impose contractual obligations on the tenant,[13] the former not least by virtue of being embodied in a deed. A breach by the tenant does therefore give rise to a claim for damages, and if the lease also contains a proviso for re-entry, the landlord can also forfeit the lease.[14]

Dispositions valid   Although a disposition in contravention of a restrictive clause may result in the termination of the lease, the disposition itself is not void.[15] It seems that despite the contractual restriction, the tenant retains his common law power to assign but must bear the consequences if he exercises it:

"It is of the nature of the creation of a term of years that the owner of the term is capable of dealing with it as a piece of property. The only way that he can be prevented or hampered is by virtue of the common form clause that he covenants not to do it and there may be a forfeiture of

---

[8] *Per* Lord Eldon, *Church* v. *Brown, supra* n. 2.

[9] ss.86(1), 89(1) and 144; *infra*, Chap. 4.

[10] s.19(1); *infra*, Chap. 4.

[11] ss.33, 37 and 139(1) and Sched. 6, Pt. III; see *infra*, Chap. 7.

[12] See *infra*, Chap. 4; in theory termination is automatic in the case of a limitation but by s.146(4) a limitation is to be treated as a condition and thus as merely enabling the landlord to terminate.

[13] As do stipulations: see *Doe d. Henniker* v. *Watt* (1828) 8 B. & C. 308, 315.

[14] Subject, again, to s.146. The restriction can be drafted in the form of a condition and a covenant. See *Doe d. Henniker* v. *Watt* (1828) 8 B. & C. 308, 315 but this would not seem to have any advantage over a covenant, or agreement, coupled with a right of re-entry. See generally Law Commission No. 141, Covenants Restricting Dispositions, Alterations and Changes of User, paras. 2.5–2.6.

[15] *Property and Blood Stock Ltd.* v. *Emerton* [1967] 3 All E.R. 321, 329, *per* Danckwerts L.J.

the term if he does it. But I stress 'if he does it' and unless he has effectively transferred the term to the assignee, there has been no breach of the covenant not to assign."[16]

There are statutory exceptions to this rule[17] and it may also be that the assignment is void for other reasons[18] in which case there may have been no breach of the restriction upon which to found a forfeiture action.[19]

Absolute, qualified and fully qualified restrictions

Whichever form the contractual provision takes, the restriction which it imposes can be absolute, qualified or fully qualified. In theory the first of these is the most severe in that it involves an express prohibition with no express provision as to its lifting. However it is, of course, open to the tenant to seek a waiver from his landlord.[20] A qualified restriction, on the other hand, is expressed to prohibit only those dispositions which have been carried out without the landlord's consent. Despite the differences in form, both types of provision admit of the possibility that the tenant will be able to effect the disposition with the landlord's consent and in both cases the landlord can refuse his consent for any reason. A qualified covenant becomes fully qualified if it is additionally provided that the landlord's consent shall not be unreasonably withheld. It is important to note that this further qualification may be express, but that if it is not, it may be implied under the Landlord and Tenant Act 1927, section 19(1)(a) which applies to all but agricultural tenancies.[21] As a consequence of this it is clear therefore that most provisions restricting disposition are of the absolute or fully qualified type.[22] Amongst other factors,[23] market forces will be influential in determining which of these is appropriate in a particular case. It has been noted[24] that the presence of an absolute covenant[25] is liable to depress the rent which the property can command. The reasons for this are outlined in the Law Commission Report No. 141. The tenant risks being burdened with sole responsibility for the obligations of the tenancy, including the rent, for the remainder of the term even though because of changed circumstances he may be unable to use the property. In such a situation he cannot rely upon the landlord's agreeing either to waive the restriction on alienation or to accept a surrender. Furthermore a business tenant subject to such an absolute restriction risks the loss of the goodwill built up during the currency of the tenancy and

---

[16] *Per* Lord Russell of Killowen *Old Grovebury Farm Ltd.* v. *W. Seymour Plant Sales and Hire (No. 2) Ltd.* [1979] 1 W.L.R. 1397, 1399 (C.A.); and see *Peabody Donation Fund* v. *Higgins* [1983] 1 W.L.R. 1091 (C.A.).

[17] See, *e.g.* s.37(4) Housing Act 1985.

[18] See, *e.g. Doe d. Lloyd* v. *Powell* (1826) 5 B. & C. 308.

[19] *Ibid.*

[20] A possibility recognised in the Land Registration Act 1986, s.3 which permits the registration of what were previously regarded as "inalienable" leases in recognition of the fact that they were being assigned.

[21] s.19(4).

[22] See generally Law Commission No. 141, *supra*, n. 14 paras. 2.4., 3.3.

[23] For example, the length of the lease—absolute restrictions are more common in leases not exceeding 21 years.

[24] Law Commission No. 141, para. 4.24.

[25] "Covenant" will be used henceforth to include conditions, limitations and agreements.

the inability to advantageously realise the value of his stock-in-trade and equipment.[26] The Law Commission recommend[27] that no disposition covenant other than a fully qualified one ought normally to be permitted.[28]

---

[26] Law Commission No. 141, paras. 4, 19–4, 23.

[27] Paras. 4.17 and 4.31.

[28] Subject to the exceptions set out in Part VII of the Report, *vis.* agricultural and mining tenancies, tenancies under the Leasehold Reform Act 1967, short lettings, tenancies which fall within the Rent Act 1977 but in respect of which the court is required to order possession on the basis of the mandatory grounds set out in Part II of Schedule 15 and certain other special cases.

2 TYPES OF DISPOSITION COMMONLY RESTRICTED

Variety of Restrictions Restrictions vary considerably in scope.[1] They may affect all or any of a number of potential dispositions, *e.g.* assignment, under-letting, parting with or sharing possession,[2] holding on trust or permitting another to occupy,[3] charging or assignment by operation of law. They may restrict the disposition if it relates to part of the property or the whole or indeed both. Furthermore the restriction may be absolute or qualified; sometimes it is absolute in relation to some types of restricted transaction and qualified in relation to others. Normally the qualification requires the landlord's *written* consent. Whatever rights the tenant may retain after the imposition of such restrictions may be further cut back by the effect of certain common provisos relating to surrender-back and to the provision of sureties.[4] The most usual form of covenant prohibits the tenant from assigning, under-letting or parting with possession of the whole or any part of the demised premises. It is proposed to examine these and other types of disposition commonly referred to in restrictions, and to consider the extent to which various transactions have been construed as falling within the scope of the restricted class.

General principles of construction

Not only must any restraint upon alienation be express, but also its terms will be "construed with the utmost jealousy to prevent the restraint from going beyond the express
Against the landlord stipulation"[5] As a consequence of this, many apparently straightforward words and expressions have come to have meanings both narrow and obscure. Thus Scrutton L.J. has very pertinently pointed out that it would be a mistake to approach these clauses "guided by the light of nature and unillumined by authority" because they have been "drafted, altered and gradually built up because of past decisions of the

---

[1] See, *e.g. The Encyclopedia of Forms and Precedents* (4th ed.), Vol. 11, pp. 318–321; Vol. 12, p. 754; (5th ed.) Vol. 22, p. 287; *Kelly's Draftsman*, (5th ed.) p. 369.
[2] See, *e.g.* (*ibid.*) Vol. 11, p. 318.
[3] *Ibid* Vol. 22, p. 287.
[4] See Chap. 6 Conditional Consents.
[5] *Per* Lord Eldon L.C., *Church* v. *Brown* (1808) 15 Ves. 258, at p. 265.

courts."[6] The strict approach has been justified on a number of grounds: that terms should be construed against the party seeking to rely upon them, or "that the tenant's rights are not to be cut down except by clear words."[7] While such general justifications satisfy some members of the judiciary, many more have sought further justification in the nearly universal presence of a forfeiture clause. So Bayley J. in *Doe d. Blencowe* v. *Bugby*[8] opined that "[T]he Courts have always held a strict hand over these conditions for defeating leases" and Atkin L.J. in *Russell* v. *Beecham*[9] pointed out that where the "lessor has used words which at the best are ambiguous ... he cannot complain if the court puts a strict construction on the words of a covenant which if broken entails a forfeiture." What if there is no forfeiture clause, however? In *Cook* v. *Shoesmith*[10] it was

Relevance of proviso for re-entry

argued that as there was no proviso for re-entry, there was no place for the strict rule of construction but Somervell L.J. was not convinced by this:

> "In certain circumstances there might be force in that: on the other hand, it would be very inconvenient if words which had been construed in a certain sense over a great number of years were to be given a different meaning according as whether there was or was not a proviso for re-entry"[11]

He then proceeded to apply the strict rule on the basis of the more general justification referred to above. The relevance of a proviso for re-entry was also questioned in *Corporation of Bristol* v. *Westcott*[12]: "for [the construction of the covenant] must be the same in an action for damages for breach of the covenant as in an action for recovery of the land." The position would seem to be, therefore, that while a strict rule of construction is especially appropriate where there is a forfeiture clause, its application can also be justified where there is none.

While undoubtedly a landlord can expect an unsympathetic construction, there have been cases where the court has refrained from imposing the most adverse construction. Thus in *Marks* v. *Warren*[13] it was argued that, as the covenant restricted only under-leasing and parting with possession, the tenant could assign with impunity, even though it would involve him in parting with possession, because the omission of any restriction upon assignment should be construed as permitting such parting with possession as was referable to assignments. This argument was rejected:

> "There is no reason to treat each limb of a covenant not to assign, not to underlet and not to part with possession as being three mutually exclusive areas. They are ... to be

---

[6] *Russell* v. *Beecham* [1924] 1 K.B. 525, 537 (C.A.).
[7] *Per* Somervell L.J., *Cook* v. *Shoesmith* [1951] 1 K.B. 752, 755 (C.A.).
[8] (1771) 1 W.Bl. 766.
[9] *Ibid.* p. 539.
[10] *Ibid.*
[11] pp. 754, 755.
[12] (1879) 12 Ch.D. 461, 465.
[13] [1979] 1 All E.R. 29.

treated as three separate covenants; but it does not follow that an act which would constitute a breach of one of these covenants, may not also constitute a breach of another of those covenants."[14]

Covenants in statutes

Finally it should be noted that where disposition covenants are referred to in statutes, their construction will not necessarily correspond with the construction which would be placed upon them when embodied in a lease.[15]

Assignment

Although assignments are usually referred to by that name, other terms are also apt to describe that particular type of transaction; they include "transfer," "part with the premises," "make over" and "barter."

Legal only

Where a covenant restricts assignment, it is taken to refer to a legal assignment of the whole unexpired term. As Romer L.J. stated in *Gentle* v. *Faulkner*[16] "a covenant . . . against assigning the demised premises, in the absence of any context showing that the covenant is to have extended meaning, covers only a legal assignment." Thus it "is beyond controversy that an agreement to assign a lease is not a breach of a covenant against assignment."[17] Nor is it a breach of such a covenant for the lessee to declare himself trustee for some third party because "an equitable assignment is not sufficient to operate as a breach of covenant."[18] A declaration of trust can therefore be used by a lessee wishing to transfer property for the benefit of his creditors (in *Gentle* v. *Faulkner*[19] the lessee declared himself trustee for the benefit of his creditors and ready to assign as that trustee should direct). It can also be used to transfer the property on sale so long as the contract provides that the purchaser is to accept an equitable title in the event of the vendor being unable to obtain the lessor's consent to assignment.[20] There is, of course, nothing to prevent the lessor

---

[14] *Per* Browne Wilkinson J. at p. 91.

[15] See for example s.14(6)(*i*) of the Conveyancing Act 1881 which dispensed with the requirement to give notice before forfeiture in the case of a covenant against "assigning, underletting, parting with possession, or disposing of the land leased" (a dispensation not continued under the Law of Property Act—see s.146(8)). In the context of a lease these words would be taken to refer to only those covenants which related to the *whole* of the land but not those which related to part. (see *infra*). Thus in *Abrahams* v. *MacFisheries* [1925] 2 K.B. 18 it was argued that as the covenant broken was one which prohibited parting with possession of part, it was outside the scope of s.14(6)(*i*) and notice should have been served on the tenant. Fraser J., however, distinguished between the construction of covenants in deeds and Acts of Parliament. The policy of the Act may override the usual rules of construction, and did so in that case, (at pp. 34–35).

[16] [1906] 2 Q.B. 267.

[17] *Per* Palles C.B. in *M'Kay* v. *M'Nally* (1879) 4 L.R.Ir. 438, 451 and see Ball L.C. at p. 445.

[18] *Per* A. L. Smith L.J. in *Gentle* v. *Faulkener, ibid.* p. 274.

[19] *Ibid.*

[20] *Pincott* v. *Moorstons Ltd.* [1937] 1 All E.R. 513; or the purchaser is otherwise agreeable: see *Southern Depot Co. Ltd.* v. *British Railways Board* (1990) 33 E.G. 45.

insisting upon a covenant which does prohibit the creation of a trust.[21] Furthermore in *Doe d. Pitt* v. *Hogg*[22] depositing the lease as security for a loan was held not to fall within the terms of a covenant restricting assignment. In fact the wording of the covenant was "not to ... transfer, set over or otherwise part with" the demised premises but this was construed narrowly as referring simply to assignment and thus only to legal assignment. As Bayley J. opined, there is no "parting with the legal interest ... because the lessee might at any time redeem the indenture by paying off the incumbrance upon it."[23] A bequest in a will does not operate as a breach of covenant because, since 1925, wills take effect only in equity and are therefore outside the scope of the covenant.[24] Any instrument relied upon as an assignment must be valid. In *Doe d. Lloyd* v. *Powell*[25] the assignment was void as an act of bankruptcy.[26] There may be other reasons why an instrument does not effect an assignment. Section 40 of the Trustee Act 1925 provides that upon an appointment of new trustees the trust property vests, either by express declaration or a declaration implied by the Act, in the new trustees. Even if this were the equivalent of an assignment, it could not give rise to a breach of a qualified covenant against assignment because, by section 40(4)(*b*), such vesting would *not occur* without the consent having previously been obtained "unless the vesting declaration ... would not operate as a breach of covenant or give rise to a forfeiture"— which seems to suggest that the vesting would only take place where consent had previously been granted, or sought and unreasonably withheld. It should perhaps be noted that subsection (4)(*b*), which prevents the vesting in breach of covenant, does so only in respect of "a lease which contains any covenant, condition or agreement against assignment or disposing of the land *without licence or consent*"[27] Whether therefore it applies to leases containing absolute covenants is open to speculation[28] though it must be noted that the *practical effect* of an absolute covenant is as described in the subsection and that the purpose of the subsection would seem to be to avoid the operation of section 40 giving rise to a breach of covenant which purpose would be defeated by the exclusion from it of leases containing absolute covenants.

    Because an assignment is by definition a transaction which relates to the whole unexpired term, a restriction upon such

---

[21] See, *e.g. Encyclopedia of Forms and Precedents*, (5th ed.), Vol. 22, 5. 9: 1.

[22] (1824) 4 Dowl. & Ry. K.B. 226; see also *Ex p. Drake* (1841) 1 Mont. D. & De G. 539.

[23] The same construction has been used in relation to a proviso for termination on assignment—see *Ex p. Cocks* (1836) 2 Deac. 14.

[24] See Barnsley, *The Lessee's Death and the Covenant not Assign*, Vol. 27, *Conveyancer*, pp. 159, 164, 177; as to the effect of the lease vesting in personal representatives, and assents by them, see *infra*.

[25] (1826) 5 B. & C. 308.

[26] See now Insolvency Act 1986, Adjustment of Prior Transactions ss.238–246 (administration and liquidation), ss.339–349 (bankruptcy) and ss.423–425 (transactions defrauding creditors).

[27] Author's emphasis.

[28] Similar wording in s.19(1)(*a*) of the Landlord and Tenant Act 1972 has been held not to encompass absolute covenants. See *infra*, Chap. 4.

transactions does not comprehend an underlease.[29] Even where the restriction upon assignment was coupled with a restriction upon "parting with . . . the premises hereby demised"[30] it was held in *Russell* v. *Beecham*[31] that, in the context in which it appeared, the additional phrase was synonymous with assignment and did not therefore prohibit underletting.[32] If

Underleases not caught

underletting does not contravene a covenant against assignment, *a fortiori* there is no contravention where the lessor has merely allowed a third party to use the premises. In *Gian Singh & Co.* v. *Devraj Nahar*[33] in the face of a covenant not to assign, the tenant took two partners into his business and under the partnership deed the business was to be carried on upon the demised premises. The landlord invited the court to find, from the terms of the partnership deed, and from the fact that the firm was using the premises, that there had been an assignment of the term, in breach of covenant, to the firm. The Privy Council found no breach. Lord Pearce pointed out that, while property used by a partnership *may* have been constituted partnership property by assignment, property used by a partnership is not necessarily partnership property and, in particular, in order to keep the tenancy safe the partners might have wished to avoid an assignment, "the tenant giving his partners a licence to trade there with him or by his constituting himself a trustee for the partnership or merely by giving the partners no express rights at all."[34]

User by third party

Assignments between joint tenants

A prohibition on assignment *has* been held to extend to an assignment by one joint tenant to another. In *Varley* v. *Coppard*[35] one joint lessee assigned his interest to the other on the dissolution of a partnership, Willes J. held this to be a breach of the covenant against assignment—which meant "neither of them shall assign the whole or any part of his interest without consent; otherwise a tenant might assign all but a 64th part . . . I cannot think that the assignment of the 63 parts would be anything but a breach of the covenant."[36] This decision was followed in *Langton* v. *Henson*[37] where Buckley J. pointed out that "when one of two joint tenants assigns to another . . . he does most effectually deal with the estate; he destroys the privity of estate between himself and his lessor; the estate has been affected; something has been parted with."[38] He refused to deal with the point that as between joint tenants the transaction was technically a release rather than an assignment, a matter raised by Jessel M.R. in *Corporation of Bristol* v. *Westcott*[39] and thus casting some doubt about *Varley*

---

[29] See *Doe d. Blencowe* v. *Bugby* (1771) 3 Wils. 234.
[30] Compare "parting with possession"; see *infra*.
[31] (1924) 1 K.B. 525 (C.A.).
[32] *Per* Bankes and Atkin L.JJ.; compare the self-confessed naïvete of Scrutton L.J.
[33] [1965] 1 All E.R. 768 (P.C.).
[34] At p. 770.
[35] (1872) VII L.R.C.P. 505.
[36] At p. 507.
[37] (1905) 92 L.T. 805.
[38] At p. 806.
[39] (1879) 12 Ch.D. 461, 465.

v. *Coppard*. A release recognises that "each joint tenant is seised of the whole of the land" and its effect is "to extinguish rather than to convey."[40] Presumably, to constitute a breach, the assignment would have to relate to the legal joint tenancy because an assignment of the beneficial interest, be it a tenancy in common or a joint tenancy, would, in accordance with the doctrine of conversion, be an assignment of a share in the proceeds of sale rather than in the land demised.

Assignments of part

It may be speculated whether an assignment of just part of the demised premises contravenes a covenant against assignment. If the covenant encompasses this type of transaction in terms, then clearly there will have been a breach.[41] If it does not, the scarcely typical case of *Grove* v. *Portal*[42] indicates that the lessee is free to assign part of the premises. The premises consisted of an exclusive fishing right and the part of it assigned was limited to two rods. While this approach is consistent with the construction put upon covenants against under-letting,[43] an assignment, unlike an under-lease, does involve a destruction of privity of estate in relation to the part assigned and it would not therefore have been surprising if the courts had adopted a construction more favourable to the landlord.[44]

In the opposite case, where assignments of part are prohibited but no mention is made of the whole, it has been held that an assignment of the whole constitutes a breach. In *Field* v. *Barkworth*[45] several contrary arguments were put on behalf of the tenant: that if the whole does not include part,[46] part should not include the whole, that the covenant should be construed against the lessor and that it was quite reasonable to suppose that a lessor could wish to control assignments of part but not of the whole. Nicolas J. rejected these arguments on the basis that, if it were intended merely to prohibit assignments of part, he would have expected to find the covenant referring to "part only" of the demised premises rather than, as it did, to "any part." "This covenant against assignment or underleasing of any part of the premises ... plainly embraces the assignment or underleasing of every part. As I see it that is the beginning and end of the case."[47]

It has been held that an assignment back to the original lessee can constitute a contravention of a covenant restricting assignment because "[t]he covenant is quite plain. It is that the lessee, the person who for the time being stands in that relation

---

[40] Megarry and Wade *The Law of Real Property*, (4th ed.), p. 428; after 1925 it is possible for a joint tenant to either release or convey his interest to other joint tenants; ss.72(4) and 36(2) Law of Property Act 1925.

[41] *Collins* v. *Sillye* (1651) Sty. 265—not to assign the land *or any part thereof*; *Anon* (1574) 3 Dyer 334b; *Gostwick's Case* (1589) Cro.Eliz. 163—covenant not to alienate any part; the lessees partitioned and one of them alienated his share giving rise to a forfeiture of the whole.

[42] [1902] 1 Ch. 727.

[43] *Infra*.

[44] Compare Buckley J.'s remarks in *Langton* v. *Henson, supra*.

[45] [1986] 1 All E.R. 362.

[46] See *supra*.

[47] At p. 364; approved by the Court of Appeal in *Troop* v. *Gibson* (1986) 1 E.G.L.R. 1.

to the lessor, shall not assign to *any person*[48] without the lessor's consent."[49] The assignee had argued that the lessee was a person already approved by the landlord and therefore no consent was required to revest the term in him.

Underleases

In some covenants a restriction on underletting is expressed by the use of words like "let," "set," "demise,"[50] "sublease." Where such a restriction exists, it refers to the grant of a lease for less than the whole of the unexpired term. It should

Legal? probably be construed as referring only to legal leases.[51] Many underleases will be legal as being by deed or will fall under sections 52(2)(*d*) & 54(2) of the Law of Property Act 1925 (taking effect in possession for a term not exceeding three years at the best rent which can reasonably be obtained without taking a fine). Equitable leases, even if not caught by a covenant against underletting would in any event fall within the scope of the usual accompanying restriction on parting with possession.[52] Despite some early doubts,[53] it is clear that a covenant against underletting *simpliciter* does not prohibit

Assignments assignment. As FitzGibbon L.J. pointed out in *Re Doyle &*
not caught *O'Hara's Contract*[54] "as an assignee subjects himself to the lessee's covenants, which run with the land, and an underlessee does not, the lessor may choose to restrain the latter species of alienation only." The wording of the covenant has to be scrutinised very carefully however. If it happens to prohibit underletting for "*all* or part of" the term, it will prohibit assignment as was held in *Greenaway* v. *Adams*.[55] A covenant not to "underlet the premises" does not prohibit underletting a part of the premises (unless followed by words such as "or any

Underleases part thereof").[56] A covenant simply not to "underlet" may be
of part similarly construed for, in the opinion of Somervell L.J. in *Cook* v. *Shoesmith*[57] "the words ... must have an object ... and the only possible object that they can be given is [the demised premises]." It had, in that case, been argued, unsuccessfully, that the covenant meant that the tenant should not assign "at all." *Cook* v. *Shoesmith* was followed, reluctantly, in *Esdaile* v. *Lewis*[58] where the condition specified "No subletting allowed." Again this was held[59] to refer to the

---

[48] Author's emphasis.
[49] *McEachen* v. *Colton* [1902] A.C. 104 (P.C.), *per* Lord McNaghten at p. 107.
[50] See *Greenaway* v. *Adams* (1806) 12 Ves. 395.
[51] Compare *Gentle* v. *Faulkener* [1900] 2 Q.B. 267; see *supra*, Assignments.
[52] See *infra*.
[53] *Per* Sir W. Grant M.R. in *Greenaway* v. *Adams, ibid.* p. 401.
[54] (1899) 1 I.R. 113, 122.
[55] *Ibid.* See also *Re Doyle and O'Hara's Contract* [1899] 1 I.R. 113; *Marks* v. *Warren* [1979] 1 All E.R. 29, 31.
[56] *Wilson* v. *Rosenthal* (1906) 22 T.L.R. 233; *Cottell* v. *Baker* (1920) 36 T.L.R. 208.
[57] [1951] 1 K.B. 752, 755 (C.A.).
[58] [1956] 1 W.L.R. 709 (C.A.).
[59] Jenkins and Hodson L.JJ.

premises as a whole, rather than to a part. Danckwerts J., dissenting, pointed out the danger of following previous cases based upon construction:

> "a case of one kind may be extended to a slightly different wording in another . . . until finally you get the result which outrages the common sense of the judge who has to decide the matter . . . 'No subletting allowed' is a perfectly plain expression which means, if the other members of the court will forgive me, exactly what it says, that there must be no subletting whatever, and that there must be no subletting of a part . . . anymore than of the whole . . . There simply must be no subletting."[60]

Multiple partial lettings

A tenant who is free to underlet part, but not the whole, may ultimately contravene the covenant by multiple partial lettings. Thus in *Chatterton* v. *Terrell*[61] the tenant sublet the top floor and then sublet the remainder. The first subletting, being a subletting of part, did not require consent but it was in fact obtained. The second subletting was not regarded as a subletting of part, but rather as completing the subletting of the whole and "she should not sublet the whole . . . without consent. Without consent to what? Without consent to subletting the whole. She has sublet the whole without consent to sublet the whole"[62] and thus contravened the covenant. *Roberts* v. *Enlayde Ltd.*[63] can be distinguished as involving a more elaborate form of covenant *vis.*, not to underlet the premises "provided that this clause shall not apply to any underletting of the said premises or any part thereof for a term not exceeding three years." The tenant underlet part on a weekly tenancy and underlet the remainder for 21 years. In neither case was consent obtained. There was held to have been no contravention because "the former was excepted from the covenant by the proviso, while the latter was not an underletting of the whole of the premises"[64] or as Scrutton L.J. expressed it, "I read the covenant to be 'not to . . . underlet . . . the whole of the premises for a term exceeding three years' . . . They have not underlet the whole of their premises for a term exceeding three years."[65] As Atkin L.J. pointed out the landlord would have been better protected had the covenant prohibited parting with possession of the premises or any part thereof[66]—a covenant against underletting does not prevent parting with possession.[67] This was demonstrated in *Horsey Estate* v. *Steiger*[68] where, in the absence of any provision against parting with possession, the landlord had to argue, unsuccessfully, that there had been a subletting. The tenant had agreed to sell the lease to a company and had allowed the

Parting with possession

[60] At p. 714.
[61] [1923] A.C. 578.
[62] *Per* Lord Wrenbury at p. 584.
[63] [1924] 1 K.B. 335 (C.A.).
[64] *Per* Bankes L.J. at pp. 338–339.
[65] At p. 339.
[66] At p. 340.
[67] —of the whole or part; see *Wilson* v. *Rosenthal* [1906] 22 T.L.R. 233.
[68] [1989] 2 Q.B. 79.

company into possession before completion[69] on condition that it should pay all the outgoings and redeliver possession if the contract was rescinded. It was held that the company were not subtenants[70]; they did not pay rent to their vendor nor did they assume any obligations of tenancy towards him; they were not tenants at will either because the vendor could not turn them out so long as they were willing to carry out the terms of purchase. There had therefore been no breach of covenant against subletting. A covenant not to underlet part does include the whole.[71]

Mortgage by subdemise

A mortgage by subdemise does contravene a covenant against underletting. It was argued in *Sergeant* v. *Nash & Co.*[72] that there had been no breach of covenant "because it was intended to refer only to [underleases] to persons intended to be let into possession, I cannot agree that such a limitation should be placed on the covenant" and in any event, "though possession does not necessarily follow on a mortgage, it may follow on very short notice."[73] The Law Commission[74] considered the present position to be "a trap for the unwary tenant" and as bringing no real benefit to the landlord, who has, in any event, to include an express provision to cover other types of charge. They recommended that covenants against underletting be deemed not to include mortgages by subdemise.

Parting with possession

This must be distinguished from "parting with the premises" which has been construed as synonymous with assignment.[75]

It has been seen that covenants against assignment and underletting do not restrain the grant to third parties of rights to use the demised premises.[76] It was the purpose of the covenant against parting with possession to give the landlord some control in this situation but as Sir Harry Gibbs pointed out in *Lam Kee Ying Sdn Bhd* v. *Lam Shes Tong*[77] the covenant "will be of little value to a lessor in many cases and will admit of easy evasion by a lessee who is competently advised." At the outset, a covenant not to part with possession *of the demised premises* does not prevent the tenant from parting with

---

[69] There was a covenant against assignment but that only covers legal assignments; see *supra*.

[70] See also Law Society's Conditions of Sale (1984 Revision) 14(2); National Conditions of Sale (20th ed. 1981) 8; Standard Conditions of Sale (First Edition) 5.2.2.

[71] As with as Assignments, see *supra*; *Field* v. *Barkworth* [1986] 1 All E.R. 362; *Troop* v. *Gibson* [1986] 1 E.G.L.R. 1.

[72] [1903] 2 K.B. 304 (C.A.).

[73] *Per* Mathew L.J. at p. 315; where a licence to sub-demise by way of mortgage is required it cannot be unreasonably withheld—s.86(1) of the Law of Property Act 1925.

[74] Law Commission No. 141, paras. 7.79—7.82.

[75] *Russell* v. *Beecham* [1924] 1 K.B. 525 (C.A.), *supra*.

[76] *Gian Singh & Co.* v. *Devraj Nahar* [1965] 1 All E.R. 768, *supra*; *Wilson* v. *Rosenthal* [1906] 22 T.L.R. 233, *supra*.

[77] [1974] 3 All E.R. 137, 143.

possession of *part* of the demised property unless this is expressed.[78] More important however is the interpretation which has been places upon the words "parting with possession.

Ouster from legal possession

> ". . . a lessee cannot be said to part with possession . . . of the premises unless his agreement with his licensee wholly ousts him from legal possession. If there is anything in the nature of a right to concurrent user, there is no parting with possession . . . the authorities show that nothing short of a complete exclusion of the grantor or licensor from legal possession for all purposes amounts to a parting with possession."[79]

> "It is quite possible for a man to permit another to occupy and at the same time himself remain in possession."[80]

While an assignment and an underlease involve a transfer of the right to exclusive possession[81] a licence does not necessarily have this effect.[82] It can of course do so, and therefore the facts of each case have to be considered. It has been held that the appearance of a stranger's name on the Register of Electors is insufficient evidence, in itself, that a breach of covenant has occurred because "the categories of person who are entitled to be registered are defined so widely . . . that it is impossible, in the absence of evidence, to be certain that any inference to be drawn from the register . . . that [a person] was present . . . constitutes presence of a nature and quality which created a breach of the tenant's covenants."[83] In *Peebles* v. *Crosthwaite*,[84] where there was a covenant against assigning, underletting and parting with possession, the tenant's executors agreed to sell the demised premises to a limited company in which the executors were large shareholders and directors. No actual assignment of the term ever took place but the company was allowed into possession, put up its name and adopted the premises as its registered office. The tenants were advised that they should retain legal possession and it was held that they had done so thus avoiding a breach of covenant. The fact that two of the executors were directors, attended at the premises and took part in the management of the business may have been an important consideration. There was a similar situation in *Rainham Chemical Works Ltd.* v. *Belvedere Fish Guano*[85] but in this case the agreement for sale went so far as to provide that the lessees retained possession despite the occupation of the company purchaser. On the basis of this, and the fact that the explosives licence, necessary for the conduct of the business on

---

[78] *Church* v. *Brown* (1808) 15 Ves. 258, *supra.*
[79] *Per* Farwell J. in *Stening* v. *Abrahams* [1931] 1 Ch. 470, 473–474.
[80] *Per* Bankes L.J. in *Chaplin* v. *Smith* [1926] 1 K.B. 198 at p. 205.
[81] *Marks* v. *Warren* [1979] 1 All E.R. 29, *supra.*
[82] *Chaplin* v. *Smith* [1926] 1 K.B. 198 (C.A.), *per* Scrutton L.J. at p. 211.
[83] *Per* Templeman L.J. in *Metropolitan Properties Co. Ltd.* v. *Griffiths* (1983) 43 P. & C.R. 138, 142 (covenant against parting with possession or sharing occupation).
[84] (1897) 13 T.L.R. 198 (C.A.).
[85] [1921] 2 A.C. 465.

Distinguish concurrent user

the premises, had never been transferred to the company, it was again found that there had been no breach of covenant. In *Chaplin* v. *Smith*[86] unlike in the two previous cases, the company was let into possession without having entered an agreement to buy because, as Bankes L.J. said,[87] "the advice came first" and so the parties entered a more limited agreement whereby the lessees were to retain possession and the company was to use. That agreement was not a "colourable" document; it expressed the real intention of the lessee who "was constantly on the premises and kept a key of them [and] . . . did business on his own account as well as business of the company"[88] and therefore there was no breach of covenant. It may have been different if the lessee had gone abroad and left the control of the premises and the management of the business to an officer of the company.[89] *Jackson* v. *Simons*[90] had rather different facts. The lessee allowed a third party to use part[91] of the premises for ticket sales, himself retaining a key. Romer J. found that there had been no parting with possession because the lessee retained legal possession of the whole at all material times. In *Stening* v. *Abrahams*,[92] allowing a third party to use the wall for an advertisement hoarding did not amount to parting with possession of part of the premises *vis.* the wall and a three-inch stratum of air outside it, because that did not prevent the tenant using the wall in any other way.

Transfer of possession

There have, of course, been cases where tenants have been found in breach of the covenant against parting with possession. In *Abrahams* v. *MacFisheries Ltd.*[93] a draft sub-lease was prepared and the key was handed over to the prospective sub-lessee who executed repairs and began to carry on business. The parties had agreed that possession should be surrendered should the head-landlord refuse his consent. He did and it was held that the lessee was in breach of the covenant against parting with possession. The evidence of a transfer of possession was equally compelling in *Lam Kee Ying Sdn Bhd* v. *Lam Shes Tong*.[94] The lessee and his partners formed a limited company and transferred the business to it as a going concern. The supply of water, telephone and electricity was transferred into the name of the company and the company tendered its own cheque for payment of rent. These circumstances indicated that the company regarded itself and was regarded by the lessee as having possession of the premises.[95] The lessee did not improve his cause by inviting the court to lift the veil of incorporation, on the basis that the company's possession (which he did not actually dispute) was the equivalent of his own, because he held the majority of shares in it.

[86] [1926] 1 K.B. 198 (C.A.).
[87] At p. 205.
[88] *Per* Scrutton L.J. at p. 211.
[89] *Per* Bankes L.J. at p. 205.
[90] [1923] 1 Ch. 373.
[91] The covenant did expressly extend to part.
[92] [1931] 1 Ch. 470.
[93] [1925] 2 K.B. 18.
[94] [1974] 3 All E.R. 137, *supra*.
[95] *Per* Sir Harry Gibbs at p. 143.

It has been established that the withdrawal from possession of one joint tenant does not amount to a parting with possession. Three justifications for this were offered in *City of Bristol* v. *Westcott*[96] that the covenant must be construed as not to part with possession to any *third* person not previously approved by the landlord,[97] that for one to withdraw does not alter the rights of the landlord, and that possession cannot be transferred to a person, *i.e.* the continuing joint tenant, who already, by virtue of the unity of possession, has full possession of the whole.[98] It may be noted that nowadays there will always be a joint tenancy at law[99] and it will be this with which the landlord is concerned, but in any event the fact that a tenancy in common partakes of the unity of possession would suggest that similar principles should apply.

Finally, it is clear that a lessee who does not have possession cannot part with it and, probably, that a lessee does **Lessees** not part with possession where it is stolen from him. In **without** relation to the first point, if a lessee has parted with possession, **possession** with the lessor's consent, to a sub-lessee, he is not then in breach of covenant if he, in his turn, consents to the sub-lessee parting with possession to a sub-sub-lessee. So it was held in *Mackusick* v. *Carmichael*[1] where the lessee had covenanted for himself and his assigns. Having already parted with possession, it could not be maintained that his present actions constituted a parting with possession by him and though he covenanted that his assigns would not part with possession, a sub-lessee is not an assign. In order to enable a lessor to retain control over possession therefore, provision should be inserted in the lease whereby a permitted subtenant enters into direct covenants with the lessor[2] or the original covenant should make the lessee responsible for the acts of not only his successors in title but also those who derive title under him.[3] The question of **Trespassers** trespassers arose in *Doe* v. *Payne*[4]. The landlord found Payne in possession of the property, carrying on his business with his name above the door. Payne asserted that the property had been let to him by persons other than the tenant. The landlord sought possession on the basis of a breach of covenant but his action was unsuccessful, Lord Ellenborough pointing out that Payne could well be a "tortious intruder" and "for ought that appears [the tenant] may have been unwilling to be turned out of possession." The covenant in this case was not to assign or underlet but His Lordship opined that the evidence would not have been sufficient even if the tenant had covenanted not to part with possession. Whether the court finds that the occupant is in possession as a result of some voluntary act of the tenant, as opposed to some trespassory act, will of course depend on

---

[96] (1879) 12 Ch.D. 461 (partners).
[97] *Per* Jessel M.R. at p. 465.
[98] *Per* Bacon V.-C. at p. 465.
[99] ss.34(2) and 36(2) of the Law of Property Act 1925.
[1] [1917] 2 K.B. 581.
[2] See *infra*, Chap. 6, Conditional Consents.
[3] Such is, in fact, the effect of s.79 of the Law of Property Act 1925 unless it is excluded.
[4] (1815) 1 Stark. 86.

the evidence, and the slightly stronger evidence of tenant
involvement in the case of *Doe* v. *Rickarby*[5] may explain the
landlord's success in that case. On the other hand the case has
been interpreted as indicating that the landlord can recover
possession on the basis of the events which have occurred even
if the tenant cannot be shown to have had any part in them.[6]

Sharing possession or occupation

It has been seen that a covenant against parting with possession
can easily be evaded by means of the lessee retaining legal
possession while permitting another to use or occupy the
premises. The answer to this, from a lessor's point of view,
may be to draft the alienation covenant in still wider terms
which comprehend sharing possession or occupation or
permitting another to occupy.[7] That such a covenant imposes a
restriction additional to parting with possession was recognised
in *Jackson* v. *Simons*[8] where allowing a third party to use part
of the premises for ticket sales was admitted to be a breach of
the covenant against sharing possession or occupation but not
of the covenant against parting with possession. Similarly in
Greenslade v. *Tapscott*[9] and *Richards* v. *Davies*[10] tenants were
held, respectively, to be in breach of a penal provision
applicable should the tenant suffer the land to be used or
occupied by any other person (third party growing potatoes
between May and October), and a covenant not to permit any
other person to use or occupy (sale of the grass keep[11] in a
specified field).[12] Covenants in these terms can clearly give rise
to argument as to what amounts to possession or occupation, as
indeed they did in the last two cases where special meanings
based upon local custom were suggested and rejected.[13] It is
doubtful whether the courts will be able to effectively employ
the rule of strict construction in the case of words which are so
wide but this would clearly be desirable should such clauses be
relied upon by the lessor in very trivial circumstances.

Charges

Although a covenant against underletting will restrict mortgages
by sub-demise, it will not cover a charge by way of legal

---

[5] (1803) 5 Esp. 4.
[6] See Foa's *General Law of Landlord and Tenant*, (7th ed.), p. 270, n. (*e*).
[7] See respectively *Encylopaedia of Forms and Precedents* (4th ed.), Vol. 12,
   p. 754 and (5th ed.) Vol. 22, p. 287, 5. 9: 1.
[8] (1923) 1 Ch. 373.
[9] (1834) C.M. & R. 55.
[10] [1921] 1 Ch. 90.
[11] Growing grass.
[12] To be taken via the mouth of the beast as distinct from agistment or
   tacking—taking in another's cattle or sheep to de-pasture them generally.
[13] Upon the basis that the insertion of the restrictions in these cases was
   thought to be specifically to exclude the type of customary third-party use
   which had occurred.

mortgage,[14] as such a chargee has no sub-term granted to him but merely has the same rights and remedies as if he had.[15] Where control over the granting of security interests *generally* is desired, it is therefore necessary to make express provision. A covenant restricting "charges"[16] is probably apt to refer to both mortgages by subdemise and charges by way of legal mortgage, as a mortgage certainly involves a charge.[17] As in the context of assignment covenants, a restriction upon mortgages[18] will only cover a legal mortgage. In *M'Kay* v. *M'Nally*[19] the lessee had deposited the lease with a letter acknowledging an agreement for a mortgage but this was held not to contravene a covenant against mortgaging for "an agreement for a mortgage is no more a mortgage than an agreement for an assignment of a lease is an assignment."[20] Finally, in the case of long leases, where a premium is paid, it will often be totally inappropriate for a landlord to seek to restrict charges of the whole absolutely, but qualified covenants[21] and covenants restricting charges of part are encountered.

Legal

Involuntary assignments

Where a general covenant against alienation[22] is used—not to assign, sub-let or part with possession—it will not restrict involuntary assignments. The types of alienation expressly referred to are considered to be of a voluntary nature and the court will not extend the operation of the covenant to involuntary dispositions.[23] A number of transfers potentially within the involuntary category are considered next.

Compulsory purchase

It is no breach of a covenant against assignment for the lessee to submit to compulsory acquisition under the provisions of an Act of Parliament. When notice has been served upon him he cannot therefore refuse to complete on the ground that the landlord has not given his consent; "as soon as land is required . . . and notice is given to take it under the Act, the licence to assign is no longer required, being virtually taken away by the

Submit to compulsory acquisition

---

[14] See *Grand Junction Co. Ltd.* v. *Bates* [1954] 2 Q.B. 160, 168.
[15] See s.87(1) of the Law of Property Act 1925.
[16] See, *e.g. Encyclopaedia of Forms and Precedents* (5th ed.), Vol. 22, p. 287, 5. 9: 3.
[17] A liability to pay money laid upon a person or an estate—*The Shorter Oxford Dictionary.*
[18] And also, presumably, upon "charges."
[19] (1879) 4 L.R.Ir. 438.
[20] *Per* Lord Chancellor Ball at p. 445.
[21] Made fully qualified by Landlord and Tenant Act 1927, s.19(1).
[22] Provisions dealing specifically with involuntary assignment are considered below.
[23] *Doe d. Mitchinson* v. *Carter* (1798) 8 Term. Rep. 57.

Act of Parliament . . . The lessor can neither refuse the licence to assign, nor assent to the assignment, for he has nothing to do with it."[24]

Vesting orders

In *Marsh* v. *Gilbert*[25] an order vesting the lease in new trustees[26] was held not to fall within a covenant restricting assignment.

> "In normal legal usage an 'assignment' is an *inter vivos* disposition made by one party in favour of another as an act of their joint volition . . . A vesting order is a transfer of the legal estate which takes effect by operation of law . . . a transfer which takes effect under an order of the court cannot normally be described as an assignment by an individual."[27]

Involuntary The fact that in this case the lessee had disappeared and knew nothing at all about the order highlighted the involuntary nature of the transfer. Equally involuntary would be the vesting of a lease in a mortgagee by foreclosure order absolute (though the granting of the mortgage in the first place may have occasioned a breach of covenant).[28] Although section 9 of the Law of Property Act 1925 provides that vesting orders are to operate as conveyances by the estate owners, this is not thought to justify the conclusion that they should be treated as if they were the estate owners' voluntary act.[29] Where a lease constitutes settled land any vesting of it under the powers conferred by the Settled Land Act 1925 "shall not operate as a breach of covenant or condition against alienation or give rise to forfeiture"[30]

Taking in execution

If a creditor obtains judgment against the lessee and the lease is taken in execution of that judgment, this will not usually constitute a breach of the general form of alienation covenant.[31] The fact that the lessee consented to judgment being entered against him, does not, *of itself*, make any difference. As Lord

---

[24] *Per* Lord Romilly M.R. in *Slipper* v. *Tottenham and Hampstead Junction Railway Co.* (1867) L.R. 4 Eq. 112, 114.

[25] (1980) 256 E.G. 715.

[26] Compare the appointment of new trustees by deed; no vesting, and therefore no breach of covenant, will occur unless consent has previously been obtained or sought and unreasonably withheld: s.40 of the Trustee Act 1925; *supra*, Assignment.

[27] *Per* Nourse J. at p. 717.

[28] See *supra*, Charges.

[29] See J. T. Farrand, *Emmet on Title*, (19th ed.), 26, 151.

[30] s.14(1) of the Settled Land Act. Presumably, the transaction whereby the lease became settled land may constitute a breach.

[31] Though if there is an express proviso for termination in this event, it will be activated: *R.* v. *Topping* (1825) M'Cle. & Yo. 544.

Kenyon C.J. stated in *Doe d. Mitchinson* v. *Carter*[32] "judgments in contemplation of law always pass *in invitum* and I see no difference between a judgment that is obtained in consequence of an action resisted and a judgment that is signed under warrant of attorney, since the latter is merely to shorten the process and to lessen the expense of the proceedings."[33] He went on to point out that the warrant of attorney did not operate specifically on the lease "but it only gave the creditor power to enter up judgment against the tenant and, *non constat*, that it would be followed up by the term being taken in execution of that judgment."[34] However it was later found by a jury that the debtor's motive in signing judgment was not the fatalistic one initially ascribed to him by Lord Kenyon but was specifically to allow the creditor to get possession of the lease in the face of an absolute covenant against assignment.[35] This additional fact did turn it into a voluntary assignment, a fraud on the covenant, giving rise to forfeiture. For

Fraud on covenant

> "it would be ridiculous to suppose that a court of justice could not see through such a flimsy pretext as this. Here the maxim applies that that which cannot be done *per directum* shall not be done *per obliquum*. The tenant could not by any assignment . . . have conveyed his interest to a creditor and consequently he cannot convey it by an attempt of this kind . . . "[36]

Vesting in a trustee in bankruptcy

It was stated *obiter* in *Doe d. Blencowe* v. *Bugby*[37] that becoming bankrupt did not amount to an assignment for the purposes of an ordinary clause restricting assignment.[38] This was followed in *Doe d. Goodbere* v. *Bevan*[39] and in *Re Riggs*[40] where Wright J. considered that an adjudication of bankruptcy, even on the lessee's own petition, did not contravene the bankrupt's covenant not to assign for "the words 'assign or underlet' are used in their ordinary or popular sense and refer only to such assignments as are directly made by the lessee as distinguished from such assignments by law as result by the statute from a petition of bankruptcy followed by adjudication."[41] Though adjudication results in assignment to the trustee in bankruptcy[42] such an assignment cannot be regarded as the act of the bankrupt, and therefore voluntary, because on presentation of his petition there is no certainty that

[32] (1798) 8 Term. Rep. 57.
[33] At p. 61.
[34] *Ibid*.
[35] (1799) 8 Term. Rep. 300.
[36] *Ibid*. 302.
[37] (1771) 3 Wils. 234.
[38] Though the additional prohibition on "doing or putting away with . . . the demised premises" did cover, amongst other things, bankruptcy.
[39] (1815) 3 M. & S. 353, 355, 359.
[40] [1901] 2 K.B. 16.
[41] At p. 21.
[42] See s.306 of the Insolvency Act 1986.

it will follow.[43] This view has been adopted not only in relation to alienation covenants but also in relation to provisos which effect a termination of the lease should the tenant assign it. Thus in *Re Griffiths*[44] Romer J. opined that:

> "[t]he adjudication was the act of the court, which had a discretion in the matter, and though the presentation of the petition by the debtor was an act by him setting the court in motion, I cannot . . . understand how the adjudication and the consequent divesting of his property can be said to be an alienation by him. If the adjudication had been on the petition of a creditor, could it truthfully be said that the creditor had alienated the debtor's property?"[45]

Proviso for re-entry on bankruptcy

While bankruptcy does not constitute a breach of a general covenant against alienation, it may result in the termination of the lease under an express proviso to that effect.[46] Early arguments to the effect that such clauses allowed the tenant to hold out false colours or were contrary to public policy as being tantamount to a provision that the lease was not to be available to the bankrupt's creditors were rejected in favour of the landlord's "right to guard against the estate's falling into the hands of any . . . person [other than the original tenant]."[47] That a landlord could so protect himself by an ordinary covenant against assignment was accepted and bankruptcy was a form of assignment in relation to which "[p]erhaps it is more necessary for the landlord to guard . . . as there is greater danger to be apprehended by him in this . . . case."[48] In *Smith v. Gronow*[48a] it was established that a proviso for termination on the bankruptcy of the tenant could only be exercised upon the bankruptcy of the current tenant not upon that of a former tenant. The lease contained a right of re-entry "if the lessee, his executors, administrators or assigns shall become bankrupt." The lessee, with the lessor's consent, assigned the lease and thereafter became bankrupt whereupon the lessor sought to re-enter against the assignee. It was held however that the proviso did not operate in these circumstances because it only referred to "the bankruptcy of the person holding the estate, that is the bankruptcy of the lessee, his executors or assigns if there has been no assignment, or if there has been an assignment, then the bankruptcy of the assign."[49]

---

[43] *Cohen v. Popular Restaurants Ltd.* [1917] 1 K.B. 480, 483.
[44] [1926] 1 Ch. 1007.
[45] At p. 1014; *Re Cotgrave* [1903] 2 Ch. 705 doubted and distinguished.
[46] See, *e.g.s Re Walker* (1884) 13 Ch.D. 454 (becoming bankrupt or filing a petition); *Civil Service Co-operative Society* v. *McGrigor's Trustee* [1923] 2 Ch. 347 (becoming bankrupt); for examples of such express provisos see *Conveyancer and Property Lawyer Precedents for Conveyancers*, Vol. 1, 5–3, p. 2523, *Encyclopaedia of Forms and Precedents* (4th ed.), Vol. 11, p. 346 (where it is pointed out that some mortgagees will not accept a lease containing such a proviso as a security), *Kelly's Draftsman*, (15th ed.), p. 371.
[47] *Per* Buller J. in *Roe d. Hunter* v. *Galliers* (1787) 2 T.R. 133, 140.
[48] *Per* Ashurst J., *ibid* at p. 139.
[48a] [1891] 2 Q.B. 394.
[49] *Per* Wright J. at p. 397.

Finally, while the vesting of the lease in the trustee in bankruptcy consequent upon adjudication does not occasion a breach of the normal form of covenant against assignment, a disposal by the trustee himself may do so. This is considered in Chapter 3, The Running of the Burden of Disposition Covenants.

Vesting in personal representatives on death

Transmission to the personal representatives of a deceased lessee by virtue of section 1 of the Administration of Estates Act 1925 does not constitute a breach of the normal form of covenant restricting assignment because, again, it is not voluntary. "It is an alienation by the act of God."[50] The addition to the covenant of words prohibiting "doing or putting away with" the term will encompass such a transmission, however.[51] Whether disposals *by* personal representatives occasion breach of the normal form of covenant will be considered in Chapter 3.

Assignments to company liquidators, etc.

It would be unusual for a lease to vest in a company liquidator because there is no automatic *cessio bonorum* to a company liquidator.[52] While section 145 of the Insolvency Act 1986 gives power to the court to order that "all or any part of the property ... belonging to the company" shall vest in the liquidator,[53]

Involuntary order in relation to company

such orders are not common.[54] Where such an order has been made the vesting would probably be considered to be involuntary in relation to the company notwithstanding the fact that it was consequential upon the application of its agent, the liquidator.[55] The property of a company does not vest in an administrator, administrative receiver or receiver (Scotland). It should not be forgotten that while the events referred to above may not constitute a breach of covenant, they may trigger a separate proviso for termination.[56] Disposals by company liquidators and others will be considered in Chapter 3.

---

[50] Lord Thurlow L.C. *Seers* v. *Hinds* (1791) 1 Ves. 294; *Doe d. Blencowe* v. *Bugby* (1771) 3 Wils. 234, *supra*.

[51] *Ibid*.

[52] See *Palmer's Company Law*, para. 88–37 and compare the position of a trustee in bankruptcy *supra* and s.306 of the Insolvency Act 1986.

[53] This section applies to a winding-up by the court, but a vesting order could be made in relation to a voluntary winding-up under s.112. *Palmer*, para. 89–58; it would also appear to apply to an unregistered company, see s.221 of the Insolvency Act 1986 and compare *Re Birkbeck Permanent Benefit Building Society* [1913] 2 Ch. 34.—property vested by order of the court in the Official Receiver as liquidator.

[54] Current Law Statutes Annotated, Insolvency Act 1986, n. to s.145.

[55] As with the vesting in a trustee in bankruptcy despite the adjudication following after the bankrupt's own petition, see *supra*.

[56] Compare *supra* "Vesting in Trustees in Bankruptcy."

Adverse possession

It is manifest that adverse possession is neither voluntary nor an assignment, and will not therefore constitute breach of a covenant against assignment. Whether it breaches a covenant against parting with possession has previously been discussed.

3 RUNNING OF THE BURDEN OF DISPOSITION COVENANTS

Touch and concern the land

If a covenant "touches and concerns" the land demised, the burden of it will run with the land to an assignee by virtue of privity of estate.[1] A covenant not to assign without the landlord's consent has been held to touch and concern the land "for it is a covenant as to who shall have occupation of the land, and it is inserted with a view that the landlord shall not be deprived of a voice as to who shall be substituted for the original lessee in possession of the landlord's premises."[2] The same reasoning would seem to apply to absolute covenants not to assign[3] and covenants which restrict under-letting, parting with possession and charging and to provisos for re-entry on bankruptcy, etc.[4] If the covenant was intended to be personal, the burden of it will not run but there is little in the usual form of alienation covenant to encourage the belief that it is personal.[5] Where the covenant takes absolute form it can be

Absolute covenants

argued that "so far from being meant to reach assigns . . . it is inserted to prevent there ever being any assigns at all." In *In Re Robert Stephenson & Co. Ltd.*,[6] however, that argument was disregarded in view of the widespread and accepted practice of applying for a licence to assign in such cases.[7]

Capacity of the covenantor

The capacity in which the lessee covenanted usually takes the matter beyond all doubt. A covenant made on behalf of the lessee's assigns or successors in title indicates that these are intended to be bound. The absence of such words is not, however, necessarily supportive of an argument that the covenant was intended to be personal; their absence may be explicable upon some other basis. In *In Re Robert Stephenson & Co. Ltd.*[8] where the lessee was defined in the lease as including merely executors and administrators, it was argued that the covenant was intended to be personal to the lessee and his personal representatives and that a subsequent assignee was free to assign. Sargant J. opined that while it

---

[1] See Megarry & Wade, *Modern Law of Real Property* (5th ed.), p. 743.
[2] *Per* Lush J. in *Williams* v. *Earle* (1868) L.R. 3 Q.B. 739 at p. 749; *Goldstein* v. *Sanders* [1915] 1 Ch. 549; *McEacharn* v. *Colton* [1902] A.C. 104 P.C.—where the same was admitted.
[3] See *infra*.
[4] See *Williams* v. *Earle* (*ibid.*); *Smith* v. *Gronow* [1891] 2 Q.B. 394; see also Elphinstone, *Covenants Affecting Land*, p. 32.
[5] Compare *In Re Royal Victoria Pavilion, Ramsgate* [1961] 1 Ch. 581.
[6] [1915] 1 Ch. 802.
[7] *Ibid. per* Sargant J. at p. 809.
[8] *Ibid.*

was possible for the parties to indicate an intention that the burden of the covenant should not run, the fact that the lessee did not covenant on behalf of himself and his assigns was insufficient evidence of such an intention. The failure to mention assigns was explicable, in this case, upon the basis of an "unfounded apprehension that the recognition of the possibility of there being assigns might be held to be inconsistent with the prohibition or restriction on assignment."[9] The learned judge was also influenced by the fact that it was a long lease and if the absence of a reference to assigns prevented the disposition covenant running it could equally have that effect in relation to others. Because, now, by the operation of section 79 of the Law of Property Act

s. 79 Law of Property Act 1925
1925, the lessee is deemed to have covenanted "on behalf of himself, his successors in title and the persons deriving title under him or them," it will rarely be possible even to argue that the covenant was intended to be personal. Even if the operation of the section is excluded, as it may be, such exclusion would not necessarily be sufficient evidence of an intention to make the covenant personal. It would depend on

Exclusion of section 79
the manner and purpose of the exclusion. The exclusion of section 79 is typically to ensure that the lessee is free from the continuing contractual liability to which that section gives rise,[10] rather than to register any intention that the covenant should be personal to the covenantor—indeed a personal covenant in these circumstances would be unlikely to be acceptable to the lessor. Where the exclusion of section 79 is achieved by the lessee covenanting on behalf of a more limited class of person than that contemplated by the section, *e.g.* executors and administrators, in the absence of some other explanation for the failure to mention successors in title, it could be concluded that the covenant was intended to be personal to that limited extent.[11]

Accepting that disposition covenants touch and concern the land (unless they are personal), the burden of them will pass to those who fall into the relationship of privity of estate with the lessor: persons who take a legal assignment of the whole unexpired term.[12] That ordinary assignees *inter vivos* come within this class is clear. The position of other types of successor is discussed below.

Personal representatives

As persons taking the whole unexpired term by operation of law, one would expect personal representatives to be affected

Liability
by the burden of the covenant. They will clearly be liable for any breaches committed by the deceased in his lifetime; to these they succeed in the same way that they succeed to his

---

[9] At p. 809.
[10] *Tophams Ltd.* v. *Earl of Sefton* [1967] A.C. 50, 81; Megarry & Wade, *The Law of Real Property*, (5th ed.), p. 742.
[11] But see *In Re Robert Stephenson & Co. Ltd.* [1915] Ch. 802, *supra.*
[12] See Megarry & Wade, *The Law of Real Property*, (5th ed.), p. 746.

debts. They will generally also be liable for their own breaches: an intention that the burden should run to them will be demonstrated either by virtue of their being expressly mentioned in the covenant or through the implication made under section 79 of the Law of Property Act 1925.[13] In *Sir William More's Case*[14] the covenant referred to the lessee "his executors or assigns" and in *Roe d. Gregson* v. *Harrison*[15] the covenant expressly referred to the lessee "his executors or administrators." In both cases an administrator was bound, being regarded in the former as an assign. As mentioned above, even in the absence of such express mention, the lessee will be deemed to have covenanted on behalf of himself, his successors in title and those deriving title under him, by virtue of section 79—thus indicating that personal representatives, successors in title, are intended to be bound.

If the section has been excluded, it may be possible to argue that the covenant was intended to be personal to the lessee—indeed Ashurst J. in *Roe d. Gregson* v. *Harrison* suggested that this might have been so in that case had the lease failed to make express mention of administrators.[16]

Effect of exclusion of section 79
Such an argument would be particularly persuasive where the exclusion of section 79 took the form of nominating a more limited class of successor than that referred to by the section. It would be correspondingly weak where the exclusion took the form of indicating that the lessee was not to be liable for breaches occurring after the lease had ceased to be vested in him[17]—thus making it clear that the purpose of the exclusion was to avoid continuing contractual liability of the lessee rather than to indicate that the burden was not to run to a successor. Where the section is excluded *as a section* the intention may be rather more difficult to ascertain and it has been suggested that the presumption is in favour of a covenant which touches and concerns the land running:

> "doubts have been expressed whether, when the lessee covenants only for himself, his executor may not assign after his death without committing a breach of covenant; but having regard to the fact that an executor is in the position of an assignee, and that the covenant runs with the land, this doubt would scarcely appear to be well founded."[18]

General arguments to the effect that the personal representatives should not, in principle, be bound by alienation

---

[13] See also Williams, Mortimer & Sunnocks, *Executors, Administrators & Probate*, (16th ed.), p. 666. " ... it seems on principle that even without express mention of the personal representatives, a covenant or condition will now be binding because the contract made by a deceased person, unless personal to him, binds his personal representatives ... " citing ss.79 & 80(2) of the Law of Property Act 1925, and see A. R. Mellows, *The Law of Succession*, (4th ed.), p. 293.

[14] (1584) Cro. Eliz. 26.

[15] (1788) 2 Term Rep. 425.

[16] He used the word "executors" in fact but that was clearly inappropriate.

[17] Compare *Tophams Ltd.* v. *Earl of Sefton* [1967] A.C. 50, *supra*.

[18] See Foa's, *General Law of Landlord and Tenant* (7th ed.), p. 257.

covenants because they come in "by act of God"[19] or, at the very least, by operation of law, would not appear to have great force.[20] In the first place, though the assignment is by operation of law, both executors and administrators can choose whether to be at the receiving end of it—the former can renounce and the latter is not bound to put himself forward.[21] In the second place, regardless of how they came in, there would appear to be little justification for vesting in them a term more valuable than that of which the deceased died possessed.

Assents

Where the personal representatives have the burden of a covenant against assignment it clearly restricts a sale of the lease; does it also restrict assents to beneficiaries? It is very convincingly argued by Professor Barnsley[22] that as an assent operates to convey the legal estate it would come within the terms of a covenant against assignment; if the covenant extended to parting with possession it would be broken in that respect also by an assent because "at some time the personal representatives must part even with the legal possession to the beneficiary; at the very latest this will be when the assent is made, and it may possibly be that a parting can be effected before, or even in the absence of, an assent."[23] He further suggests that it would be possible to exclude transmissions to beneficiaries from the ambit of an alienation covenant by an appropriate proviso.

Trustees in bankruptcy

Question of construction

Whether a trustee in bankruptcy is bound by an alienation covenant depends upon its terms. In *Goring* v. *Warner*[24] the covenant referred only to the lessee, his executors or administrators; in *Doe d. Goodbere* v. *Bevan*[25] it referred additionally to his assigns but consistent with *Doe d. Mitchinson* v. *Carter*[26] that was held to refer only to voluntary assigns not those who took by operation of law.[27] In both cases it was held that the trustee was not bound. That it is a matter of construction appears from *Re Johnson*[28] where the trustee in bankruptcy was bound by a covenant which expressly extended to assigns *by operation* of law.[29]

---

[19] *Seers* v. *Hinds* (1791) 1 Ves. 294.

[20] Compare the position of trustees in bankruptcy, *infra*.

[21] *Doe d. Goodbere* v. *Bevan* (1815) 3 M. & S. 353, 358.

[22] Vol. 27 Con.N.S. 159, 177.

[23] *Ibid*. p. 178.

[24] (1724) 2 Eq.Cas.Abr. 100.

[25] (1815) 3 M. & S. 353.

[26] (1798) 8 Term Rep. 57, *supra*.

[27] And see *Re Birkbeck Permanent Benefit Building Society* [1913] 2 Ch. 34, 38, *supra*; *Re Farrow's Bank Ltd*. [1921] 2 Ch. 164 "what was decided was that the trustee was not the assign of the bankrupt within the meaning of the covenant, because the covenant related only to voluntary assigns and not assigns in law," *per* Lord Sterndale M.R. at p. 175; *Re Wright* [1949] Ch. 729, 735, 736.

[28] (1894) 70 L.T. 38.

[29] That the parties could so stipulate was also recognised in *Re Birkbeck*, *ibid*.

Most significantly, in *Re Wright*[30] the tenant was defined to include "successors in title," which a trustee in bankruptcy certainly is, and it was held that the trustee was bound. The importance of this is, of course, that by section 79 of the Law of Property Act 1925 the covenantor is deemed to have covenanted on behalf of his successors in title, unless a contrary intention is expressed. In many cases therefore the trustee in bankruptcy is, as a matter of construction, going to be bound by the covenant, in spite, it is submitted, of the attempts in early times to establish a general principle to the contrary.

Outdated attitudes   Such attempts were based on a fear that the trustee would be left "encumbered with the engagement belonging to the property which he takes"[31] and also upon the notion that the trustee was under a duty to dispose of the lease for the benefit of the creditors and that this duty overrode any contractual restriction on disposition which might limit or prevent a proper realisation.[32] In relation to the first matter, it has very pertinently been pointed out that since 1869, a trustee in bankruptcy has been able to disclaim an onerous lease and "is no longer in the position of finding himself involuntarily landed with an onerous lease and unable to dispose of it except by assignment to another person" and since 1927 his position has been further eased by the transformation of qualified covenants into fully qualified by section 19(1) of the Landlord and Tenant Act of that year.[33] The second proposition was viewed with some scepticism as early as 1806 when Sir William Grant M.R., referring to *Goring* v. *Warner*,[34] commented that "that decision was made ... in opposition to ... the tendency of all the old cases; and upon a strange ground: that statute supersedes agreement. How can that be if the agreement was legal?"[35] In *Re Farrow's Bank Ltd.* the Court of Appeal refused to apply these principles to the position of a liquidator of a company, Younger L.J. confessing that he could perceive no "reason of law or equity why those interested in the liquidation should at the expense of the lessor be dispensed from compliance with an essential condition of the company's lease" and expressing the opinion that the bankruptcy cases to the contrary were based on "no very intelligible principle."[36]

---

[30] *Ibid.*
[31] *Per* Lord Ellenborough C.J. in *Doe d. Goodbere* v. *Bevan* (1815) 3 M. & S. 353.
[32] In argument in *Re Wright* [1949] Ch. 729; see also *Re Birkbeck Permanent Benefit Building Society* [1913] 2 Ch. 34—which concerned the liquidator of an unregistered company: "a contractual restriction of assignment does not apply to the assignment by a person on whom property has devolved by operation of law and who is under an obligation to assign"—*per* Neville J. at p. 38.
[33] Aronson K.C. and Muir Hunter in argument in *Re Wright, ibid.*; and see *Williams & Muir Hunter on Bankruptcy*, (19th ed.), p. 284.
[34] (1724) 2 Eq.Cas.Abr. 100.
[35] *Weatherall* v. *Geering* 12 Ves. 504, 512.
[36] At p. 177.

Conclusion In conclusion, whether a trustee in bankruptcy is bound
by an alienation covenant is a question of construction and has
nothing to do with the general notions just referred to. Usually
the trustee will be bound because the covenant will be deemed
to have been made on behalf of successors in title[37]; if it was
made on behalf of a more limited class of successor, e.g.
assigns, executors and administrators, this may exclude the
operation of section 79 and free the trustee from liability
under the covenant if such trustee falls outside the class
nominated. If section 79 is excluded more directly with no
more limited class nominated, it is likely that it was so
excluded to avoid the continuing contractual liability of the
lessee[38] rather than as an indication that the covenant was
intended to be personal and in these circumstances it is
submitted that the burden of the covenant should run to the
trustee.

Liquidators

It has already been mentioned that liquidation does not
generally result in the company's property vesting in the
liquidator.[39] The powers of the directors to manage the
company cease[40] in favour of the liquidator and an assignment
by the latter therefore would be on behalf of the company and
thus regarded as an assignment by the company itself and "as
plain a breach of the covenant as could possibly be."[41]

Sublessees

The burden of covenants touching and concerning the land,
entered into on the part of the lessee, runs only to those who
take a legal assignment of the whole unexpired term—they do
not therefore run to sublessees. Thus, where the lessee
covenants not to sublet without consent and thereafter obtains
the lessor's consent to a sublease, the sublessee is free to sub-
underlet (or otherwise contravene the terms of the restriction)
without consent.[42] As was pointed out by Atkin J. in
Mackusick v. *Carmichael*[43] "the first under-tenant licensed is
free from the control of the superior landlord" but "means

---

[37] See s.79 and *Re Wright*.
[38] See *supra*.
[39] See *supra*, Assignments to Company Liquidators, etc.
[40] See ss.9 (members' voluntary winding-up), 103 (creditors' voluntary
winding-up) and ss.144, 167 Insolvency Act 1986; *Pennington's Company
Law* (5th ed.) pp. 625 and 892 and the cases there cited; Farrar, *Company
Law*, p. 563 (winding-up by the court).
[41] *Per* Lord Sterndale M.R. in *Re Farrows Bank Ltd.* ([1921] 2 Ch. 164, 174)
where the suggestion, derived from *Cohen* v. *Popular Restaurants Ltd.*
((1917) 1 K.B. 480), that it could make a difference whether the
liquidation was voluntary or compulsory was dismissed (*per* Younger L.J.
at p. 178.
[42] See *Villiers* v. *Oldcorn* (1903) 20 T.L.R. 11.
[43] [1917] 2 K.B. 581.

exist which by proper expedients the control of the superior landlord can be retained."[44] The effectiveness of such expedients will be considered in relation to conditional consents in Chapter 6. However, in many cases, the lessee will be responsible for the sublessee's actions by virtue of having covenanted on behalf of himself and *inter alios* those deriving title under him.[45]

---

[44] At p. 586.
[45] See s.79 of the Law of Property Act 1925 and compare *Mackusick* v. *Carmichael*.

4 FULLY QUALIFIED COVENANTS AGAINST DISPOSITION

Construction
In a large number of cases the tenant covenants, not that he will not alienate the demised property at all, but that he will not do so without the consent of the landlord. Such a qualified covenant becomes a fully qualified covenant where it is further provided that "such consent is not to be unreasonably withheld".[1] As a matter of construction, the effect of these words is to "limit the generality of the covenant"[2]; the tenant does not covenant that he will never assign etc. without consent, but rather that he will not assign without consent where the landlord has been reasonable in withholding it. If the landlord is unreasonable in withholding it the tenant reserves his common law right[3] to assign at will. The usual form of covenant does not therefore create a cross-covenant by the landlord not to unreasonably withhold consent[4] and consequently does not provide the tenant with a remedy in damages. The covenant can be drafted to provide such a remedy; in *Ideal Film Renting Co.* v. *Neilson*[5] the lessee covenanted not to assign without consent "*and the lessor covenants with the [lessee] not unreasonably withhold such consent.* . . . It was held that on an unreasonable refusal of consent, the tenant was free to assign but had the additional remedy of proceeding against the landlord for breach of covenant. Where the Landlord and Tenant Act 1988 applies, the tenant may sue the landlord for damages for breach of statutory duty; this is dealt with in Chapter 5.

The origin of the fully qualifying phrase

Sections 86 & 89 Law of Property Act 1925
The fully qualifying phrase may be expressed[6] in the lease but if it is not, it will often apply nevertheless. Section 86(1) of the Law of Property Act 1925 provides that where a disposition covenant requires the lessor's consent to a mortgage by

---

[1] See Chapter 1.
[2] See Amphlett B. in *Treloar* v. *Bigge* (1874) L.R. 9 Ex 151, 156—who compared it to a covenant by the tenant to repair "provided the lessor shall allow the timber."
[3] *Re Gibbs and Houlder Bros. & Co. Ltd.* [1925] All E.R. Rep. 128, 133.
[4] See *Treloar* v. *Bigge ibid.* and also *Sear* v. *House Property and Investments Society* (1880) 16 Ch.D. 387.
[5] [1921] 1 Ch. 575.
[6] As to whether, under the general law, it may be implied. See Chapter 9, p. 184.

**Section 19(1)(a)
Landlord &
Tenant Act
1927**

subdemise[7] that consent shall not be unreasonably withheld; s.89(1) of the same Act states that where a lease is subject to a legal mortgage or charge and the mortgagee needs the lessor's consent to exercise his power of sale, again, such consent shall not be unreasonably withheld. Section 19(1)(a) of the Landlord and Tenant Act 1927 is of more general application and operates by way of implied proviso. It provides as follows:

> In all leases whether made before or after the commencement of this Act containing a covenant condition or agreement[8] against assigning, underletting, charging or parting with the possession of the demised premises or any part thereof without licence or consent, such covenant, condition or agreement shall notwithstanding any express provision to the contrary, be deemed to be subject: (a) to a proviso to the effect that such licence or consent is not to be unreasonably withheld, but this proviso does not preclude the right of the landlord to require payment of a reasonable sum in respect of any legal or other expenses incurred in connection with such licence or consent.

The scope of section 19(1)(a) Landlord and Tenant Act 1927

**"Leases":
agricultural
holding
excluded**

The implication is made into "leases" a word defined in section 25 as including a lease, underlease or other tenancy, an assignment operating as a lease or underlease (a reference perhaps to an "assignment" of less than the whole unexpired term), or an agreement for such lease, underlease tenancy or assignment. The section is not applicable to agricultural holdings within the meaning of the Agricultural Holdings Act 1986[9] or to certain covenants referred to in section 30 of the Leasehold Reform Act 1967. This section contains special provisions relating to extended leases[10] acquired under the Act from specified landlords (*vis*. The Commission for New Towns, the Development Board for Rural Wales, a development corporation within the meaning of the New Towns Act 1965 and a local authority in respect of houses provided by them by virtue of section 5 of the Towns Development Act 1952).[11] Such landlords can require the inclusion in the extended lease, of a qualifed covenant against subleasing[12] and such covenant will not be subject to the section 19 implication.[13]

**Section 30
Leasehold
Reform Act
1967**

---

[7] See *supra*, Chapter 2.

[8] *Supra* Chapter 1.

[9] See s.19(4); *infra* Chapter 7: though there may be express provision to the like effect.

[10] S.30(2).

[11] See s.30(7).

[12] s.30(1)(a) and (2)—this is the only type of disposition referred to though such a landlord can additionally require the inclusion of "such covenant as appears to [him] requisite for securing that in the event of any proposal to sell the property or any part of it, the landlord will have a right of pre-emption at the price mentioned in (4)—see s.30(1)(b) and (2).

[13] See s.30(5).

Applies to Qualified Covenants

It is clear that section 19 applies where the lease contains a covenant against assignment etc. "without licence or consent". While its main field of operation is in relation to such covenants which do not go on to express the fully qualifying phrase, it also operates where the covenant *expressly* provides that such consent is not to be unreasonably withheld. In the latter case, the implication has no practical impact where the express clause is identical in effect to the proviso implied by the Act; however where the express clause is to a different effect, it is an attempt to make an "express provision to the

"Notwithstanding express provision to the contrary

contrary" and is therefore overridden by the statutory implication.[14] Thus where attempts have been made to expressly provide in the lease that consent will not be unreasonably withheld but that a refusal on certain listed grounds should be deemed reasonable, such provisions have been held to be ineffective. The statutory implication goes in instead. In *Balfour* v. *Kensington Gardens*[15] it was specified that the failure of a proposed sub-tenant to enter into direct covenants with the landlord would render it reasonable for the landlord to withhold his consent. Macnaghten J. found that such failure was not a reasonable ground upon which to withhold consent and evidently accepted the argument of counsel for the tenant that it did not become reasonable just because the lease said so—any other view would destroy the protection which the tenant was intended to enjoy under the Act. In *Re Smith's Lease*[16] again there was a fully qualified covenant with the proviso

> "that any refusal by the lessor to consent ... shall not be deemed an unreasonable withholding of consent by reason only that the lessor at the time of intimating any such refusal may offer to accept ... a surrender of the tenancy ... and in the event of any such offer being made by the lessor the lessee shall surrender the tenancy hereby created."

Roxburgh J. found that the proviso was ineffective and the refusal unreasonable.[17] He commented that "if it were possible for the parties to stipulate in the lease that certain things should not be deemed unreasonable, they could surely stipulate that nothing should be deemed to be unreasonable and that would be a complete stultification of the Act".[18] The point also arose in *Creery* v. *Summersell & Flowerdew & Co. Ltd.*[19] where a fully qualified covenant was followed by a stipulation that the lessor "reserves the right to decline to give his consent if in his opinion the proposed underlessee is for any reason in his discretion undesirable as an occupant or underlessee". Harman

---

[14] See generally Law Commission No. 141, para. 3.24.
[15] (1932) 49 T.L.R. 29.
[16] [1951] 1 All E.R. 346.
[17] Compare valid surrender provisions, *infra*, p. 36.
[18] p. 348.
[19] [1949] 1 Ch. 751.

Provisions referring to a respectable and responsible person

J. considered the stipulation invalid in so far as it went beyond section 19(1)(*a*) which made reasonableness the only touchstone. Equally invalid, it is submitted, is the attempt to provide that "such consent will not be unreasonably withheld *in the case of a respectable and responsible person*". This form of covenant is still to be found in precedent books,[20] though less commonly than formerly, in spite of the fact that the reference to a respectable and responsible person is as ineffective as it is unnecessary. The effect of the section 19 implication[21] is that the landlord cannot *unreasonably* withhold his consent in *any* case and the attempt to give him the liberty to do so in relation to a disreputable assignee must be ineffective. It is also unnecessary because if the proposed assignee is a disreputable person the landlord could withhold his consent upon grounds which the court would find reasonable. This type of covenant would appear to have its origin in cases prior to the Act[22] and has nothing now to recommend it. However a clause in identical terms but omitting the word "unreasonably" is a completely different matter.[23]

Condition precedent to a right to assign

While it is clear that the parties cannot settle between themselves what is, or what is not, to be deemed a reasonable withholding of consent, they can agree that the tenant is to have no right to dispose of the term at all, unless he complies with a specified procedure designed to protect the landlord's interests. Such an arrangement was first considered in *Adler* v. *Upper Grosvenor Street Properties Ltd.*[24] where the tenant had covenanted

Proviso for surrender

> "not to assign ... without the previous consent in writing of the landlords such consent (*subject as hereinafter provided*) not to be unreasonably withheld ... Provided that should the tenant desire to assign ... he shall before doing so offer in writing to the landlords to surrender the lease ... without any consideration and the landlords may accept such offer at any time within 21 days from the receipt thereof ... but shall otherwise be deemed to have rejected it"

Inflation

The purpose of this provision is to secure a surrender in the landlord's favour should inflationary pressures make it expedient. As Denning M.R. explained in *Greene* v. *Church Commissioners for England*[25]

> "If rents rose during the [term]—so that a higher rent was obtainable ... the lessee would himself be able to assign the remainder of his term at a premium—because the assignee would pay money to get the flat at the lower rent

---

[20] See, *e.g. Encyclopaedia of Forms and Precedents*, Vol. 11, 2: 26.
[21] As to the construction of such clauses *prior* to the Act, see A. L. Smith L.J. in *Bates* v. *Donaldson* [1896] 2 Q.B. 241, 246 and Kodilinye (1988) Conv. 45.
[22] *Willmott* v. *London Road Car Co. Ltd.* [1910] 2 Ch. 525; *Associated Omnibus Co. Ltd.* v. *Idris etc. Ltd.* (1919) 148 L.T. Jo. 157; *Ideal Film Renting Co. Ltd.* v. *Neilson* [1921] 1 Ch. 575.
[23] See *Moat* v. *Martin* [1950] 1 K.B. 176, *infra*, p. 41.
[24] [1957] 1 All E.R. 229.
[25] [1974] 3 All E.R. 609, 611.

contained in the lease. But by means of this proviso . . .
the lessor could insist on surrender and let at the higher
rent. In short, the lessor would get the benefit of the rise
in rents and not the lessee"

The clause in *Re Smith's Lease*[26] was designed to serve a similar
purpose but was ineffective as seen above. The *Adler* clause was
successful. The surrender was secured by a condition precedent
to any right to assign—rather than by an agreed gloss upon the
meaning of "unreasonably".[27] Hilbery J. opined that if the
landlord accepted the surrender, the tenant had no right to
assign at all and that that state of affairs was countenanced by
the Act which, as previous decisions[28] had established, "is not
applicable to and is not to be read into a clause which
absolutely prohibits assignment."[29] If the landlord refuses the
surrender, the tenant can seek permission to assign and it is
then expressly provided that consent shall not be unreasonably
withheld. At the stage when it becomes relevant therefore,
section 19(1)(a) is satisfied. He construed the proviso as a
covenant by the tenant by way of a condition precedent which

> "operates on matter which is anterior to the coming into
> operation of the covenant against underletting or assigning
> without the previous consent of the landlords."

He continued

> "if it is put into operation and the landlords refuse the
> surrender, the tenant has not lost his right under the
> covenant against assigning or underletting without the
> landlords' previous consent; if the landlords accept the
> surrender, then the whole lease goes and the situation is no
> worse than, and no different from, what it would be if he
> had a covenant against assigning which was absolute."[30]

Status of proviso considered

The decision was followed by the High Court of Australia in
Creer v. *P. & O. Lines of Australia Pty. Ltd.*[31] where the
general status of a proviso was considered. It was argued that it
is something which "bears upon" what goes before. The
proviso therefore bears upon the earlier qualified covenant, as is
evidenced by the appearance in the qualified covenant in
question of the phrase "(subject as hereinafter provided)." Via
this reasoning it seems that the court was being invited to
construe the clause as a whole as if it stipulated that a refusal of
consent on the ground that the tenant had not offered a
surrender was not to be deemed unreasonable and this, being
indistinguishable from *Re Smith's Lease*, was invalid. This

---

[26] *Supra*, p. 35.
[27] The unfortunate bracketed phrase "(*subject as hereinafter provided*)" seems to
have been disregarded but has been commented on in subsequent cases see
infra.
[28] These have never been identified but subsequent decisions certainly support
his point, see *infra*.
[29] At p. 231.
[30] At p. 233.
[31] (1971) 45 A.L.J.R. 697 at p. 699.

argument met with considerable sympathy from Menzies J., who did doubt the correctness of the *Adler* construction, but he finally accepted that construction, because it was a *possible* construction, because both before and after that case, such clauses had been in common use and assumed to be effective and finally because "upon a matter of conveyancing, I consider conformity to be more important than originality,"[32] Barwick C.J. and Windeyer J. followed *Adler* more readily. In *Greene* v. *Church Commissioners for England*[33] the Court of Appeal questioned the *Adler* construction, Denning M.R. pointing out that "[n]o matter how the clause is wrapped up, it means that the landlord can always refuse his consent to an assignment if he thinks he can get a higher rent. . . . That may be considered to be unreasonable—no matter that it is concealed under the cloak of the proviso."[34] Sir Eric Sachs commented that it was rather odd that a landlord could not refuse consent on the ground that he wanted a surrender[35] or on the ground that the tenant had refused to pay a premium for a licence[36] yet "under the terms of the proviso, if valid, he may demand the surrender of the residue and thus obtain for himself the value of the premium (if any) . . . [37] These criticisms were *obiter*, the case having been decided on the basis that, even if valid, the proviso could not be enforced against an assignee of the tenant because it had not been protected by registration as a class C (vi) land charge under the Land Charges Act 1972. In 1979 the Court of Appeal considered the validity of a surrender clause directly in

Validity of a surrender clause

Bocardo S.A. v. *S. & M. Hotels Ltd.*[38] and, while admitting that the "distinction between the *Adler* formula and *Re Smith's Lease* formula is semantic" because the "practical result is the same"[39] refused to declare the former void. This was partly due to the very great respect accorded to the decision in *Creer* and to the realisation that the critical remarks in *Greene* had been made without the court having had the benefit of a citation of *Creer*. It was also based, to some extent, upon a reluctance to disturb the long standing expectations of conveyancers. More than anything however, the court did not wish to interfere with freedom of contract except where essential and as the policy of the 1927 Act did not require interference where the landlord and tenant had agreed that there shall be no right of assignment at all, there was no logical reason why it should require interference where the tenant was to have a right to assign limited by a condition precedent.[40] Lawton L.J. indicated that even Parliament had assumed that

---

[32] At p. 699.
[33] *Supra.*
[34] At p. 614.
[35] See *infra* Chap. 6; *Bates* v. *Donaldson* [1896] 2 Q.B. 241.
[36] See *infra* "Payments to the Lessor," at p. 45.
[37] At p. 616.
[38] [1979] 3 All E.R. 737.
[39] *Per* Megaw L.J. at p. 742.
[40] *Per* Megaw L.J. at pp. 742, 3; Browne L.J. at p. 746; it has been argued however that the policy of the 1927 Act in general was, by enabling the tenant to apply for a new lease, to secure for himself the goodwill in the premises which his efforts had created and the *Adler* clause cuts across this; (1972) L.Q.R. 31.

surrender clauses were valid in referring to them in section 127 of the Rent Act 1977. There would now appear to be no doubt about the validity of surrender clauses though they can operate very harshly in some circumstances.[41] Thus in *Greene* the result would have been that the tenant would lose the valuable chance of obtaining a reasonable price for tenants fittings—curtains and carpets—for which an assignee would pay but which would have to be removed on a surrender to the landlord. In *Cardshops Ltd.* v. *Davies*[42] the Court of Appeal refused to permit inclusion of a surrender proviso in a new lease under the Landlord & Tenant Act 1954, in substitution for the fully qualified covenant in the old lease, because it was "a harsh term when applied to business lettings in which considerations of the sale of goodwill may arise"—"it imperilled the whole existence of such goodwill as these tenants had built up."[43]

Provisos for surrender and business tenancies Section 38 Landlord & Tenant Act 1954
In the case of a business tenancy to which Part II of the Landlord and Tenant Act 1954 applies[44] however a surrender proviso, though valid, may be ineffective. This is because of the impact of section 38(1) of that Act which provides that "[a]ny agreement relating to a tenancy to which this Part of this Act applies ... shall be void ... in so far as it purports to preclude the tenant from making an application or request under this Part of this Act."[45] In *Allnatt Properties* v. *Newton*[46] a lease of business premises contained a typical surrender clause except that the landlord agreed thereunder to pay for the surrender "a sum representing the net premium value (if any) of the lease for the unexpired residue of the term." This still leaves a tenant worse off than he would be if he disposed of the lease to a third party because (i) a third party may well pay not only a premium but also an amount for goodwill[47] and (ii) the landlord's limited generosity in agreeing to pay the tenant something for any surrender may result in him being able to command a higher rent on a rent review than would otherwise

[41] Compare Hilbery J. in *Adler* "it is not particularly hard on him if he wishes to get rid of the term that he should afford the landlords the opportunity of accepting a surrender ... " at p. 231.

[42] [1971] 2 All E.R. 721.

[43] *Per* Widgery L.J. at p. 727 and Edmund Davies L.J. at p. 726; on striking a balance between the interests of the tenant in the goodwill he has built up and that of the landlord in any increase in the value of the property, whether resulting from inflation or a planning change, see J. R. King-Smith, "*Restrictions upon Alienation and Use of Leasehold Property—Good Estate Management or Unfair Practice?* The Blundell Memorial Lectures 1977.

[44] *vis.* where the property comprised in the tenancy is or includes premises which are occupied by the tenant and are so occupied for the purposes of a business carried on by him or for those and other puposes: s.23(1); on ceasing to occupy see *Morrison Holdings Ltd.* v. *Manders Property Ltd.* [1976] 2 All E.R. 205.

[45] "Or provides for the termination or the surrender of the tenancy in the event of his making such an application or request or for the imposition of any penalty or disability on the tenant in that event" see *Encyclopaedia of Forms & Precedents* (5th ed.), Vol. 22, 55.4, n. 2 for a short and very tentative exploration of methods of rendering surrender agreements enforceable.

[46] [1981] 2 All E.R. 290.

[47] See though *Encyclopaedia of Forms and Precedents* (5th Ed.,) Vol. 22, 55.5 where the possibility of providing that the landlord should pay an amount equal to that which would have been received from an assignee on the open market, is examined.

be the case. In *Allnatt* the tenant made the required offer of surrender which the landlord accepted. The tenant later tried to withdraw his offer when it became apparent that the landlord would be paying just £10,000 instead of the £45,000 which could be commanded from a third party purchaser. The landlord sought specific performance of the agreement but the tenant claimed a declaration that it was void under section 38(1) because, if it went through, he would be prevented from applying for a new tenancy when the existing one would have expired. Clearly this was the case, but section 38 only applies to agreements which "purport to preclude" the tenant from making such an application and if that were construed to mean that the agreement must *profess in terms* to preclude a tenant's application, it did not do so. Sir Robert Megarry V-C following *Joseph* v. *Joseph*[48] held that the phrase included not only "an agreement which in terms prevents the tenant from making an application or request" but also to one which "in fact operates to prevent the tenant from doing this."[49] The agreement was therefore declared void and the landlord could not have specific performance.[50] It was, however, only the *agreement*—the accepted offer—which was void. The proviso for surrender before assignment did not offend section 38. It did require the tenant to offer a surrender

Distinguish the proviso and the agreement

> "but an offer to surrender is not an agreement, nor does an agreement to make an offer to surrender, by itself, preclude the tenant from making an application or request . . . until it be known whether the landlords have accepted or rejected the offer to surrender, it cannot be known whether there is any agreement which will preclude an application or request within the meaning of the subsection: there may or may not be."[51]

Tenant must offer surrender

As the proviso for surrender escaped the section, the court refused the tenant a declaration that, for the future, he could apply for consent (not to be unreasonably withheld) without first offering a surrender. The position of the tenant is, therefore, that he must offer a surrender. If the landlord refuses or does not accept within 21 days, the tenant can proceed as with an ordinary fully qualified covenant. If however the landlord accepts the surrender, while *he* cannot enforce the resultant agreement, the tenant cannot claim the benefit of the fully qualified covenant; his restricted right to assign under that covenant is expressed to be conditional upon the landlord having refused the offer or having failed to accept it within 21 days and of course the landlord has accepted it, albeit that he has failed to accept effectively. It is as if the

---

[48] [1966] 3 All E.R. 486.
[49] At p. 294.
[50] See also [1984] 1 All E.R. 423, C.A. (Appeal Dismissed); the only way therefore to ensure that a surrender proviso will be enforceable in relation to a business tenancy, is to seek the approval of the court under s.38(4).
[51] At p. 295.

tenant had entered an absolute covenant.[52] Thus "although the decision in *Allnatt* appears to give the tenant of business premises greater protection than the *Adler* and *Bocardo* cases give to tenants of residential premises, ... in reality this is not so."[53] Where the offer to surrender is not accepted, they are similarly placed. Where it is accepted, in the case of residential property the tenant has to surrender; in the case of business premises, he does not have to surrender but he has no right to assign to a third party.

In conclusion, it can be seen from the above, that the use of a condition precedent to the right to assign as a drafting device to avoid the operation of section 19(1)(a) is a success.[54] There is therefore scope to extend its use to cover other types of demands made by landlords, demands which if expressed as reasons for refusal would remain unsatisfied because they may be found to be unreasonable.[55]

Provisions stating that the landlord's consent is not to be unreasonably withheld in the case of a respectable and responsible person have been discussed above, and it has been submitted that they amount to an "express provision to the contrary" and are therefore ineffective. However a clause in identical terms but omitting the word "unreasonably" is treated quite differently. From the tenant's point of view it confers, and confers effectively, a very desirable degree of protection

Moat v. Martin clauses

exceeding that which flows from the statutory proviso. In *Moat v. Martin*[56] the Court of Appeal refused to countenance the argument that such an express clause was ousted by the statutory proviso. In that case the tenant covenanted "not to assign ... without the consent ... of the landlord *such consent will not be withheld in the case of a respectable and responsible person.*" The tenant sought permission to assign to a respectable and responsible person and the landlord refused to give it arguing that the statutory proviso had to be substituted for the express words thus allowing him to withhold his consent, if he had reasonable grounds for doing so, *even* to a respectable and responsible person. Evershed M.R. noted that the purpose of the section was to relieve tenants and that it would therefore be surprising to find that it cut down their rights.[57] Denning L.J. pointed out that the section only negatived provisions "to the contrary" of the provision implied by statute. The provision in this case was not to the contrary of a provision that consent is not to be unreasonably withheld because "[i]t supports it and goes beyond it."[58] Therefore the tenant was free to assign to a

---

[52] See Blake, (1983) 47 Conv. 158; who also suggests that the surrender proviso could be modified, in the tenants interests, by expressing *non-completion of a surrender* to amount to a refusal; and see, *e.g. Encyclopaedia of Forms and Precedents* (5th Ed.), Vol. 22, Form 75 where the tenant's freedom to assign under the qualified covenant arises upon the landlord failing to accept and subsequently being able and willing to complete the surrender.

[53] Sheldon & Friend (1982) 98 L.Q.R. 14, 16.

[54] Subject to what has been said about business tenancies.

[55] See also Conditional Consents, *infra* Chapter 6, p. 115.

[56] [1950] 1 K.B. 175.

[57] At p. 179.

[58] At p. 181.

respectable and responsible person notwithstanding that the landlord might have reasonable objections. The precise manner in which a *Moat* v. *Martin* clause operates in relation to the statutory proviso, would appear to be uncertain. Perhaps the court considered that there was no need for the implication of the statutory proviso in these circumstances, and therefore one is left simply with the express words of the clause.[59] This is rather unsatisfactory. It would mean that in the case of an assignment to someone other than a respectable and responsible person, the landlord could refuse his consent upon any ground he liked, reasonable or not. As mentioned above, the purpose of the section is to prevent the landlord unreasonably withholding his consent in all cases, even in those involving possibly questionable assignees. Furthermore the opening words of the clause clearly classify it as a covenant not to assign without consent; it is therefore within the terms of section 19 and subject to the statutory implication that consent shall not be unreasonably withheld. The clause should therefore be construed as a covenant not to assign without consent, such consent not, in any case, to be unreasonably withheld and in the case of a respectable and responsible person, not to be withheld at all. Thus in any case, even that of a disreputable person, the refusal must be reasonable—and in the nature of things it usually will be. In the case of a respectable and responsible person it is not enough that the refusal is reasonable—there must be no refusal at all. This would appear to be the construction put upon a similar clause in *Cowan* v. *Beaumont Property Trusts Re Cooper's Lease*[60] "not to assign the said premises or any part thereof without the previous consent in writing of the lessor but so that such consent shall not be withheld to an assignment ... of the said premises to a respectable and responsible person." The respectable and responsible person phrase was applicable only to dealings with the whole, as no reference was made to part in the second section of the clause. Cross J. stated that

> "if the dealing in question is to be an assignment or underlease of the whole of the premises, then whether one is acting reasonably or unreasonably does not matter. You can assign or underlet the whole premises provided only that the man who is put forward is respectable and responsible. If on the other hand you are contemplating only granting an assignment or underletting part of them ... then the landlords can refuse consent provided that they are reasonable in doing so."

He thus implies that the requirement of reasonableness is to be imported into the first part of the covenant. Even so understood, there remains the question of whether the resultant clause is to be construed as a *single* covenant by the tenant which creates a limited obligation not to assign, an obligation which is inapplicable should the landlord withhold his consent

---

[59] This would seem to be the view of Evershed M.R.
[60] (1968) 19 P. & C.R. 541.

unreasonably or, in the case of a respectable and responsible person, at all or whether there are *two* covenants—one by the tenant, which creates a limited obligation, not to assign without consent, an obligation inapplicable if the landlord unreasonably withholds his consent and one by the landlord not to withhold consent to a respectable and responsible person.[61] In the latter case the tenant's freedom derives from the fact that the restriction upon assignment does not apply where the landlord is being unreasonable and he would be acting unreasonably if the refusal of consent by him was a breach of the express covenant he had entered into with regard to respectable and responsible persons.[62]

Definition of a respectable and responsible person

Whether the assignee is such a person will be a question of fact. "Responsible" refers to financial capacity[63] in the sense of being able to discharge all obligations in relation to rent and covenants under the lease.[64] "Respectable" refers to the general reputation of the person in relation to behaviour "primarily in carrying on his business but probably also in the carrying on of the whole of his external relations."[65] A limited company is a "person" for these purposes, albeit legal rather than natural, and it can, if it has the necessary attributes, come within the phrase under discussion. In *Willmott* v. *London Road Car Co.*[66] the suggestion that while a company could be responsible it could not be respectable, because the latter was an attribute to which only a natural person could aspire, was rejected.[67] When deciding whether a company is responsible, the court will take a broad view. In *Re Greater London's Property Ltd.'s Lease*[68] the lessor required a guarantee from the holding company of the proposed assignee because the latter's accounts showed that it had borrowed a large sum repayable on demand. Danckwerts J. pointed out that:

(1) the lender was in fact the holding company which, on the facts, was not likely to call in the loan

(2) if it did, the proposed assignee could realise its fixed assets to discharge it

(3) the proposed assignee was currently trading at a profit and this was likely to continue and

(4) the relationship between the holding company and the subsidiary company was to be regarded as a source of

---

[61] Evershed M.R. in *Moat* v. *Martin* considered both possibilities.

[62] It may also be noted that where a *Moat* v. *Martin* clause is used, the consent of the landlord has been held to have been withheld where he had failed to consider the tenant's request within a reasonable time. *Lewis, Allenby (1909) Ltd.* v. *Pegge*; See also the Landlord & Tenant Act 1988, *infra* Chapter 5.

[63] See Farwell L.J. in *Willmott* v. *London Road and Car Co.* [1910] 2 Ch. 525 at p. 537.

[64] *Per* Cozens-Hardy L.J. *ibid.* at p. 531.

[65] *Ibid. per* Fletcher-Moulton L.J. at p. 535.

[66] *Ibid.*

[67] There are, of course, limits upon the extent to which a company can be equated with a natural person—see, *e.g. Jenkins* v. *Price* [1908] 1 Ch. 10 where a company could not bring itself within a covenant to "at all times reside upon the premises" and the Court of Appeal held that the lessor had therefore been reasonable in refusing consent because the covenant was in effect one not to assign to a limited company.

[68] [1959] 1 W.L.R. 503.

strength, not weakness, to the subsidiary. He considered the lessor's anxieties worthy of "a pedantic chartered accountant" and opined that "figures must not be treated as a theoretical exercise without any reference to the probable facts." It was held that the lessor had unreasonably withheld his consent.

Absolute covenants   Section 19(1)(a) does not, on its face, apply to absolute covenants.[69] However in *Property & Bloodstock Ltd.* v. *Emerton*,[70] Danckwerts L.J. rather cryptically reserved his opinion upon the matter. Others have been more forthcoming. In *Bocardo S.A.* v. *S.M. Hotels Ltd.*[71] Megaw L.J. found it "hard to see how the words of section 19(1) . . . could fairly be construed as applying to leases which contain a simple covenant against assignment with no reference whatever to 'without licence or consent.'"[72] He was of the opinion that the parties remained free to agree to forbid assignment altogether. Exactly the same point arises in relation to section 19(2) (covenants against making improvements [see Chapter 8]) and was considered in *F.W. Woolworth Ltd.* v. *Lambert*.[73] It was there argued that every covenant not to make improvements, etc., was a covenant not to do so without the landlord's consent because every such covenant can be released by the landlord if he so thinks fit. Both absolute and qualified covenants therefore came within the terms of the section. Romer L.J. rejected this line of reasoning on the basis that the difference between absolute and qualified covenants was well known when the Act was passed and had both sorts been intended to be covered by the section, the words "without licence or consent" would have been omitted. To hold on the present wording that the section covered both sorts "would be to disregard the words 'without licence or consent.' If every covenant not to make improvements and every covenant not to assign and every covenant against alteration of use of the demised premises is to be deemed to be a covenant not to make improvements or not assign or not to make alterations of user, as the case may be, without the licence or consent of the landlord, then the words 'without licence or consent' in the sub-section would be otiose and useless."[74]

Building leases   Where the qualified covenant is contained in a building lease, described in section 19(1)(b) as a lease for more than 40 years made in consideration wholly or partially of the erection or substantial improvement, addition or alteration of any buildings where the lessor is not a government department or local or public authority, or a statutory or public utility company, the covenant, etc., is subject not only to the proviso that consent is not to be unreasonably withheld but also to the further proviso that "in the case of any assignment, under-letting, charging or parting with the possession (whether by the

---

[69] See *supra*.
[70] [1967] 3 All E.R. 321.
[71] [1979] 3 All E.R. 737.
[72] At p. 741.
[73] [1937] 1 Ch. 37.
[74] At pp. 58, 59.

holders of the lease or any undertenant whether immediate or not) effected more than seven years before the end of the term no consent or licence shall be required, if notice in writing of the transaction is given to the lessor within six months after the transaction is effected". The liberty which this provision confers is not total; while the requirement in the lease for consent can be disregarded, other requirements may still have to be fulfilled. In *Vaux Group plc.* v. *Lilley*[74a] the tenant had covenanted, if the landlord so required, to obtain an acceptable guarantor for the assignee and direct covenants by him. Knox J held that these obligations were not struck down by section 19(1)(*b*): a statute must not be construed as interfering with freedom of contract any more than its terms require. The Law Commission have recommended the repeal of section 19(1)(*b*) should their major recommendation, which would ensure that tenants were never subject to disposition covenants stricter than a fully qualified one, be enacted.[75] They point out that if this is the case the tenant is adequately protected and in fact tenants who would otherwise have fallen within the section 19(1)(*b*) concession can often refuse to accept a lease containing any restriction on powers of disposition.[76]

Types of disposition affected

The implication under section 19(1)(*a*) is applicable to the types of alienation referred to—presumably whether or not the precise words of the provision are used in the covenant.[77] If the covenant encompasses other types of alienation, for example sharing occupation or possession,[78] declaring a trust in favour of a third party,[79] doing or putting away with the demised premises[80] these would not be affected by the implication.

Payments to the lessor

Lessor's expenses in relation to consent

The implication under section 19(1)(*a*) does not preclude the landlord from requiring a reasonable sum "in respect of any legal or other expenses incurred in connection with such licence or consent"[81]; where such expenses are paid by a lessee in relation to a licence to underlet, the lessee can only pass that cost on to the underlessee if there is agreement in writing to that effect.[82] There is no similar provision for expenses in

In relation to section 19(1)(*b*) notices

relation to the implication, under section 19(1)(*b*), in connection with long building leases, that the tenant does not have to get consent so long as notice in writing is given in accordance with the section. The landlord's costs in receiving

---

[74a] [1990] EGCS 102.
[75] See Law Commission No. 141, paras. 7.4–7.6.
[76] Law Commission No.141, paras. 7.73–7.78.
[77] Equivalent words and phrases are considered in Chap. 2.
[78] *Supra* p. 19.
[79] *Supra* p. 9.
[80] *Supra* p. 24.
[81] In fact the landlord's solicitor may request an undertaking from the tenant's solicitor to pay the landlord's costs whether or not the matter proceeds. This is not considered to be improper. See 1984 Vol. 81 L.S.G. 3556.
[82] See ss.1 & 2 Costs of Leases Act 1958.

and registering section 19(1)(b) notices would appear to be irrecoverable although where a lease expressly provides for registration of assignments, it is very often stipulated that such costs be paid.[83]

Fines unreasonable

Should the landlord require payment over and above his expenses for giving his consent, this would almost certainly amount to an unreasonable refusal of consent on his part entitling the tenant to assign without consent. If it was *reasonable* for the landlord to turn the power to refuse consent into a "source of profit"[84] there would have been no need for section 19(1)(a) to expressly preserve his right to claim expenses. That section 19(1)(a) precludes the landlord from demanding payment beyond his expenses, is commonly accepted but it is possible to construe it otherwise. It may endorse as reasonable a demand for a reasonable sum in respect of expenses etc. *without* condemning out of hand demands in excess of that sum. Where a demand exceeds the landlord's expenses whether it is reasonable is a question of fact and one important consideration would be the terms of the lease—the parties may have agreed that a fine be payable in which case the demand would be in accordance with the landlord's covenanted rights and therefore perhaps reasonable.[85] If this was the correct view, then it would be possible to make express provision for the payment of a fine in the lease, under section 19(1)(a), just as it is under section 144 of the Law of Property Act which more explicitly prohibits fines.

Section 144 Law of Property Act 1925

The relationship between section 19(1)(a) and section 144 of the Law of Property Act 1925 is not considered to be a very happy one.[86] Section 144 pre-dates section 19(1)(a), and like it, applies to covenants not to assign etc. without consent. Neither applies to absolute covenants, in respect of which, therefore, the lessor is free to require a fine. The effect of section 144 is limited to incorporating into the lease, *unless there is express provision to the contrary*, a proviso to the effect "that no fine or sum of money in the nature of a fine shall be payable for or in respect of such licence or consent; but this proviso does not preclude the right to require payment of a reasonable sum in respect of any legal or other expense incurred in relation to such licence or consent." It is not easy to perceive what additional protection this offers to the tenant. Indeed in most cases it offers less. There is no doubt, here, that the parties can contract out of its effect. Even if there has been no contracting out, unlike section 19, it would seem only to concern itself with covenants against disposing of the whole, the implication against fines being, therefore, apparently inapplicable in

---

[83] See, *e.g. Encyclopaedia of Forms and Precedents*, (4th Ed.) Vol. 11, p. 315, 2: 26; and (5th Ed.) Vol. 22, p. 288, 5.9: 10.

[84] *Per* Fletcher Moulton L.J. in *Waite* v. *Jennings* [1906] 2 K.B. 11 at p. 17.

[85] Compare *Bromley Park Garden Estates Ltd.* v. *Moss* [1982] 2 All E.R. 890; see also Chapter 8 where a similar view is explored in relation to alteration covenants; note also Law Commission No. 141, para. 3.16 where the prospect of such an interpretation being placed upon s.19(1)(a) was viewed with some dismay.

[86] A close analysis of these two sections may be found in Law Commission No. 141, 3.8. *et seq.*

relation to dispositions of part.[87] This conclusion has been reached because the section does not refer to covenants restricting dispositions of the whole "*or any part*" and upon the authority of *Grove* v. *Portal*[88] and *Wilson* v. *Rosenthal*[89] which hold respectively that a covenant against assigning or underletting does not extend to assigning or subletting part only.[90] These decisions are of course a product of the strict rule of construction against the landlord which the courts have employed when considering covenants which restrain the tenant in the exercise of his common law right of free alienation.[91] It does not follow that the same strict view should be taken of the same words when they appear in a statutory provision intended to benefit tenants and where the result would be to the tenant's disadvantage. Where it applies, section 144 does explicitly preclude the landlord from demanding a fine, a matter to which section 19 does not refer save by way of powerful implication, but it has been doubted whether in the generality of cases

Agricultural tenancies

section 144 serves any useful purpose; its only relevance being in relation to leases of agricultural holdings which by section 19(4) are excluded from the operation of section 19. Here, if its provisions have not been expressly excluded, it would seem to · afford agricultural tenants some protection against demands for a fine.[92]

Fines irrecoverable

If, despite these provisions, a tenant pays a fine, he will have difficulty in recovering it. Even the more explicit section 144 does not make the request for a fine illegal and in the absence of fraud, duress or undue influence the tenant could not recover it.[93] In *Andrew* v. *Bridgman*[94] the lessor requested a fine of £45 in relation to a licence to assign and the lessee paid it after having drawn the lessor's attention to the statutory proviso. It was found as a fact that she had not paid under protest and she could not recover it. The Act did not make the payment illegal but the demand, being contrary to the tenant's rights under the lease as modified by the statute, "relieves the lessee from the necessity of obtaining the lessor's consent, and enables [her] to ignore the restriction on assignment contained in the lease."[95] If the tenant has entered any arrangement

---

[87] See Law Commission 141, para. 3.9.

[88] [1902] 1 Ch. 727.

[89] [1906] 22 T.L.R. 238.

[90] See *supra* Chap. 2.

[91] See *supra* Chap. 2.

[92] Assuming the covenant was not absolute, in which case s.144 will not apply; even if it was qualified, in the absence of an express fully qualifying phrase, the lessor could effectively get a fine—by refusing his consent, even on an unreasonable ground, and insisting that the tenant surrenders his lease in return for a new one which will be granted at a premium and will permit the disposition. Law Commission No. 141, para. 3.9.

[93] *Per* Stirling L.J. in *Waite* v. *Jennings* [1906] 2 K.B. 11 at p. 16 with whose opinion the other members of the Court of Appeal agreed; there was disagreement over whether the section, then s.3 of the Conveyancing Act 1892, included benefits in the nature of a fine—the case concerned a request that the proposed assignee enter into direct covenants with the landlord (the majority considered that it did not).

[94] [1908] 1 K.B. 596.

[95] *Per* Cozens Hardy M.R. at p. 599; The Law Commission recommend that the tenant should be able to recover, *ibid.* paras. 8.26–8.27.

which involves payment of a fine, he can withdraw. In *Comber* v. *Fleet Electronics Ltd.*[96] a tenant agreed, in return for a licence to assign and change the use, to assign to the landlord certain local authority compensation rights. The landlord granted the licence but the tenant refused to assign the compensation rights. Vaisey J. refused to enforce the tenant's undertaking on the ground that the legislation[97] was passed to protect the tenant and therefore it was "the landlord who had to suffer."[98]

Consent must be sought

Whatever the nature of the disposition covenant, consent must be sought. This is obviously so in relation to absolute covenants and in relation to the few qualified disposition covenants which survive the operation of section 19(1)(a) of the Landlord and Tenant Act 1927. In the case of a fully qualified covenant it could be argued, though not successfully, that as the landlord could not have reasonably withheld consent, there was no need to seek it. However under a fully qualified covenant, the tenant is only free to assign, etc., without consent where the landlord has been unreasonable in withholding it and it cannot be maintained that he has withheld it at all if it has not even been sought. In *Barrow* v. *Isaacs & Son*[99] the landlord was entitled to re-enter because consent had not been sought despite the fact that no objection could reasonably have been made by him to the proposed sub-tenant. This case was approved in *Eastern Telegraph Co. Ltd.* v. *Dent*[1] Kay L.J. explaining that he could not bring himself to say that "a judge could run his pen through part of that contract, which is that consent should be asked for, and render it of no effect"[2] and Romer L.J. relying upon the fact that the proviso—such consent not to be unreasonably withheld—"has no application in this case, for it cannot be said that the lessors unreasonably withheld their consent . . . because no consent was asked for."[3] Some covenants restrict disposition without the "previous" consent of the landlord or without the consent of the landlord "first had and received" but such additions add nothing to the sense of the covenant which already requires that a request for consent should precede the disposition. The fact that a disposition has been the subject of negotiations between the parties will not necessarily be construed as a request for consent. In *Creery* v. *Summersell & Flowerdew & Co. Ltd.*[4] the underlease had been

---

[96] [1955] 2 All E.R. 161.
[97] Referring to s.144 of the Law of Property Act and s.19(1)(a) of the Landlord and Tenant Act 1927.
[98] At p. 165.
[99] [1891] 1 Q.B. 417.
[1] [1899] 1 Q.B. 835.
[2] At p. 838.
[3] At p. 839. *Hyde* v. *Warden* (3 Ex.D. 72) in so far as it suggests otherwise, was disapproved. In *Burford* v. *Unwin* (1885) (Cab & El 494) Huddleston B. regarded himself as bound by *Hyde* but expressed an opinion adverse to it.
[4] [1949] Ch. 751.

discussed by the parties but the tenant had never expressly sought consent and the written indication of the lessor that he would be satisfied with a bankers reference was held not to amount to a consent.[5] In relation to such pre-disposition negotiations care must also be taken to seek consent to a disposition to the correct person. In *David Blackstone Ltd.* v. *Burnetts (West End) Ltd.*[6] the defendants thought that the sublease was to be granted to two individuals acting as a firm and sought consent on this basis. In the event it was granted to a limited company connected to these individuals, the rent being guaranteed by one of them. It was presumed that the consent to the individuals would not cover the sublease to the company and that the defendants were therefore in breach of covenant.

The request

Writing

Disclosures

The request for consent should be in writing; under the Landlord & Tenant Act 1988, section 1(3), the service of a *written* application for consent gives rise to duties on the part of the landlord, breach of which may entitle the tenant to damages.[7] It should be accompanied by the information necessary to enable the landlord to make his decision. He will not be deemed to have unreasonably withheld his consent if he was not supplied with the means to make it. Thus, in *Isow's Restaurant Ltd.* v. *Greenham*,[8] where the tenant brought an action for a declaration, having refused to supply the landlord with the further information which he sought, it was held that as the landlord's enquiries were reasonable, consent had been reasonably withheld. However in *City Hotels Group Ltd.* v. *Total Property Investments Ltd.*[9] the landlord, having been supplied with full information, sought, at a late date, even more and it was held that consent had been unreasonably withheld. What information the tenant has to supply depends on the facts of the case but would include details of the disponee, evidence of his financial status, character references, the true[10] nature of the proposed transaction (including in the case of a sub-letting, its terms),[11] the extent of the property affected and the proposed user. In *Re Sparkes Lease*[12] the landlord, who had taken a covenant which restricted the uses to

---

[5] At p. 760.
[6] [1973] 3 All E.R. 782.
[7] See *infra*, Chapter 5.
[8] (1969) 213 E.G. 505.
[9] (1985) 1 E.G.L.R. 253.
[10] See, *e.g. F. W. Woolworth plc* v. *Charlwood Alliance Properties Ltd.* (1987) 282 E.G.L.R. 585, 590.
[11] Even if, though the landlord's consent is needed, he has covenanted not to withhold his consent if that of the superior landlord was forthcoming: *Fullers Theatre & Vaudeville Co.* v. *Rofe* [1923] A.C. 440. Here the covenant was construed as binding the landlord not to object *in principle* leaving him still able to object to the terms of the sub-letting in so far as they may allow the sub-tenant to do something inconsistent with the landlord's own lease and put him at risk of forfeiture.
[12] [1905] 1 Ch. 456.

which the tenant could put the property and who occupied part
of the premises himself, refused his consent to a sub-lease *inter
alia* unless he was told the purpose for which the proposed
subtenant would use the property and his refusal of consent
was found to be reasonable. Even if there is no restraint on
user in the lease, the landlord can sometimes refuse consent on
the basis of user[13] and is therefore entitled to know what it is
to be. If the tenant has provided adequate information, it is
then up to the landlord, if he requires more, to make his own
enquiries or to ask the tenant for further information.[14] If he
fails to do this, he cannot later justify a refusal simply on the
basis that he would have liked more information. Where a
landlord considers that he has enough information to justify a
refusal, he may do so safe in the knowledge that the
reasonableness of that refusal will be judged on the basis of the
information he then had.[15] It must be appreciated however that
the relevance of this proposition is limited to cases where the
landlord has come by further information, favourable to the
proposed disposition, in circumstances where it was
unaccompanied by a renewed request, express or implied, for
consent. Where there has been an initial refusal and the tenant
has come back with further information, the initial request for
consent has very sensibly, been construed as continuing,
demanding that the landlord enter into a fresh consideration on
the basis of the current information. As Eve J. pointed out in
Ideal Film Renting Co. v. *Neilson*[16]

> "I have to consider the ... knowledge of the lessor at the
> date when the request was made, but in this connection it
> must not be overlooked that the request was a continuing
> one, down to the commencement of the action and that a
> good deal happened between [the initial request] and when
> the writ was issued."[17]

Information acquired after consent If, on the other hand, the landlord has given his consent, on
the basis of available information, it is not necessarily open to
him, later, to revoke it when factors come to light which would
have entitled him to withhold it. In *Mitten* v. *Fagg*[18] the
landlord had given his consent to the assignment of a lease
relating to a restaurant; after the tenant had contracted to
assign but before he had actually done so, the landlord read in
the newspaper that the proposed assignee had been convicted
on numerous counts under the Food Hygiene Regulations
1970. The landlord could not revoke the consent; the tenant
had had no knowledge of the offences, indeed it was the

---

[13] See, *e.g. Bridewell Hospital Governors* v. *Fawkner* [1892] 8 T.L.R. 637. *Bates*
v. *Donaldson* [1896] 2 Q.B. 241, C.A. *per* Kay L.J. at p. 244; and *infra*
Chapter 6, at p. 79.
[14] *Mitten* v. *Fagg* (1978) 247 E.G. 901.
[15] *British Bakeries (Midlands) Ltd.* v. *Michael Testler & Co. Ltd.* [1986]
E.G.L.R. 64.
[16] [1921] 1 Ch. 575 at p. 582.
[17] Compare *Woodfall, Landlord and Tenant*, Vol. 1, where it is suggested (at
para. 1.1180) that information possessed by the landlord up to the date of
hearing should also be of relevance.
[18] *Ibid.*

landlord who informed him of them, and had changed his position on the basis of the consent. Goulding J. expressly left open what the position would have been, had the landlord made the discovery before the tenant had changed his position.

Sufficient time

The landlord must also be given sufficient time to digest the information if it is later going to be asserted that he has withheld his consent unreasonably. In *Goldstein* v. *Sanders*[19] the sublessor was held to have reasonably withheld his consent to an assignment on discovering that the premises were in a state of serious disrepair necessitating an investigation of the legal position in relation to himself, the assignor and the head-landlord. However the circumstances may require the landlord to respond with despatch: "if too long a time is allowed, the object of the request would be defeated because these are matters in which if a man cannot get the premises quickly, he may go elsewhere."[20]

The licence

Written

Where a written licence is required, a parol licence will not suffice because "a person who stipulates for a written licence . . . wisely stipulates for evidence in writing of his consent . . . in order that the contest which often arises where there is only parol evidence can be avoided; the writing is to be an end to all strife between the parties."[21] If there has been an oral consent, the court may be willing to grant relief against forfeiture. In relation to a breach occurring before 1926, this was possible if there had been fraud, as where the parol licence had been used as a snare.[22] The court's jurisdiction to grant relief in relation to breaches occurring after 1925 was extended in section 146 of the Law of Property Act.[23] It is also possible that the landlord has waived the requirement for writing[24] in which case forfeiture would not arise. Where willingness to consent is conveyed in writing with an indication that a formal licence is to be prepared, the court will not necessarily construe the initial consent as being "subject to contract." In *Bader Properties Ltd.* v. *Linley Property Investments Ltd.*[25] the lessor wrote saying that he was willing to consent to an underlease and would forward the licence in due course if in the meantime the tenant would confirm that he would be responsible for the

Conditional licences

costs. On the basis of this the tenant made the underlease. Forfeiture proceedings were subsequently brought against him—unsuccessfully because "the language used was clear and unequivocal and the defendants were then free to go ahead on the basis that what would follow would be no more than a

[19] [1915] 1 Ch. 549; see *infra* Chapter 6, p. 000.
[20] *Per* Neville J. in *Lewis & Allenby (1909) Ltd.* v. *Pegge* [1914] 1 Ch. 785 (proposed residential letting); see also s.1(3) of the Landlord and Tenant Act 1988, *supra*, Chapter 5.
[21] *Per* Fry L.J. in *Willmott* v. *Barber* (1880) 15 Ch.D. 96, 105.
[22] See *Richardson* v. *Evans* (1818) 3 Mad. 218; *Willmot* v. *Barber, ibid.*
[23] See *infra.*
[24] *Millard* v. *Humphreys* (1918) 62 S.J. 505.
[25] (1968) 19 P. & C.R. 620.

formality."[26] On the other hand, in *Venetian Glass Gallery Ltd.* v. *Next Properties Ltd*[26a] the correspondence between the parties was initiated and continued 'subject to contract' and a written statement that the lessors were prepared in principle to consent was held not to amount to a consent. However the engrossment and sealing of the formal licence by the lessors was held to be a delivery in escrow and thus became a valid consent upon the tenant complying with the conditions of the escrow—delivery of the counterpart and payment of the rent deposit. In *West* v. *Dobb*[27] the landlord consented to W going into possession of the premises at once but made it clear in his letter that he expected a formal assignment to be drawn up in due course. The tenant allowed W into possession but made no formal assignment to him. It was held that there had been no breach of the covenant not to part with possession because it was too technical to say the consent was conditional upon a formal assignment being executed. The letter of consent in this case was loosely phrased and more technical wording would undoubtedly give rise to a more technical construction.[28]

No general waiver

It is now clear that a licence only sanctions the particular transaction and does not operate as a waiver of the covenant for the future.[29]

Forfeiture and relief

Where a breach of covenant has been occasioned by a failure to seek consent in circumstances where the landlord could not reasonably have withheld his consent, it may be thought that Equity would readily grant relief against forfeiture but this is not so. In *Barrow* v. *Isaacs & Sons*[30] it was admitted that Equity could relieve against fraud, accident or mistake but "mere forgetfulness" was regarded as a state of mind distinct from being mistaken[31] and reluctantly the court refused to grant relief despite the fact that the landlord "has no valid ground of objection; that he never would have objected; that no reasonable man could have objected; and that if he had been asked and had objected, his objection would have been wholly unreasonable ... more than that the omission to ask his leave under those circumstances has not had any possible effect whatever upon his rights or upon what he would have done or upon what he would not have done."[32] Kay L.J. drew attention to the danger of granting relief in cases of

Equity

Refusal to grant relief

---

[26] Roskill J. at p. 638; see also *Rutter* v. *Michael John* (1967) 201 E.G. 299.
[26a] [1989] 30 E.G. 92.
[27] (1870) 5 L.R. Q.B. 460.
[28] See, *e.g. The Encyclopaedia of Forms & Precedents* (5th Ed.) Vol. 22. Form 142, which makes it clear that the licence does not authorise an assignee to go into possession prior to the execution of the assignment.
[29] See s.143(1)(*a*) and (2) of the Law of Property Act 1925, previously s.1 of the Law of Property (Amendment) Act 1859 which negatived the common law rule in *Dumpor's Case* (1603) 4 Co. Rep. 1196 that covenants were not severable. See also *Halsbury's Statutes* (4th Ed.) Vol. 37, p. 27.
[30] [1891] 1 Q.B. 417.
[31] *Per* Esher M.R. at p. 420.
[32] At p. 419.

forgetfulness: "It is impossible not to see that such relief would be an incentive to negligence. If we were to grant it, hereafter lessees might avoid looking at their leases lest they should be reminded by them of obligations which it would be more convenient to forget."[33] Similarly and equally reluctantly in *Eastern Telegraph Co. Ltd.* v. *Dent*[34] no relief was granted where the omission to seek consent was "due to thoughtlessness or because he thought the breach unimportant." The sublease was to a person who already held a part of the premises on a direct lease from the landlord and the sublease was immediately cancelled when the landlord pointed out the need for consent. Prior to 1926 the court *could* only rely upon the equitable jurisdiction to grant relief in relation to breaches of alienation covenants and this, as has been shown above, does not extend to forgetfulness. The Conveyancing Act 1881 extended the jurisdiction to grant relief in relation to certain types of breach of covenant but not in relation to breaches of alienation covenants.[35] This deficiency was remedied in relation to breaches of such covenants occurring on or after January 1, 1926[36]; section 146 of the Law of Property Act 1925 enables the court to grant relief as it thinks fit "having regard to the proceedings and conduct of the parties [under section 146(1)] and to all other circumstances."[37] This new jurisdiction was recognised and exercised in *House Properties Investments Ltd.* v. *James Walker Ltd.*[38] where Lord Goddard C.J. noted that as a result of section 146 of the Law of Property Act, the court now had additional jurisdiction in these cases and he granted relief to a tenant who had underlet without asking for the landlord's consent. The facts were, admittedly, a little unusual in that the proposed sub-tenant, a government department, had requisitioned the premises and the landlord had acted "in a thoroughly unreasonable manner."[39] In *Creery* v. *Summersell & Flowerdew & Co. Ltd.*[40] Harman J. accepted that as a result of section 146 and the previous case he had the jurisdiction to grant relief but he was of the opinion that it should be sparingly exercised because granting relief to the subtenant, who was asking for the term to be vested in him, "would thrust upon the landlord a person whom he has never accepted as tenant." Furthermore in this particular case, in contrast to the other cases mentioned above, the landlord *could* have reasonably refused his consent and the case for relief was not therefore so compelling. Relief was granted, however, in *Scala House Ltd.* v. *Forbes*[41] where the tenant's

Relief can be granted

---

[33] At p. 429.
[34] *Supra* [1899] 1 Q.B. 835.
[35] See *Jackson* v. *Simon* [1923] 1 Ch. 373, 381.
[36] s.146(8).
[37] Under s.146(1) notice of the proceedings should be served on the "lessee", who in an assignment case, will be the assignee, and as breaches of alienation covenants are incapable of remedy (see *infra*) there is no need for the notice to call upon the lessee to remedy the breach; *Scala House Ltd.* v. *Forbes* [1973] 3 W.L.R. 14.
[38] [1948] 1 K.B. 257.
[39] At p. 261.
[40] *Supra* [1949] Ch. 751.
[41] [1973] 3 W.L.R. 14.

solicitor having been asked to prepare a management agreement
in respect of a restaurant in fact produced a document which
rendered the managers subtenants, on a 12 year term, without
any thought having been given to the necessity for the lessor's
consent. Russell L.J. found the tenant free of blame in the
matter and considered that had consent been sought, the lessor
could not reasonably have refused it. The subterm had already
been surrendered and to forfeit the lease would enable the
lessor to renegotiate terms at a higher rent reflecting the
increase in goodwill which was attributable to efforts of the
tenant and the subtenants in building up the business: "truly
pennies from heaven."[42] That was a result which the court

Section 146 Law
of Property Act
1925

would not countenance. In *David Blackstone* v. *Burnetts (West
End) Ltd.*[43] the question of relief did not actually come up
because it was found that the lessor had waived the breach but
Swanwick J., having noted that relief was granted in *Scala*,
opined that, nonetheless, attention should be paid to the
cautionary observations expressed in *Barrow* v. *Isaacs*[44] and in
Shiloh Spinners v. *Harding*[45] where Lord Wilberforce
commented that wilful breaches should not, or at least should
only in exceptional circumstances, merit relief.[46]
Caution did not, however, prevent the Privy Council granting
relief in *Lam Kee Ying Sdn Bhd* v. *Lam Shes Tong*[47] where
there had been a breach of a covenant against parting with
possession. The lessee, as the lease permitted him to do, took
two partners into the business. The three then formed a
company, in which the lessee held the majority of shares, and
parted with possession of the premises to that company.[48] Sir
Harry Gibbs pointed out that the same business was being
conducted as before and it was still controlled by the same
partners and therefore had consent been sought, the lessor
could not reasonably have refused it. Thus it appears that relief
may now be granted in respect of a breach occasioned by
a failure to seek consent if such consent could not reasonably
have been withheld and the failure was due to a bona fide
oversight. Even if the failure was deliberate, or "wilful",
despite Lord Wilberforce's comments in *Shiloh*, relief may
still be granted and according to *Southern Depot Ltd.* v.
British Railways Board[49] it is not confined to "exceptional
circumstances" but will be granted where the damage to
the lessor from the breach is slight as compared to the
advantage which would accrue to him should relief be refused.
Where a breach of covenant arises not from a failure to
seek consent but from a disposition effected despite a

[42] At p. 23.
[43] *Supra* [1973] 3 All E.R. 782.
[44] *Ibid.*
[45] [1973] 1 All E.R. 90.
[46] Because the lessor should not be compelled to remain in a relationship of
neighbourhood with a person in deliberate breach of his obligations" at
p. 103; however, the case did not concern a disposition covenant and the
court was confined to the more limited equitable jurisdiction, the covenants
being contained in an assignment rather than a lease.
[47] [1974] 3 All E.R. 137.
[48] See *supra* p. 17.
[49] [1990] 33 E.G. 45.

reasonable refusal, the availability of relief is unclear. However one could envisage a deserving case as where, perhaps, the landlord advanced new reasons at a late stage.[50]

Breach incapable of remedy

Where there has been a breach of a disposition covenant, the question of relief against forfeiture would not even arise if such breach were capable of remedy and the tenant upon receipt of the section 146 notice, remedied it. In such circumstances the proviso for re-entry is not enforceable. The better view, though, would seem to be that breach of a disposition covenant is not capable of remedy[51] and that the lessor can proceed to exercise his right of re-entry after service of the section 146 without giving the tenant the opportunity to remedy the breach. In *Scala House Ltd.* v. *Forbes*[52] it was argued that the 14 days between the service of notice and the issue of the writ was insufficient to allow the tenant to remedy the breach, *e.g.* by assigning the lease to the subtenant with consent or entering a proper management agreement and that the writ was therefore premature. It was held that as the breach was incapable of remedy,[53] the lapse between the notice and the writ sufficed and the tenants only course was to seek relief against forfeiture, Russell L.J. considered *Capital & County Property Co. Ltd.* v. *Mills*[54] to be wrongly decided. In that case Browne J. thought that a breach by way of a short term sublease was capable of remedy by the effluxion of time or by the lessor granting his consent. As the sublease did not expire for a few weeks the lessor had been premature in issuing his writ within 14 days of the notice of forfeiture. Russell L.J. in *Scala* refused to adopt this reasoning:

> "First, I find it difficult to see how a breach is said to be capable of remedy because the lessor can waive the breach, which would be involved in the suggestion that he could *post hoc* consent to the subletting. Second, I do not see how a breach by unlawful subletting can be said to be remedied by the lessee when he does nothing except wait for the subterm to come to an end by effluxion of time."[55]

He went on to say that where the sublease had already determined, the breach was obviously incapable of remedy and the lessor was not hampered in the issue of his writ by the necessity of allowing the tenant time—the tenant had to rely upon his right to apply for relief. How therefore could "it be otherwise if the lessee has failed to get rid of the subterm until after notice was served? Is the lessee then in a stronger position and the lessor in a weaker position? In my judgment not so."[56] James L.J. after some initial doubts, expressed himself even

---

[50] It is argued in Chapter 5, p. 60 that such new reasons should not be taken into account in determining whether there has been a breach of covenant; if they are taken into account and result in the disposition constituting a breach of covenant, it may well be an appropriate case for relief.
[51] See, *e.g. Abrahams* v. *MacFisheries Ltd.* [1925] 2 K.B. 18 *per* Fraser J. at pp. 34, 35.
[52] *Supra* [1973] 3 W.L.R. 14.
[53] *Per* Russell L.J., Plowman J. and James L.J.—the latter a little reluctantly.
[54] [1966] E.G.D. 96.
[55] At p. 22.
[56] At p. 23.

more strongly: "The breach of this class of covenant is a one-and-for-all breach; whatever events follow the breach, they cannot wipe the slate clean."[57]

---

[57] At p. 25.

5 LANDLORD AND TENANT ACT 1988

The need for change

In 1985 the Law Commission[1] drew attention to a number of areas in which the law and practice relating to the operation of disposition covenants hindered leasehold conveyancing and fell short of providing adequate protection for the tenant. They referred to these matters again two years later[2] quoting also the observations of Dillon L.J. in 29 *Equities Ltd*. v. *Bank Leumi (UK) Ltd*.[3]

> "One of the difficulties which arose in this case and arises in many cases where there is a sale of leasehold property subject to the landlord's consent to assign is that neither the vendor nor the purchaser has any real leverage on the landlord to give his consent or even to act speedily in going through any formalities. What so often happens is that the landlord takes a very long time before giving his mind to the matter. Surveyors and managing agents have other things to do and are in no hurry. Ultimately the matter is passed to the landlord's solicitors to prepare a formal deed of licence or consent, and rather a large meal is made of it over a considerable period of time at the expense ultimately of the vendor or purchaser of the leasehold interest."[4]

Specific areas of concern

The form of the covenant

Where consent has been unreasonably withheld, it is the landlord who, in a general sense, is in the wrong and he should therefore be liable to make recompense to the tenant for any loss which his decision has occasioned. However, the usual

---

[1] Law Commission No. 141, Covenants Restricting Dispositions, Alterations and User.
[2] Law Commission No. 161, Leasehold Conveyancing to which a draft Bill was appended.
[3] [1987] 1 All E.R. 108.
[4] At p. 111.

No damages where consent unreasonably withheld

form of fully qualified covenant does not produce this result.[5] It merely dictates that if the consent is unreasonably withheld, the tenant is entitled to assign without it. However an assignee will be justifiably cautious about accepting an assignment without consent in view of the risk of subsequent forfeiture proceedings and may not be willing to wait for the tenant to apply to the court for a declaration of unreasonableness. The lack of consent "appreciably diminishes the value of the lessee's property"[6] and often means that the tenant loses the transaction. As the landlord did not covenant not to unreasonably withhold consent,[7] he cannot be sued for damages. The Law Commission recommended that the landlord be under an "inescapable obligation" to pay damages for unreasonably withholding consent[8] and this has been implemented in sections 1 and 4 of the Landlord and Tenant Act 1988.[9]

The dilatory landlord

While delays in reaching and communicating decisions can sometimes amount to an unreasonable withholding of consent,[10] as has been noted above the tenant's remedies for such withholding were inadequate. The proposed assignee was not likely to go ahead with the transaction without consent or to wait around for the tenant to obtain a declaration, with the result that the tenant often lost the sale and had no remedy against the landlord in respect of his loss. A delay in communicating one sort of decision does not amount to unreasonable withholding at all and in these circumstances the tenant is left completely without redress. The circumstances referred to arise where the landlord reaches a decision in a reasonable time and upon reasonable grounds to withhold consent and then keeps it to himself. He cannot be said, at any stage, to have unreasonably withheld consent within the covenant.[11] He may well have unreasonably withheld his *decision* but that is not conduct which releases the tenant from the obligations of his covenant. The Law Commission recommended that the landlord be liable to pay damages to the tenant for such conduct[12] and this is implemented in section 1(3)(*b*) of the Landlord and Tenant Act 1988.[13]

Failure to communicate a reasonable withholding

Multiple consents

Sometimes a proposed disposition will require more than one consent: that of the immediate landlord and that of one or more superior landlords. The responsibility for obtaining such

---

[5] See *supra*, p. 33.
[6] *Per* Cozens-Hardy L.J. in *Young* v. *Ashley Gardens Properties Ltd.* [1903] 2 Ch. 112, 116.
[7] See *supra*, p. 33.
[8] Law Commission No. 141, paras. 8.65, 8.11.
[9] See *infra*.
[10] See Law Commission 141, para. 8.52.
[11] *Ibid.* para. 8.57.
[12] Law Commission No. 141, paras. 8.65, 8.112.
[13] See *infra*.

consents depends upon who has covenanted with whom and in what terms. For example, if a sub-tenant has covenanted in the sub-lease to obtain the consent of the tenant *and* a superior landlord, should he wish to sub-underlet, it is his responsibility to seek the tenant's consent and also to apply direct to the superior landlord for his consent. Such superior landlord may also receive an application for consent from the tenant. This would be so where the tenant himself has in the lease covenanted with the landlord not to sub-let without consent. He will be deemed in the absence of contrary provision to have covenanted on behalf of himself and those deriving title under him,[14] to have covenanted in effect that his sub-tenant would not sub-let without the *landlord*'s consent. The tenant will therefore apply for the landlord's consent to meet the terms of his extended covenant. Thus in relation to one proposed disposition there may be two separate channels for the processing of applications for consent to the superior landlord resulting in the undesirable situation that an individual landlord is faced with "two separate applications, coming at different times from different people."[15] In practice, this inconvenience is minimised if the tenant as the *immediate* landlord receives from the sub-tenant both of the applications which the sub-tenant is required to make—that which is directed to the tenant himself and that which is directed to the superior landlord and then passes the latter on to the superior landlord. This is more convenient for the superior landlord and also for the sub-tenant who without the co-operation of the tenant as his immediate landlord may have difficulty in ascertaining the identity and whereabouts of the superior landlord (*e.g.* in cases where the sub-tenant covenanted simply with "the superior landlord" or with a named person who has subsequently sold his reversion to another). The channelling of all applications systematically up the leasehold ladder becomes even more important where the chain of lettings is long and the Law Commission regarded it as "the best available means of dealing with the chain problem."[16] They recommended that it be encouraged by the imposition of a positive duty to pass on applications. This has been implemented in section 2 of the Landlord and Tenant Act 1988.[17]

Giving reasons

No duty Where a tenant is unreasonably refused consent, he has the option of assigning, or whatever, without it. However, he can only judge whether the landlord has been unreasonable in refusing if the latter discloses some reasons, which in the past he was not obliged to do.[18] In these circumstances the tenant

---

[14] s.79 of the Law of Property Act 1925.
[15] Law Commission No. 141, 8.122.
[16] Para. 8.117.
[17] See *infra*.
[18] *Young* v. *Ashley Gardens Properties Ltd.* [1903] 2 Ch. 112 at p. 115, *per* Vaughan Williams L.J.; *Parker* v. *Boggan* [1947] K.B. 346 at p. 348, *per* Macnaghten J. Compare s.94(6) of the Housing Act 1985 in relation to secure tenancies (*infra* Chap. 7).

dared not risk going ahead with the transaction because if the undisclosed reasons later turned out to have justified the refusal, forfeiture proceedings may successfully be brought. He could seek a declaration of unreasonableness, inviting the court to infer that the landlord has no reasons and that therefore the refusal was arbitrary[19] and this might elicit a more reasoned response from the landlord but the delay and uncertainty involved in such a course of action made it impractical in most circumstances.

A provision requiring the landlord to give a statement of his reasons, as recommended in Law Commission No. 141[20] and enacted in section 1(3)(b)(ii) of the Landlord and Tenant Act 1988 does not however necessarily put the tenant in a position to make an informed decision whether or not to

New reasons proceed without consent. The tenant also needs the security of knowing that new reasons cannot be advanced by the landlord subsequent to the assignment, thus possibly invalidating the whole basis of his previous decision to go ahead. In *Bromley Park Garden Estates Ltd.* v. *Moss*[21] Slade L.J.[22] reluctantly opined that the landlord could produce further reasons for his refusal, even after the tenant had assigned, etc., upon the basis of previously stated, and demonstrably bad reasons, so long as those further reasons were genuine and actually influenced his

Influence on mind at the relevant time.[23] The tenant had to accept the risk
refusal that he may not be aware of all the landlord's motives for refusing his consent. As the court found that the landlord had put forward no reasonable ground for his refusal *at any stage*, the views expressed may be regarded as *obiter*[24] but it is clear that Slade L.J. considered the point to have been established by earlier decisions like *Sonnenthal* v. *Newton*[25] and *Welch* v. *Birrane*.[26] In the former, Lord Upjohn stated that he "knew of no reason" why the landlord should be confined to reasons given in earlier correspondence, but it should be noted that the case concerned an action for a declaration by the tenant (rather than an action for forfeiture by the landlord) and the tenant had not therefore "burned his boats." In the latter, which did concern a forfeiture action, Lawson J.[27] opined that the trial judge could consider reasons not put forward in the notice of refusal but the Court of Appeal could not. He relied in particular upon the judgment of Denning M.R. in *Lovelock* v. *Margo*.[28] It is hard to see how. Lord Denning was concerned

[19] *Frederick Berry Ltd.* v. *Royal Bank of Scotland* [1949] 1 K.B. 619 at p. 623, *per* Slesser L.J.
[20] Para. 8.16.
[21] [1982] 1 W.L.R. 1019 (C.A.).
[22] With whom Cumming-Bruce L.J. agreed.
[23] At p. 1033 *et seq.* and see also *Lovelock* v. *Margo* [1963] 2 Q.B. 786; *British Bakeries (Midlands) Ltd.* v. *Michael Testler & Co. Ltd.* [1986] E.G.L.R. 64; *Rossi* v. *Hestdrive Ltd.* (1985) 274 E.G. 928; see *infra*, p. 70 for discussion of the relevant time.
[24] As may a similar view put forward by Macnaghten J. in *Parker* v. *Boggan* [1947] K.B. 346, 348.
[25] (1965) S.J. 333 (C.A.).
[26] (1975) 29 P. & C.R. 102.
[27] At p. 107.
[28] [1963] 2 Q.B. 786.

with a more straightforward issue: whether the reasons advanced had to be those which in fact influenced the landlord's mind when refusing or whether reasons subsequently thought up by her legal advisers ("objective good reasons") were admissible.[29] He did not directly consider whether the landlord was at liberty to advance his genuine reasons up to and including the hearing. If he had, there are indications that he would have sympathised with the tenant's plight. It is submitted that at least in actions for forfeiture for breach of covenant, where consent has been sought and refused and the tenant has thereupon proceeded with the transaction, reasons advanced subsequent to the alleged breach should be excluded.[30] Even in an action for a declaration it cannot be assumed that the landlord will have complete freedom to depart from his pleadings. This point was made by Megaw L.J. in *Berenyi* v. *Watford Borough Council*[31]:

> "I would ... disagree with any suggestion ... that, in proceedings [for a declaration] in the county court, it is open to the landlord, having served the notice required by the rules, materially to depart from it, as a matter of right. It is a matter which should be dealt with by amendment of the pleadings ... and it would have to be dealt with in accordance with the requirements of justice."

He points out that if the tenant is not prejudiced by the amendment or if such prejudice can be cured by an adjournment or costs, leave to amend may be granted. It may be noted that the Law Commission did not recommend the enactment of a provision whereby the landlord would be tied to his reasons[32] and the Landlord and Tenant Act 1988 contains no such provision. It has been demonstrated above however that the authorities do not warrant the conclusion that the landlord has carte blanche to introduce reasons right up to the hearing: even if they genuinely affected his mind at the time of refusal. It should also be remembered that the court may doubt whether late reasons did influence him at the time of refusal,[33] and that late reasons may constitute a breach of the duty under section 1(3)(*b*)(ii) of the Landlord and Tenant Act 1988 and give rise to a claim in damages.[34]

The burden of proof

It was clearly established that it was not for the landlord to prove that he was reasonable in refusing consent: it was for the

---

[29] See *supra*.
[30] If they are not excluded, the tenant should certainly get relief against forfeiture; see *supra* Chap. 4.
[31] [1980] 256 E.G.L.R. 271, 279.
[32] See Law Commission No. 141, para. 8.16.
[33] J. T. Farrand, *Emmet on Title*, (19th ed.), para. 26.161; Hill and Redman's *Law of Landlord and Tenant*, (18th ed.), Vol. 1, p. 1183, n. 10.
[34] See *infra*.

tenant to establish that he was unreasonable.[35] In only two
situations could the contrary be argued. First, Slesser L.J. in
Lambert v. *F. W. Woolworth & Co. Ltd.*[36] considered that the
burden may be reversed where "the landlord gives no reason at
all but merely refuses"—under those circumstances he would
owe a duty to show that his action was reasonable—but in
Frederick Berry Ltd. v. *Royal Bank of Scotland*[37] Lord Goddard
C.J. interpreted this as meaning merely that "if the landlord
gives no reason the Court would more readily imply that the
withholding was unreasonable." Second, in *R. M. Cole* v.
Russells (Tulse Hill) Ltd.[38] it was pointed out that if the tenant
established a prima facie case that the refusal was unreasonable,
the burden then shifted to the landlord. The Law Commission
was critical of the rule that, in general at least, the tenant had
to shoulder the burden. "It seems to us wrong that, although
the landlord is the only person who knows what are his reasons
for withholding consent, it should be for the tenant to prove
that they must be bad ones."[39] If the landlord knew that he
would have to justify his refusal "he would concentrate his
mind on his reasons before he makes his decision" rather than,
as sometimes happens, refuse automatically and only formulate
reasons if challenged by the tenant. A reversal of the burden of
proof, coupled with the other recommendations requiring the
landlord to serve notice of his reasons and be liable in damages
for delay and unreasonable withholding, would eliminate some
of the delays which occur in connection with the disposition of
leases. Such a reversal is now accomplished by section 1(6) of
the Landlord and Tenant Act 1988.[40]

The Landlord and Tenant Act 1988

The Law Commission proposals referred to above were enacted
as the Landlord and Tenant Act 1988. Other changes
recommended in their Report No. 141, "Covenants Restricting
Dispositions, Alterations and Changes of User" have yet to be
implemented. The measures incorporated into the 1988 Act
were brought forward for urgent action as a result of a
subsequent Law Commission Report (No. 161) entitled
"Leasehold Conveyancing" which was issued as a response to
the anxieties expressed by the Conveyancing Standing
Committee in 1985 in relation to delays in leasehold
conveyancing. It was admitted that the implementation, in

---

[35] *Shanley* v. *Ward* (1913) 29 T.L.R. 714; *Mills* v. *Cannon Brewery Co. Ltd.*
[1920] 2 Ch. 38; *Frederick Berry Ltd.* v. *Royal Bank of Scotland* [1949] 1
K.B. 619, 623; *Pimms Ltd.* v. *Tallow Chandlers in the City of London* [1964] 2
Q.B. 547; *British Bakeries (Midlands) Ltd.* v. *Michael Testler & Co. Ltd.*
(1986) 1 E.G.L.R. 64; *Rayburn* v. *Wolf* (1986) 18 H.L.R. 1; compare
Housing Act 1985, s.94(2), *infra* Chap. 7.
[36] [1938] 1 Ch. 883.
[37] *Ibid.* p. 623.
[38] [1955] E.G.Dig. 133.
[39] Law Commission No. 141, para. 8.11.
[40] See *infra*.

isolation, of the proposals referred to, may have disadvantages[41]; in particular it had been recommended that absolute covenants be converted, in future, to fully qualified ones.[42] The fact that this has yet to be enacted may mean that landlords will resort to absolute covenants in order to avoid the statutory duties[43] now imposed upon them in the case of fully qualified covenants. The Law Commission felt that the risk of this was slight however because of the unwillingness of tenants to accept such covenants. Should it happen, implementation of the remainder of their recommendations would become pressing. The draft Bill appended to Law Commission No. 161 received the Royal Assent on July 29, 1988 and came into force two months later.[44] It applies only to England and Wales. Its provisions can be consulted at Appendix 1, and are summarised in flow chart form at Appendix 2.

Tenancies to which the Act applies

The Act applies to tenancies[45] whether made before or after the Act came into force, (but not to secure tenancies as defined in section 79 of the Housing Act 1985[46]). The word tenancy includes sub-tenancy and an agreement for a tenancy.[47] To fall within the Act the tenancy must contain a covenant[48] on the part of the tenant which restricts assigning, underletting, charging or parting with possession of the demised premises or any part[49] without the consent of the landlord "or some other person" (*e.g.* a superior landlord) subject to the qualification that consent is not to be unreasonably withheld.[50] The fully qualifying phrase "such consent not to be unreasonably withheld" may be express or it may be implied into the covenant as a result of section 19(1)(*a*) of the Landlord and Tenant Act 1927[51] or sections 86(1) and 89(1) of the Law of Property Act 1925. As long as the fully qualifying phrase is there, qualifying the tenant's obligation, it does not matter that his obligation is also qualified in some other way.[52] It is submitted that this may be a reference to a *Moat* v. *Martin* clause which has elsewhere[53] been construed as a covenant not to assign without consent, such consent not in any event to be unreasonably withheld and in the case of a respectable and responsible person not to be withheld at all. An absolute

Fully qualified disposition covenant necessary

[41] Law Commission No. 161, para. 1.4.
[42] See Pt. VII, Law Commission No. 141.
[43] See *infra*.
[44] s.7(2); referred to in *Venetian Glass Gallery Ltd.* v. *Next Properties Ltd.* [1989] 30 E.G. 92 as "the curious little Act."
[45] s.1.
[46] s.5(3).
[47] *Ibid.*
[48] This includes a condition or agreement, see *supra*, Chap. 1.
[49] See Chap. 2.
[50] s.1(1).
[51] This section does not apply to leases of agricultural holdings though they may be subject to express full qualification.
[52] s.1(1)(*b*).
[53] *Supra*, p. 41.

disposition covenant is outside the Act and therefore gives rise to none of the duties referred to hereafter.

Written application by tenant required

The duties to which the Act gives rise are dependent upon the service[54] by the tenant upon the person who may consent of a *written application* for consent.[55] The application will be treated as served for the purposes of the Act if (a) served in any manner provided in the tenancy or, (b) in respect of any matter for which the tenancy makes no provision, served in any manner provided by section 23 of the Landlord and Tenant Act 1927.[56] There is no prescribed form because such a form "might lead some people into believing that a completed form was by itself always a sufficient and comprehensive application"[57] whereas in fact in many cases the form would have to be accompanied by supplementary information, *e.g.* accounts.[58] Nor is it provided that the application should contain a warning to the landlord of his potential liability in damages under the Act.

No prescribed form

Performance within a reasonable time

All the duties imposed by the act must be performed within a reasonable time.[59] 28 days was suggested by the Law Commission in their earlier Report[60] but either side was to be allowed to show that that period was, in the particular circumstances, too long or too short. They finally concluded that a provision incorporating such elasticity was not worth having.[61] Once the tenant has supplied the landlord with full information, the latter should deal with the application "expeditiously"[62] and seeking further information from the tenant which could not assist in deciding the application will not be effective to disguise delay.[63]

The basic duties

  1. "to give consent, except in a case where it is reasonable not to give consent."[64]

---

[54] Which service must take place after the Act came into force—s.5(4).
[55] s.1(3).
[56] s.5(2).
[57] Law Commission No. 161, para. 2.4. Compare Law Commission No. 141, para. 8.128.
[58] See *supra*, Chap. 4, p. 49.
[59] ss.1(3), 2(1), 3(1).
[60] No. 141, paras. 8.123–8.127.
[61] Law Commission No. 161, para. 2.5.
[62] See *City Hotels Group Ltd.* v. *Total Property Investments Ltd.* [1985] 1 E.G.L.R. 253.
[63] *Ibid.*; see also Chap. 4, p. 51; and *Midland Bank plc* v. *Chart Enterprises Inc.* [1990] 44 E.G. 68.
[64] s.1(3)(*a*).

The general scope of this duty involves a consideration of the very extensive case law on the distinction between reasonable and unreasonable withholding of consent. In relation to this, reference should be made to Chapter 6. Two matters can however be mentioned here. First, giving consent subject to a condition which is not reasonable is not a compliance with the present duty.[65] Second, in the case of one type of disposition covenant, a withholding of consent which would otherwise be reasonable is deemed to be unreasonable.[66] This is where there is a *Moat* v. *Martin* covenant, *i.e.* where the landlord covenants that in the case of a respectable and responsible person, he will not withhold his consent at all, even reasonably.[67] In such a case, it may be that, were it not for the very strict covenant which he has made, the landlord could have reasonably withheld his consent. This fact will not however enable him to discharge his duty under section 1(3)(*a*); section 1(5), the meaning of which is by no means obvious,[68] provides that a refusal of consent *can* only be reasonable if, should the tenant disregard it and carry on with the disposition, he would be in breach of the covenant. Where the landlord, having bound himself by a *Moat* v. *Martin* clause, refuses consent to a disposition to a respectable and responsible person, the tenant is released from his covenant and completion of the disposition is no breach on his part.

2. "to serve on the tenant written notice of his decision whether or not to give consent specifying in addition:

    (i)   if consent is given subject to conditions, the conditions,

    (ii) if consent is withheld, the reasons for withholding it.[69]

Communication

Conditions

To avoid liability under this subsection the landlord must serve notice of his decision upon the tenant. Even when he is confronted with an application so manifestly preposterous that refusal is inevitable, he has to notify the tenant of his decision to withhold consent or he may incur liability to the tenant under section 4.[70] Failing to communicate a refusal, even a reasonable one which the tenant could be said to have anticipated, amounts to a breach of duty.[71] The communication of a consent must be accompanied by any conditions to which it is subject and the communication of a refusal must be accompanied by the reasons for it. The communication must be in writing to enable the tenant to have as clear a picture of his position as is possible and to avoid the misunderstandings which are an inherent difficulty with oral dealings. It has previously been noted[72] with some regret that the tenant

---

[65] s.1(4).

[66] s.1(5).

[67] See *supra*, Chap. 4, p. 41.

[68] See, *e.g.* annotation in Current Law Statutes 1988, Chap. 26, and also the virtually incomprehensible explanatory note to the draft Bill in Law Commission No. 161.

[69] s.1(3)(*b*).

[70] See *infra*.

[71] Compare *supra*, p. 58.

[72] *Supra*, p. 60.

Reasons

remains subject to uncertainty because, in the case of a refusal, the Act does not limit the landlord to the reasons he initially communicated. New reasons may, if admissable, invalidate the basis of the tenant's decision to assign, etc., without consent.

The burden of proof

As has been noted above,[73] the burden of proof has, in the past, save in exceptional circumstances, been upon the tenant to establish that a withholding of consent is unreasonable. For the reasons there referred to, the Law Commission recommended a reversal of the burden, and in relation to all aspects of the duties imposed by the Act,[74] the burden of proof is placed upon the landlord.[75] If delay in granting consent or in communicating a decision is alleged, it is for him to prove that he satisfied his duties in these respects in a reasonable time. If he attaches a condition to the consent, it is for him to prove that it was a reasonable condition. If he refuses consent, it is up to him to show that the refusal was reasonable.

Superior landlord's consent required to a disposition

Duty to consent, communicate decision, etc.

Where a landlord receives a written application from his tenant it may be for his consent, it may be for the consent of one or more superior landlords or it may be for the consent of all of them. It will depend upon the covenants which have been entered into.[76] If it is for his consent and he has no knowledge of anyone else's consent being required, he will just owe the section 1(3) duties above referred to. If, on the other hand he "believes that another person, other than a person who he believes has received the application or a copy of it, is a person who may consent to the transaction"[77] he owes a further duty to the tenant "to take such steps as are reasonable to secure the receipt within a reasonable time by the other person of a copy of the application."[78] The person to whom such application or copy is passed himself then owes the duties to the tenant which arise under section 1(3)[79] and, possibly, the duty under section 2 to pass the application on up the leasehold ladder if he believes another may need to consent. It may be that in the course of this procedure applications for consent are served upon the immediate or a subsequent landlord in respect of

[73] p. 61.
[74] Save perhaps in relation to the duty under s.2 to pass on applications, see *infra*.
[75] s.1(6).
[76] See *supra*, p. 58 "Multiple Consents."
[77] s.2(1)(*b*).
[78] s.2(1).
[79] See s.2(2).

which their consent is not required: in such a case the only duty which will be owed is the duty under section 2 to pass the application on if it is believed necessary. In relation to the section 2 duty it seems unclear upon whom lies the burden of proof. Section 1(6) refers only to the duties arising under section 1(3) and not that arising under section 2. Presumably therefore it will be for the party alleging breach, the tenant, to establish that reasonable steps to ensure receipt were not taken in a reasonable time. If a particular landlord believes that though his *immediate* landlord does not need to consent, the consent of a superior one is required he can pass the application direct to that superior landlord and this would appear to be what the section primarily envisages in such a case. It may be however that he does not know the identity or address of the superior landlord and in these circumstances the Law Commission considered that he should be able to discharge his duty by passing the application to his immediate landlord for onward transmission.[80] If he does this, he can surely be said to have "taken such steps as are reasonable" within section 2(1).

Superior landlord's approval required to a consent

The consent of a superior landlord may be required not only for a disposition but also as a prerequisite to the granting of consent by an inferior landlord to his tenant.[81] The inferior landlord may have covenanted that he would not give his consent to a disposition by the tenant without the approval of the superior landlord, such approval not to be unreasonably withheld. A covenant of this sort does not fall within the terms of section 1(1) and would therefore not give rise to the duties on the part of the superior landlord under section 1(3) (in relation to responding in a reasonable time, giving consent except where reasonable not to, communicating decisions, etc.). However, section 3 provides that where there is a fully qualified covenant[82] on the part of an inferior landlord not to consent to a disposition without the approval of the superior landlord, in relation to that approval, duties equivalent to those arising under section 1(3) are imposed upon the superior landlord and in respect of such duties the superior landlord shoulders the burden of proof.

The tenant's mortgagee

The duties under the Act are owed not only to the tenant, but, where he has mortgaged the demised property and it is the

---

[80] Law Commission No. 141, para. 8.118.
[81] See, *e.g. Viennit Ltd.* v. *Williams & Sons (Bread Street) Ltd.* [1958] 3 All E.R. 621.
[82] Full qualification will have to be express, the covenants under discussion being outside the terms of s.19(1) of the Landlord and Tenant Act 1927.

mortgagee who is proposing to exercise the statutory or express power of sale, to the mortgagee also.[83]

The consequences of breach of duty

Damages

Breach gives rise to liability in damages. The possibility of breach leading to deemed consent was examined closely by the Law Commission[84] but it was not pursued because it was felt that "it would involve a good deal of complexity, some risks and a certain amount of what may best be described as rough justice."[85] The mechanism by which the landlord would become liable in damages was considered in Law Commission Report No. 161.[86] The duties could have been implied into the lease as statutory covenants on the part of the landlord. This option was rejected for a number of reasons. First, it would mean that the original landlord would remain liable on the covenants even after he had assigned the reversion,[87] a continuing liability which, where it presently applies, is considered undesirable.[88] Second, there is no way that an implied covenant of this sort could be enforceable against a superior landlord by a sub-tenant or by a mortgagee of the tenant and both of these were intended to have the benefit of the duties. The release of the landlord from his obligations on assignment of the reversion and the wider enforceability which was desired could, however, be achieved by the imposition of statutory duties and this is the effect of section 4 of the Act which imposes upon a landlord who is in breach, liability in

Liability in tort for breach of statutory duty

tort for breach of statutory duty. The tenant may thus be able to recover damages wherever he can establish loss as a result of a breach of any of the duties imposed by the Act—be it loss of the transaction or, possibly, having to drop the price or, in the case of a delayed but reasonable refusal or a failure to give reasons, abortive legal costs. It was contemplated that damage might be difficult to prove and assess (presumably the tenant would have the right to be placed in the position he would have been in, had the tort not been committed) but the Law Commission took the view that it should not need to be assessed very often because the existence of the liability would be enough to deter landlords from incurring it.[89] The damages

---

[83] s.5(1).

[84] Law Commission No. 141, paras. 8.69–8.109.

[85] Para. 8.106; in the case of assignments by way of exchange between secure tenants and sub-lettings of part by a secure tenant (see ss.92 & 94 of the Housing Act 1985) deemed consent provisions have been enacted but the Law Commission opined that many of the difficulties of such schemes were minimised by the fact the landlord would be either a local authority or, at least, an institution: para. 8.104; a deemed consent provision can be inserted in the lease if desired: see R. W. Ramage, *Kelly's Draftsman*, (15th ed.), p. 369.

[86] Paras. 2.1–2.3.

[87] s.79 of the Law of Property Act 1925.

[88] Law Commission Working Paper No. 95, 1985 and Law Commission No. 174 (1988).

[89] Law Commission No. 141, para. 8.66.

remedy[90] is additional to the existing remedies available to the tenant, namely, disposing of the property without consent where it has been unreasonably withheld or applying for a declaration of reasonableness. To this extent it increases the potential for litigation relating to conveyancing transactions.

---

[90] Which may presumably be combined with a claim for an injunction requiring the landlord to carry out his statutory duties: see Current Law Statutes Annotated, 1988 note to s.4 of the Landlord and Tenant Act 1988 (C. Hunter); see also Chap. 11.

6 UNREASONABLE WITHHOLDING OF CONSENT

Burden of Proof

It has been seen[1] that so long as the tenant makes written application as required by the Landlord and Tenant Act 1988,[2] the burden of proof will be upon the landlord to establish that the withholding of consent was reasonable. He will, it is submitted, have to satisfy the court:

(1) Relevant date

(1)   that the reasons he gives actually affected his mind at the relevant date.[3]

The relevant date

If the tenant has brought an *action for a declaration* that consent has been unreasonably withheld, the relevant date, where the landlord has actually *refused* his consent, is the date of the refusal[4] but where the landlord is merely *withholding* his consent, it is the date of the issue of the writ.[5] If the tenant has *assigned* etc. without consent and the landlord has instituted proceedings for forfeiture for breach of covenant, the relevant date would appear to be that of the assignment. Where the landlord is withholding rather than refusing, the assignment date is clearly the crucial one. Where, however, the landlord has actually refused consent, it is less obviously so. It may well be thought that the refusal date is the one that then matters. Such a thought would run contrary to the opinion of Slade L.J. in *Bromley Park Garden Estates Ltd.* v. *Moss*[6] who opined that a "tenant who decides to proceed with an assignment following an unqualified refusal of consent on the part of the landlord, must be entitled to take

---

[1] Chapter 5.
[2] s.1(3), see Appendix I.
[3] For the position where they did, but were not then communicated to the tenant see *supra*, Chapter 5, p. 60.
[4] *Rossi* v. *Hestdrive Ltd.* (1985) 274 E.G. 928, 931; *British Bakeries (Midlands) Ltd.* v. *Michael Testler & Co. Ltd.* (1986) 1 E.G.L.R. 64.
[5] *City Hotels Group Ltd.* v. *Total Property Investments Ltd.* (1985) 1 E.G.L.R. 253, 257.
[6] [1982] 2 All E.R. 890, 901.

this course in the light of the facts as they exist at the date of the *assignment*."[7] It may well be, however, that the learned judge was concerned to reinforce a concession, made on behalf of the landlord, that the relevant date was not the still later date, that of the hearing and that in so doing he did not intend to directly address the question of the relative merits of the date of the refusal on the one hand and the assignment on the other. It may be noted that he had no need to address it because, in the case, the refusal was followed immediately by the assignment.

The three remaining issues, namely,

(2) that the reasons related to some relevant interest,

(3) that the apprehension of harm which he entertained in regard to that interest should the disposition proceed, was reasonable, and

(4) that that harm was not outweighed by the detriment which would be suffered to a relevant interest of the tenant should consent be refused, will be considered in turn.

(2) Relevant interests

General principles   The whole point of a fully qualified (as oppose to an absolute or merely qualified) covenant is that it limits the matters to which the landlord may have regard when withholding his consent. These matters are here described as "relevant interests." There can be no absolute certainty about them for the reasons given by Lord Denning M.R. in *Bickel* v. *Duke of Westminster*[8] who, having commented that previous

Propositions of good sense, not law

cases lay down no propositions of law, went on to point out that:

"[t]he words of the contract are perfectly clear English words: 'such licence shall not be unreasonably withheld.' When those words come to be applied in any particular case, I do not think the court can or should, determine by strict rules the grounds on which a landlord may, or may not, reasonably refuse his consent. He is not limited by the contract to any particular grounds. Nor should the court limit him. Not even under the guise of construing the words. The landlord has to exercise his judgment in all sorts of circumstances. It is impossible for him, or for the courts, to envisage them all. ... Seeing that the circumstances are infinitely various, it is impossible to formulate strict rules as to how a landlord should exercise

---

[7] Author's italics.

[8] [1976] 3 All E.R. 801, 804.

his power of refusal. The utmost that the courts can do is to give guidance to those who have to consider the problem. As one decision follows another, people will get to know the likely result in any given set of circumstances. But no one decision will be binding precedent as a strict rule of law. The reasons given by the judges are to be treated as propositions of good sense—in relation to the particular case—rather than propositions of law applicable to all cases."[9]

It must not however be forgotten that the need for what Lord Denning called "guidance" is very great. The existence of some general principles has always been of crucial importance to the tenant, because he cannot exercise his option of assigning etc. without consent, safe from forfeiture, unless he can assess the reasonableness of the landlord's refusal. Since the Landlord and Tenant Act 1988, the landlord himself needs to consider seriously the reasonableness of his response in order to avoid liability in damages.[10]

Early formulations of principle

Early attempts to formulate principles focused upon the landlord's interest in the personality of the proposed assignee or his user of the property. A. L. Smith L.J. in *Bates* v. *Donaldson*[11] opined that the purpose of the clause was to "protect the lessor from having his premises used or occupied in an undesirable way or by an undesirable tenant" and this theme was echoed by Warrington L.J. in *Re Gibbs & Houlder Bros. & Co. Ltd.'s Lease*[12] when he said "I think you must find in the objection something which connects it either with the personality of the intended assignee who is suggested as the new tenant of the property, or the user which he is likely to make of the property to be assigned to him."[13] The words of Warrington L.J. have been quoted frequently over the years—at the expense of another, and more important, insight which

Relevance of lease

was shared by all three judges, namely that the suitability of the assignee and his user have to be viewed *in the context of the arrangements agreed in the lease.*

> "An act must be regarded as reasonable or unreasonable in reference to the circumstances under which it is committed, and when the question arises on the construction of a contract the outstanding circumstance to be considered is the nature of the contract to be construed, and the relations between the parties resulting from it."[14]

---

[9] The view of Joyce J. in *Premier Rinks Ltd.* v. *Amalgamated Cinematograph Theatres Ltd.* (1912) W.N. 157 who is reported to have asked "what was the good of cases being reported and cited on a question of this sort? [They] should [be] obliterated from the books. Authorities had nothing to do with the question he had to decide and did not affect his mind at all" is clearly a little extreme.

[10] ss.1(3) and 4.

[11] [1896] 2 Q.B. 241, 247.

[12] [1925] All E.R. Rep. 128, 133.

[13] It has been plausibly suggested (Kodilinye, 1988 Conv. 45, 48) that the concentration upon the personality and user of the proposed assignee was the result of the form which the disposition covenant took in these early cases and the manner in which they were then construed.

[14] Warrington L.J. at p. 133.

"I think we must look at these words in their relation to the premises, and to the contract made in reference to the premises between the lessor and the lessee; in other words one must pay attention to the relation of landlord and tenant *inter se*."[15]

" . . . you have to consider what was within the reasonable contemplation of the parties to the lease . . . the reason must be something affecting the subject-matter of the contract which forms the relationship between the landlord and the tenant, and . . . it must not be something wholly extraneous and completely dissociated from the subject-matter of the contract."[16]

More recently similar sentiments were expressed by Roskill L.J. in *West Layton* v. *Ford*[17] when he commented that "the right approach . . . is to look first of all at the covenant in order to see what its purpose was when the parties entered into it." This approach was emphatically endorsed by the Court of Appeal in *Bromley Park Garden Estates Ltd.* v. *Moss.*[18]

Bromley etc. v. Moss Cumming-Bruce L.J.[19] characterised the landlord's reason in that case as "wholly extraneous to the intention of the parties to the contract when the covenant was granted and accepted." Dunn L.J. opined that a landlord is not entitled to refuse his consent "in order to acquire a commercial benefit for himself by putting into effect proposals outside the contemplation of the lease under consideration, and to replace the contractual relations created by the lease by some alternative arrangements more advantageous to the landlord . . . "[20]; such a "collateral **Collateral** purpose" would render the refusal unreasonable. Slade L.J. **purposes** proceeded upon the same basis.[21] The effect of this approach is *not* to make considerations of personality, user (or, as in the *Bromley Park Case* itself, good management) irrelevant; rather it is to limit the relevance of such considerations to those situations where they can be shown to relate to some right enjoyed by the landlord under the lease—typically his right to receive rent, to secure performance of the other covenants on the tenant's part and to recover possession at the expiration of the term granted.[22] Thus, for example, a refusal of consent is not made reasonable merely because of the impecuniosity of the proposed assignee but because that impecuniosity is likely to imperil the landlord's covenanted right to rent. In the *Bromley Park Case* the landlord refused his consent to an assignment and justified it as being in the interests of "good estate management" (a factor recognised as relevant by Sir Ernest Pollock M.R. in *Re Gibbs & Houlder Bros.*).[23] In particular, he

[15] Sir Ernest Pollock M.R. at p. 132.
[16] Sargant L.J. at p. 134.
[17] [1979] Q.B. 593, 605.
[18] [1982] 2 All E.R. 890; 1983 Conv. 140 Licences to Assign—A New Deal?
[19] At p. 899.
[20] At p. 900.
[21] At p. 902.
[22] Or other more specific rights referred to in the lease or in some collateral agreement; compare *Wilson* v. *Flynn* [1948] 2 All E.R. 40.
[23] [1925] All E.R. Rep. 128.

asserted that he could now let that part of the premises, a flat, to the existing tenant of the shop below, and having the property subject to a single, instead of a multiple, letting would increase its investment value. He would accept a surrender or he would be willing to consent to an assignment to the existing tenant of the shop on condition that the latter thereupon surrendered both leases in exchange for a new lease of the whole. However the lease contained no hint that the return of the property to unified possession was a matter in the contemplation of the parties when it was entered into. "It cannot be relied upon merely because it would suit the plaintiff's investment plans. It may well enhance the financial interests of the plaintiffs to obtain a single tenant holding the whole building ... but that intention and policy is entirely outside the intention to be imputed to the parties at the time of the granting of the lease,"[24] and, one may add, totally inconsistent with the tenant's manifest right to enjoy the property for the term granted, which right of enjoyment, in this case, included a right to assign which, though limited, was greater in extent than the landlord was prepared to recognise.

Further statements of the "contractual" approach

Subsequent cases have reflected the "contractual" approach and its terminology. In *International Drilling Fluids Ltd.* v. *Louisville Investments (Uxbridge) Ltd.*[25] Balcombe L.J. included in his seven propositions[26] "(2) a landlord is not entitled to refuse his consent to assignment on grounds which have nothing whatever to do with the relationship of landlord and tenant in regard to the subject-matter of the lease. ... "[27] In *F.W. Woolworth plc* v. *Charlwood Alliance Properties Ltd.*[28] His Honour Judge Finlay Q.C. noted that "a landlord's interests, collateral to the purposes of the lease, are in any event ineligible for consideration[29] and in *Rayburn* v. *Wolf*[30] it was pointed out that a landlord would be unreasonable to the extent that he was "trying to extract an uncovenanted benefit."[31]

"Uncovenanted benefits"

The intention to be imputed to the parties at the time of the lease—what interests they were seeking to protect—is a question of construction to be determined upon the basis of the knowledge which they then had. The facts which are alleged subsequently to have an adverse effect upon a relevant interest need not have been foreseen by the parties. Thus in *Leeward Securities Ltd.* v. *Lilyheath Properties Ltd.*[32] it was clearly within the intention of the parties to protect the landlord's reversion but the danger which materialised, in the form of a tenant who would have Rent Act protection, could not have been foreseen because it was the result of legislation subsequent to the lease. The landlord's refusal of consent was reasonable. Thus if the

[24] *Per* Cumming-Bruce L.J. at p. 899.
[25] [1986] 1 All E.R. 321.
[26] See Appendix III.
[27] At p. 325.
[28] (1987) 282 E.G. 585.
[29] At p. 589.
[30] (1986) 18 H.L.R. 1 C.A.
[31] At p. 4.
[32] (1984) 271 E.G. 279.

intention to protect the interest is clear, the direction of attack need not be.

Specific cases.   Bearing in mind the general issues referred to above, it is proposed now to consider the wide range of reasons which may be asserted as justifying a refusal or withholding of consent and the manner in which they have been regarded by the courts.

Objections based upon anticipated user

(i) Where there is a provision restricting user.   The observance by the disponee of a provision in the lease restricting the purposes for which the demised premises can be used, would, it may be thought, constitute a relevant interest which the landlord is entitled to protect in considering an application for consent to assign etc. This is not always the case. Where the disposition and change of use are already a *fait accompli* at the time consent is sought, it **Breach already** seems that the landlord can reasonably refuse his consent. **occurred** Thus in *Wilson* v. *Flynn*[33] the subtenant had already been let into possession and was making kitchen equipment contrary to a covenant restricting user to the practice of accountancy and in *Creery* v. *Summersell & Flowerdew & Co. Ltd.*[34] the subtenants, law stationers and process servers, were in a similar position in regard to a covenant limited to surveyors and valuers. The landlord will also be acting reasonably where though breach of the user covenant has not yet **Breach inevitable** occurred, it is *inevitable*. Thus in *Jenkins* v. *Price*[35] a lessor was held reasonable in refusing consent to an assignment to a limited company which could by no means comply with a covenant requiring the tenant "at all times to reside" upon the demised premises and carry on the business of licensed victualler. In *Packaging Centre Ltd.* v. *Poland Street Estate Ltd.*[36] the landlords were held reasonable in withholding consent to a sublease for use *exclusively* as offices when the lease contained a covenant to use the premises for the *combined* purposes of offices and showrooms, Lord Evershed M.R. opining that the landlords could reasonably say: "We object to an exercise of the power of subletting which will inevitably involve a breach of the specific obligation you entered into." The inevitability in this case may have flowed from the fact that the sublease had already been made and the subtenants allowed into possession, as in the cases initially mentioned, or from the fact that the sublease bound the sublessee to use the premises in breach of the lease.[37]

---

[33] [1948] 2 All E.R. 40.
[34] [1949] Ch. 751.
[35] [1908] 1 Ch. 10 C.A.
[36] (1961) 178 E.G. 189.
[37] See *Killick* v. *Second Covent Garden Property Co. Ltd.* [1973] 2 All E.R. 337, *per* Stamp L.J. at p. 339.

Pennyquick J. took the same line in *Granada T.V. Network Ltd.* v. *Great Universal Stores Ltd.*[38] when he said:

> "I can see no reason why a landlord who was entitled to restrain his tenant from using the demised premises except for a specified purpose should be regarded as acting unreasonably in refusing consent to a disposition in favour of a party who would *necessarily*[39] be unable to use the premises for the specified purpose."

The user covenant in that case was very narrow indeed limiting use to office occupation by the *original tenant and his surety and any associated or subsidiary company of either*; the proposed sublessee had no links with either the tenant or the surety and could not therefore comply.[40] It is, of course, possible for a user clause to be so narrowly drawn as to make breach of it a necessary consequence of *any* disposition and indeed only a liberal construction of the user clause prevented this situation from arising in *Granada*. A user clause of this very restrictive type sits unhappily with a qualified disposition covenant. The user clause effectively constitutes an absolute bar on dispositions and renders the lease inalienable while the disposition covenant prohibits merely those dispositions to which the landlord could reasonably withhold his consent. Where this conflict is the result of indiscriminate use of precedent books and the matter has been imperfectly considered by the parties, the conflict may be capable of resolution by construing the user clause so as to allow user by subsequent disponees.[41] However this course is not open where the user clause is in unequivocally narrow terms. Possibly one could argue that both parties have a relevant interest to protect—the landlord in securing compliance with the user clause and the tenant in maintaining the status of the lease as basically assignable—and that these interests should be balanced to ascertain whether harm to the landlord caused by the disposition was or was not outweighed by the harm to the tenant should the disposition not go ahead.[42]

Link with waiver
The significance of the fact that the user provision has already been contravened or will inevitably be contravened, was hinted at by Harman J. in *Creery* v. *Summersell & Flowerdew Co. Ltd.*[43] when commenting upon the relationship between the user clause and the application for consent, in the circumstances of that case: "if the lessor does give his consent ... then the obligation of the lessee under the [user provision] is necessarily waived or suspended for the period of a valid assignment or underletting."[44] Giving consent where breach of the user clause has occurred or is inevitable will amount to

---

[38] (1962) 187 E.G. 391.
[39] Author's italics.
[40] It is mentioned in *Killick ibid.* that the sublease in this case too bound the subtenant to a user which would constitute a breach of the lease.
[41] *Per* Evershed M.R. in *Granada*, as quoted by Pennyquick L.J. in *Packaging, supra.*
[42] See *infra*, p. 123.
[43] [1949] Ch. 751.
[44] At p. 760.

waiver by the landlord of his rights under that clause and would therefore preclude him from enforcing it. Fear of raising an estoppel makes it reasonable for the landlord to refuse his consent.

This reasoning was accepted as "well-founded" by Stamp L.J. in *Killick* v. *Second Covent Garden Property Co. Ltd.*[45] However he found that it was not applicable to the facts in the case before him where breach of the user clause had not

Breach not inevitable occurred nor was it inevitable. The lease contained a covenant "not to use (the premises) for any purpose other than the trade or business of printer." There was some dispute as to whether this covenant was absolute or permitted a change of use with the landlord's consent, such consent not to be unreasonably withheld. Stamp L.J. dealt with the case on both bases though, as a matter of construction, holding that it was fully qualified. On the basis that it was an absolute covenant, the assignment would not necessarily result in breach because the assignee *could* comply, albeit that he intended to apply for planning permission for offices. As the assignee could comply, consenting to the assignment need not preclude the landlord from enforcing the covenant against him subsequently. Such a situation did not *per se* give rise to an estoppel and the risk that the landlord may estop himself by some incautious action could be guarded against by the landlord expressly reserving his rights in relation to enforcement of the user covenant when granting his consent to the disposition. In the result therefore, the assignee

> "would step into the shoes of the lessee ... and would thereupon become subject to the user covenant. The landlords would be in the same position, neither better nor worse, to enforce the user covenant as would be the case if the present (lessees) were themselves proposing to seek planning permission for use of the premises as offices and proposed so to use them."[46]

On the basis that the user covenant was fully qualified, the landlord did not have a leg to stand on. There could then be no question of the assignment "inevitably" involving a breach of the user clause and raising an estoppel against the landlord— all that the assignment involved was that the assignee may in the future, as the user covenant envisaged, ask for consent for a change of use. He had every intention of seeking consent and there was no evidence that he would disregard a reasonable refusal (which was the only circumstance under which a breach would arise).[47]

The idea to which this case gives rise, namely, that the landlord can only reasonably withhold his consent where to consent would constitute a waiver of the user clause thus

[45] [1973] 2 All E.R. 337, 339.
[46] At p. 339.
[47] See also *British Bakeries (Midlands) Ltd.* v. *Michael Testler & Co. Ltd.* [1986] 1 E.G.L.R. 64, 65 where, in the light of *Killick* it was conceded that "even if the landlord did expect there to be a breach of the user covenant, it would not be a sufficient reason for withholding consent."

disabling him from subsequently enforcing it, was further considered and to some extent qualified in *F.W. Woolworth plc v. Charlwood Alliance Properties Ltd.*[48] It may be that though consent would not give rise to a waiver and would therefore not preclude the landlord from enforcing the user covenant, the remedy that he could expect from such an action would be inadequate. What he wants is compliance with the covenant and in the case of a restrictive user covenant, as in *Killick*, this can be secured by means of a prohibitory injunction. In *Woolworth* however there was a positive user covenant compliance with which was dependent upon the court's readiness to grant a mandatory injunction in the event of future breach, a matter which could not be taken for granted. Future enforcement may therefore be limited to a remedy in damages and this additional factor may make a refusal of consent reasonable.

Distinguish positive and restrictive user covenants

The *Woolworth* case concerned a 99-year lease of a substantial part of the Arndale Centre, Middleton, to the tenant, F.W. Woolworth, for use as a Woolco store. The lessors, Charlwood Alliance Properties Ltd., had included in the lease a positive covenant by the tenant "to keep the shop portion of the demised unit open for retail trade at least during the normal trading hours at the Centre." Some years later the tenant contracted to sell 11 Woolco stores, including the lease of the Middleton store, to the Dee Corporation. Rumours reached the lessors that the Middleton store would be closed down and when they received an application for consent to the assignment to the Dee Corporation, they sought an assurance from the tenant and the proposed assignee that the store would be kept open in compliance with the covenant. No assurance was forthcoming, despite repeated requests. The tenant did cease to carry on business at the store and issued an originating summons claiming a declaration that the lessors had unreasonably withheld consent. It was argued on his behalf, on the basis of *Killick*, that the lessor would only be reasonable in refusing consent, on the ground that the proposed assignee would not comply with a user covenant, where it could be shown that breach of the user covenant would be a necessary consequence of the assignment. His Honour Judge Finlay did consider factors from which he could, perhaps, have concluded that breach *was* inevitable, namely, that the actual company to which the assignment was to be made "had no practical capacity and very possibly no legal capacity to run a retail business."[49] However "lack of practical capacity" would not appear to involve the same degree of impossibility exhibited in the earlier cases and the lack of legal capacity was only a supposition. It seems preferable therefore to explain his decision that the withholding of consent was reasonable upon the basis that, although breach was not a necessary consequence of the assignment and the lessors would therefore be able to enforce the covenant against the proposed assignees subsequently, their remedy may well be limited to damages. In

[48] (1987) 282 E.G. 585.
[49] At p. 590.

Killick where the covenant was restrictive in nature " . . . an injunction either obtained *ex parte* or *inter partes* would prevent breach before it happened" and the lessor could insist that "the terms of the covenant be strictly complied with."[50] Specific enforcement of a positive covenant like the one in *Woolworth*, raised the question of the availability of a mandatory injunction and while the judge was prepared to assume "that there is no rule of law or settled practice which would militate against the grant of a mandatory injunction"[51] nevertheless in this particular case the lessor could entertain reasonable doubts as its availability, not least because of the "situation" and "character" of the proposed assignee—a reference no doubt to the legal and practical incapacity of the proposed assignee to comply with the positive covenant. If this is the correct interpretation of the case, the principle that the landlord refuses consent unreasonably if he will subsequently be able to enforce the user covenant against the assignee has been limited; he is now unreasonable only if he will subsequently be able to enforce *strict compliance*. Whilst one applauds the refinement of the *Killick* principle to meet the obvious needs of justice in the *Woolworth* case, it may be questioned whether one really has to become involved in estoppel and the availability of mandatory injunctions in order to settle cases of this type. It would be more straightforward to recognise that the landlord is protecting a relevant interest when he withholds consent because a breach of the user covenant is *likely*.

(ii) **Where there is no provision restricting user or such provision as there is will be complied with.**   Even where the landlord cannot point to an apt user restriction in the lease, he can still successfully refuse consent on the basis of anticipated

Refusal may still be reasonable

user. Thus, Kay L.J. in *Bates* v. *Donaldson*[52] opined that "if the proposed assignee intended to use the house for some purpose to which the landlord might reasonably object, *though such purpose was not forbidden by the lease, nor by any rule of law*,[53] the landlord might reasonably refuse to permit the assignment."[54] This statement was *obiter dicta*, the landlord in that case having refused consent upon grounds other than user. The more general statement by Warrington L.J. in *Re Gibbs & Houlder Bros. & Co. Ltd.'s Lease*[55] as to the sufficiency of an objection on the basis of the user which the proposed assignee is to make of the property is also illustrative of this point.[56] The argument that to allow the landlord to successfully object in these circumstances would enable him to secure an uncovenanted advantage in the form of the imposition, *ex post facto*, of a user restriction, has, as will be seen, made only

---

[50] At p. 590.
[51] *Ibid.* This point was considered further in connection with the lessors' counterclaim against the tenant actually seeking a mandatory injunction requiring the tenant to keep the store open, see p. 593.
[52] [1896] 2 Q.B. 241.
[53] Author's italics.
[54] At p. 244.
[55] [1925] All E.R. Rep. 128, 133.
[56] *Supra* p. 72.

limited progress. In *Bridewell Hospital (Governors)* v.
Faulkener[57] the landlord withheld consent because the proposed
assignment was to General Booth for use as offices for the
Salvation Army. The lease contained no provision preventing
such a use but Kekewich J. held that the landlord was
reasonable. In *Premier Confectionary (London) Co. Ltd.* v.
London Commercial Salerooms Ltd.[58] the lessors had let a shop
and a separate kiosk, in the same vicinity, to a single tenant. In
both leases, user was limited to the business of tobacconist.
Both leases had been assigned to the plaintiff company and on
its liquidation the liquidator sought consent to assign just the
kiosk to an assignee, who was financially sound, for use as a
tobacconists. Bennett J. found the landlord's refusal of consent
to be reasonable—they bona fide considered occupation by the
proposed assignee to be undesirable and it made no difference
that such occupation was not contrary to the lease or the rules
of law.[59] The substance of their objection was that the kiosk
was let at a low rent and attracted more business than the shop.
Its separate disposal and continued use as a tobacconists would
put at risk the viability of the business carried on at the shop
and thus the landlord's entitlement to future rents therefrom.
Then again in *Whiteminster Estates* v. *Hodges Menswear Ltd.*[60]
the landlords, Hodges, refused consent to an assignment of 8
Elgin Gate to Dunn's Outfitters because the business of Dunn's
Outfitters would compete with the business which they
themselves carried on at 10. The report is very brief but there
is no mention in it of any clause which restricted the user of
number 8. Had there been one, the landlord can be expected to
have relied on it. It was held by Pennycuick V.-C. that consent
had been reasonably withheld. *Rodney* v. *Austerfield*[61] would
appear to be another case where the proposed use was not
prohibited by the lease and yet the landlord was found
reasonable in refusing consent to the use proposed—that of a
bookmakers. The landlord had a moral objection to this
business and Judge Perks opined that

> "[t]here were many activities, now lawful, which were
> unlawful a short while ago—prostitution, abortion and
> bookmaking were examples—and although the law might
> have changed there was no reason for a person's own
> morality to do so."

The statement of Kay L.J. in *Bates* v. *Donaldson* (quoted
above) was accepted as a proposition of law in the very much
more recent case of *International Drilling Fluids Ltd.* v.
Louisville Investments (Uxbridge) Ltd.[62] Balcombe L.J. did not
however choose to apply it to the facts of that particular case.
It concerned a 30-year lease (of which 16 were unexpired) of an
office building. The building was not to be used "for any

[57] (1892) 8 T.L.R. 637.
[58] [1933] Ch. 904.
[59] At p. 912.
[60] (1974) E.G. 715.
[61] 1979 C.L.Y. 1572.
[62] [1986] 1 All E.R. 321, 325.

purpose other than offices ... with ancilliary showrooms." The tenant sought consent to assign the lease to Euro Business Services Ltd., not as its own offices but to run the business of letting out, on a temporary basis, fully furnished and serviced office accommodation. It was common ground that this was within the terms of the user clause, but the landlord argued that it would depreciate the value of his reversion. Balcombe L.J., who gave the only substantial judgment, pointed out that, with the exception of *Premier Confectionary*,[63] cases where the landlord had been held reasonable in refusing consent despite the fact that the proposed disponee would comply with user clause, were all cases where the user clause left the tenant with considerable freedom. He considered that there "is all the difference in the world between the case where the user clause prohibits only certain types of use, so the tenant is free to use the property in any other way, and the case where (as here) only one type of specific use is permitted." In the latter case "it is not reasonable for the landlord to refuse consent to an assignment on grounds of the proposed user (being within the only specific type of use), where the result will be that the property is left vacant and where (as here) the landlord is fully secured for payment of the rent."[64] He refused to follow *Premier Confectionary*[65] to the extent that it suggested that "in all circumstances it is reasonable for a landlord to refuse his consent to an assignment on the grounds of the proposed user, even though the proposed user is the only user permitted by the lease."[66] He found it difficult to reconcile the decision with the proposition, which he accepted,[67] that "the landlord is not entitled to refuse his consent ... on grounds which have nothing whatever to do with the relationship of landlord and tenant in regard to the subject-matter of the lease."[68] In other words the landlord had succeeded in getting an uncovenanted advantage at the expense of the tenant—who was deprived of a covenanted right to use the property as a tobacconists. He admitted the possibility that the actual decision could be supported upon other grounds—"in that the two tenancies were originally granted to the same person and there was no certainty (as there is here) that the landlord had security for the rent of the shop for the residue of the term."[69] The possibility of explaining the case upon the basis of a collateral agreement with the original tenant that the two properties would be assigned together to a common assignee is discussed in relation to "Objections based upon harm to other property of the landlord."[70]

Distinguish narrow user clauses

Thus, if the use proposed is within the only form of user permitted by the lease, the landlord may well be unreasonable in refusing his consent on grounds of user as such will be

[63] *Supra.*
[64] At p. 327.
[65] Which as a decision of first instance did not, in any event, bind him.
[66] At p. 327.
[67] At p. 325.
[68] At pp. 325, 327 and see *Re Gibbs & Houlder, supra* p. 72.
[69] At p. 327.
[70] See *infra.*

considered a trespass upon the tenant's covenanted rights. He
should therefore consider reformulating his objection so that he
is no longer objecting to the user *per se* but rather to its effect
upon his other relevant interests. He may, for example, argue
that the proposed business was unsound and this gave rise to
the danger that the rent would not be paid throughout the
term. If, on the other hand, the use proposed is one of a
number permitted by the lease, a refusal on grounds of user
will, strangely, not be considered a trespass upon the tenant's
covenanted rights and the landlord can therefore more easily
establish that he has acted reasonably.

Objections based on harm to other property of the landlord

**Not necessarily
reasonable**

The need to protect other property of the landlord is not,
necessarily, a relevant interest which the landlord is entitled to
protect. The point is illustrated by *Re Gibbs & Houlder Bros. &
Co. Ltd.'s Lease*[71] where the landlord refused consent to an
assignment to Roneo Ltd. because he would thereby lose
Roneo as good tenants of property which adjoined the property
demised. He would find great difficulty in reletting the
adjoining property, leading to a loss of rent. The Court of
Appeal held unanimously that the tenant was entitled to a
declaration that consent had been unreasonably withheld. Sir
Ernest Pollock M.R. stressed the need to consider
reasonableness in relation

> "to the premises, and to the contract made in reference to
> the premises between the lessor and the lessee; in other
> words one must pay attention to the relation of landlord
> and tenant *inter se*, or perhaps one may add, to the due
> and proper management of the property or it may be on
> grounds which are important between the lessor and other
> tenants of that property or that estate, of which the lessee
> had cognisance."[72]

He regarded the objection in the present case as quite
independent of the relation of lessor and lessee: as being
personal to the lessor and "wholly extraneous to the lessee."[73]
Warrington L.J., also, said that the "outstanding circumstance
to be considered is the nature of the contract to be construed
and the relation between the parties resulting from it" and
went on to point out that "in cases in which an objection to an
assignment has been upheld as reasonable, it has always had
some reference either to the personality of the tenant, or to his
proposed user of the property."[74] The view of Sargant, L.J.
was similar:

---

[71] [1925] 2 All E.R. 128.
[72] At p. 132.
[73] *Ibid.*
[74] At p. 133.

"you have to consider what was within the reasonable
contemplation of the parties to the lease ... the reason
must be something affecting the subject-matter of the
contract between the landlord and the tenant, and it must
not be something wholly extraneous and completely
dissociated from the subject-matter of the contract. ...
   The result of any other view than that which I have
expressed in the present case, would be that as the
personality of the lessor varied [consequent on an
assignment of the reversion], so the reasons for refusing or
withholding consent ... might vary if those reasons might
include any circumstance that happened for the time being
to affect the pecuniary interest of the lessor. In the present
case, the reason for refusing has nothing whatever to do
with the relationship of landlord and tenant in regard to
the subject-matter of the demise. The sole reason is that, if
the property is allowed to be assigned to the new tenants,
the new tenants will desire to terminate their tenancy of
other property under the power of determination given to
them by the lease under which they hold that property ...
that is a reason wholly dissociated from, and unconnected
with, the bargain made between the lessor and the lessees
under the lease which we have to consider, and is, from
that point of view, a purely arbitrary and irrelevant
reason."[75]

Bargain between the parties

It is important to note that all regarded as crucial the
bargain between the parties when the lease was entered into.
In the above case the right to protect other property of the
landlord was not part of that bargain—but it could be
otherwise. Such a right could arise, explicitly or implicitly,
from the terms of the lease, or even, perhaps, from a
contemporaneous collateral agreement.[76] This may be what
Pollock M.R. had in mind when he referred to the validity of
grounds "which are important between the lessor and other
tenants of that property or that estate of which the lessee had
cognisance." For example, if there were several tenants in a
building or on an estate and to the knowledge of the particular
lessee the lettings had been arranged with certain ends in view,
the landlord would be entitled to refuse his consent to a
disposition which would be inconsistent with the overall
scheme. Such a contractual approach could perhaps clarify
Premier Confectionary London Co. Ltd. v. *London Commercial
Sale Rooms Ltd.*[77] Here two properties, a shop and a kiosk had
been let to a single tenant and both leases restricted the use to
a tobacconists. Both were assigned to the present tenant whose
liquidator sought permission to assign just the kiosk. Bennett J.
held that the landlord was entitled to withhold his consent
though the user would be within the only type of user
permitted in the lease (a feature of the case criticised by
Balcombe L.J. in *International Drilling Fluids Ltd.* v. *Louisville*

---

[75] At pp. 134, 135.
[76] Compare *Wilson* v. *Flynn* [1948] 2 All E.R. 40.
[77] [1933] Ch. 904—see also *supra* "Objections based upon anticipated user".

Investments (Uxbridge) Ltd.[78]). He could, perhaps more convincingly, have found that there was a collateral agreement, at the time the lease of the kiosk was entered into, that it would only be assigned together with the lease of the shop, to a common assignee. It is clear that from the beginning there was an agreed plan showing how the space on the ground floor of the building, upon which both the shop and the kiosk were situated, was to be used. There was also reference to a policy adopted by the landlord that there should not be different tenants of premises in the building carrying on trade in competition.

Harm from user or personality of assignee

Be that as it may, such a contractual approach is not capable of explaining all the cases where the landlord has been held reasonable in protecting his other property in the vicinity. Such an outcome has also been justified upon the basis that the landlord is entitled to refuse his consent if the harm to his other property would flow directly from the demised property via the personality of the proposed assignee or the use he would make of the demised property. This reasoning was certainly present in *Premier Confectionary*, Bennett J. justifying the refusal by the landlord on the basis that it was the user of the kiosk by the proposed assignee as a tobacconists which gave rise to the harm to the shop.[79] In *Bridewell Hospital (Governors)* v. *Fawkner*[80] the proposed assignment was to General Booth for the purposes of the Salvation Army. Kekewich J. held that the refusal of the landlord was reasonable because he was entitled to consider "the well-being of the whole estate."[81] "It might be that one property was intended to be held for a purpose, which however excellent in itself, might deteriorate the other properties"[82] and the belief of the landlord that this would be so in the present case was reasonable (despite the fact that the property was required solely as offices and no meetings or band playing would take place). Even where the harm alleged does flow from the use of the demised premises or the personality of the proposed assignee, it must be substantiated. The fears of the landlord in that regard must be reasonable.[83] In *Berenyi* v. *Watford Borough Council*[84] it was claimed that the disposition, a sublease, would cause over-intensification of use and would lead to traffic congestion and manoeuvering difficulties but, in fact, these factors had been discounted by an inspector on a planning appeal. In *Rayburn* v. *Wolf*[85] it was claimed that the assignment, being to a person who had no immediate intention of occupying, would lead to subleases which may be of short duration and to young people who have the wrong attitudes and may therefore cause friction with the other residents. Such harm was dependent upon too many future contingencies to justify a refusal of consent at the

---

[78] [1986] 1 All E.R. 321.
[79] And see *Whiteminster Estates* v. *Hodges Menswear Ltd.* (1974) E.G. 715.
[80] (1892) 8 T.L.R. 637.
[81] At p. 637.
[82] *Ibid.*
[83] See *infra.*
[84] (1980) 256 E.G. 271 C.A.
[85] (1986) 18 H.L.R. 1.

assignment stage but it was freely conceded that they may be of great relevance should permission subsequently be sought to sublet.

In conclusion, if the protection of other property of the landlord is reasonably apprehended and either is part of the bargain between lessor and lessee, or is associated with the personality or user of the proposed assignee of the demised premises, it may justify a refusal of consent. A desire to protect other property of the landlord can be regarded as an aspect of good estate management and references to this concept can be found in many of the above cases. Other aspects of good estate management are considered below.

Objections based on good estate management

The concept of good estate management is a vague one and cannot, without further definition, form the basis of a reasonable refusal of consent. It may be that the landlord is concerned about harm which the assignment may do to his other property. Such cases have been discussed above. Under the present heading it is proposed to deal with cases where the landlord has adopted some overall policy which he would like to see implemented in relation to the demised premises. An early case of some relevance is *Viscount Tredegar* v. *Harwood*.[86] The lease in this case contained a covenant on the part of the tenant to "keep insured the (demised premises) . . . in the Law Fire Office or in some other responsible insurance office to be approved by the lessor." The current tenant was required by his mortgage to insure with the Atlas Company and did so having failed to secure the landlord's approval. As a test case, the landlord brought forfeiture proceedings against him for breach of covenant. The House of Lords had to decide first, whether the covenant should be read subject to the qualification that such approval was not to be unreasonably withheld,[87] and secondly, if so, whether the landlord could reasonably have refused his approval. Viscount Dunedin and Lord Shaw of Dunfermline[88] did not see fit to imply the qualification but, had they done so, they would have reached the conclusion that the landlord was entitled in this case to withhold consent.

> "Lord Tredegar being the ground landlord of some 1000's of houses in Cardiff found it almost impossible, if they were insured in many different offices, to check the due renewals of the premiums. Whereas if they were all insured in the Law Fire, then by arrangement with that office, they kept his agents informed of any default so that he might apply for due renewal of the premium."[89]

(margin note:) **Estate management policies**

[86] [1929] A.C. 72.
[87] s.19 of the Landlord and Tenant Act 1927 being inapplicable to covenants to insure.
[88] Lord Blanesburgh dissented.
[89] *Per* Viscount Dunedin at p. 77.

"it would be wrong to confine the reason in such a case to the particular house exclusive of all considerations as to the management of the estate to which it belonged."[90]

Lord Blanesburgh, dissenting, noted that the Tredegar Estate policy of disallowing insurance in other offices, even when necessary to facilitate a tenant's mortgage arrangements, was recent and a departure from what was contemplated when the leases were granted.[91] In *Bromley Park Garden Estates Ltd.* v. *Moss*[92] where such a contractual approach had something of a rebirth, Cumming-Bruce L.J. noted the Tredegar Case as standing out as the only case where the landlord had succeeded despite there having been no harm to his neighbouring property and he went on to point out that the decision in relation to reasonableness, while entitled to "great respect" was *obiter*.

Bromley Park v. Moss

Bromley Park itself was another case where the landlord could not argue harm to his other property and based his objection upon interference with a policy adopted, in the interests of "estate management," after the date of the lease. The case concerned a flat above a restaurant. Both flat and restaurant were originally owned by St. John's College, Cambridge and were let by them to separate tenants. The property was subsequently sold to the plaintiffs subject to the two leases. The flat was held upon a three year lease subject *inter alia* to a fully qualified covenant against assignment and a covenant relating to interior repair. When the lease had eight months to run the then tenant applied for a licence to assign to the defendant. The licence was refused, the assignor being advised that if she wished to vacate the flat she must surrender the lease; it was not the landlord's practice to permit assignments of residential tenancies. This absolute refusal to consider assignments was manifestly unreasonable[93] and therefore the assignor, relying upon her residual common law right, assigned the lease to the defendant. The plaintiffs issued proceedings for possession against him in the county court on the ground of breach of covenant. In the action, changing ground somewhat, the plaintiffs claimed that the refusal was reasonable as being in the interests of the proper management of their estate: properties subject to multiple lettings had a lower investment value than properties in single occupation and the opportunity now existed to let the entire premises to the existing tenant of the restaurant at an increased rent and subject to a full repairing covenant. The Court of Appeal held unanimously that consent had been unreasonably been withheld. The plaintiffs had relied upon a statement in *Woodfall on Landlord and Tenant*[94] which reflected the traditional view that a refusal of consent based on the personality of the proposed assignee, the effect of the proposed

[90] *Per* Lord Shaw at p. 81.
[91] At pp. 84, 85.
[92] [1982] 2 All E.R. 890.
[93] See *Lehman* v. *McArthur* (1867) L.R. 3 Eq. 746; *Bates* v. *Donaldson* [1896] 2 Q.B. 241.
[94] 1978, Vol. 1, para. 1181.

assignment upon user and occupation of the demised premises, or, as was most relevant here, the proper management of the lessor's estate, will be reasonable. The Court of Appeal, **Uncovenanted** however, held that the issue of reasonableness did not fall to **advantages** be considered primarily upon the basis of such considerations but rather upon the basis of the contract between the lessor and the lessee and the right being asserted by the landlord in this case was,

> "wholly extraneous to the intention of the parties to the contract when the covenant was granted and accepted. It cannot be relied upon merely because it would suit the plaintiff's investment plans. It may well enhance the financial interests of the plaintiff to obtain a single tenant holding the whole building ... but that intention and policy is entirely outside the intention to be imputed to the parties at the time of the granting of the lease."[95]

While *Bromley Park* was not expressly referred to by the Court of Appeal in the later case of *Rayburn* v. *Wolf*,[96] the decision proceeded upon a similar basis. Here the landlords decided, in spite of the fact that the lease contained a fully qualified covenant allowing both assignments and subleases with consent, that they would not consent to the proposed assignment because the assignee was an American who had no plans to live in flat for 20 years and may, therefore, indulge in short term subletting to young perons whose "habits and attitudes are not the same as those of the majority of the residents" and could cause friction in the future.[97] The court concerned itself with the immediate objection namely that the particular assignment would give rise to subletting. In that connection it was stated that the landlord could take into account good estate management "so long as he is not trying to secure an uncovenanted benefit."[98] In this case, as in *Bromley Park*, the result of a refusal upon the stated ground would secure to the landlord an uncovenanted benefit. "It is quite clear that the lease itself envisages not only assignments but also underleases; therefore it is plainly within the purvue of this lease that there were to be underleases. So the mere possibility of an underlease being granted by a proposed assignee (something anticipated by the headlease itself) cannot be a ground for objection."[99] Here again therefore the landlord was trying to impose an estate management policy, the results of which would have been outside the contemplation of the parties at the time the lease was made and which would have amounted to the extraction of an uncovenanted advantage. It was pointed out by the court that upon the occasion of a future application for consent to sublet, the landlord would be able to reasonably withhold his consent if he could then establish that the subletting would give rise to estate management problems

---

[95] *Per* Cumming-Bruce L.J. at p. 899.
[96] (1986) 18 H.L.R. 1.
[97] At p. 4.
[98] *Per* Browne-Wilkinson, L.J. at p. 4.
[99] *Ibid.*

stemming from the undesirability of the subtenant or the terms of the sublease.[1]

Thus it is submitted that if the landlord's policy has no place in the contractual context in which the lease was made, its subsequent imposition upon the occasion of an application for consent to a disposition will be unreasonable. Only in *Tredegar* has the contrary been suggested and that was *obiter*.

Objections based upon the financial or business status of the assignee

Landlord's interest in future rent and value of reversion

The financial status of an assignee can affect relevant interests of the landlord[2]—in the receipt of future rent and, consequentially, in the value of the reversion, should he wish to sell it. The ability of the assignee to run the business, a separate and yet closely connected factor, can affect the same interests because lack of a sound business track record may result in future financial instability.

Factors relevant to assignee's status

The tenant will invariably have to supply references relating to the proposed assignee: bank references, trade references, accounts, etc. In *British Bakeries (Midlands) Ltd.* v. *Michael Testler & Co. Ltd.*[3] and *Ponderosa International Developments Inc.* v. *Pengap Securities (Bristol) Ltd.*[4] the references supplied were found to be sufficiently inadequate to justify a refusal of consent by the landlords. The following points are drawn from the judgments of Peter Gibson and Warner JJ. respectively in those cases.

(1)   The terms of the letter requesting the reference may need to be disclosed to properly interpret its contents,[5] unless the reference itself is very specific.

(2)   A disclaimer of liability "while common enough these days, . . . nevertheless detracts from the weight" to be given to the reference.[6]

(3)   Where an assignee authorises his bank to disclose confidential information but the bank "conspicuously" fails to give the information, an unfavourable implication may be made, *e.g.* that the assignee is overdrawn.[7]

(4)   In the case of trade references, the business standing of the referee should be clear and where a referee is exercising his profession, *e.g.* as accountant or valuer,

---

[1] See *supra* Objections based upon harm to other property.
[2] *e.g. Shanley* v. *Ward* (1913) 29 T.L.R. 714.
[3] [1986] 1 E.G.L.R. 64.
[4] [1986] 1 E.G.L.R. 66.
[5] *Ponderosa* at p. 69.
[6] *British Bakeries* at p. 65.
[7] *Ponderosa* at p. 69.

he should have and be seen to have appropriate qualifications. Thus in *British Bakeries* the judge commented that "it is impossible to place much reliance on valuations which are not stated to have been made by a professional valuer."[8]

(5) Where the obligations under the lease are greater than those which the assignee has customarily had to bear, the reference should address the assignee's ability to support the increased burden. A positive opinion offered upon this matter should reveal the facts upon which it is based.[9]

(6) A trade reference should reveal the amount of business transacted between the referee and the assignee and that business should be on a scale appropriate to the obligations in respect of which the reference was sought.[10] It should be business which is relevant to that which the assignee is proposing to carry on in the future.[11]

(7) Any accounts supplied should be up to date and audited. Unaudited accounts mean that the accountants must have been dependent on what they were told by the assignee. If the accounts make no allowance for a salary to the assignee and there is no evidence of an income from some independent source, the profit shown should be appropriately discounted. Pre-tax profits (after any such adjustment), as a rule of thumb, should be not less than three times the amount payable (in relation to rent, rates if the rent is exclusive thereof, repairs and other outgoings) under the lease being assigned. An asset valuation is less significant because "a reasonable landlord is concerned with the tenant's ability to meet the obligations under the lease as those obligations fall due. "Many a debtor is properly made bankrupt, even though he claims he has assets which when ultimately realised would be sufficient to pay his debts."[12]

(8) Any hint of vagueness may be regarded adversely, *e.g.* a failure to state whether a salary figure is before or after tax or an indication that property has been charged without disclosing the extent of the charge.

(9) Where the assignee's financial status is on the weak side, the landlord will still be held to have unreasonably withheld his consent if the assignee is backed by a strong guarantor and, in the case of a recently granted lease, the original covenantor remains liable for the rent and performance of the covenants.[12a]

These factors may be of relevance whether the assignee is an individual or a limited company, but in relation to the latter

---

[8] At p. 65.
[9] *British Bakeries, ibid.*
[10] *British Bakeries, ibid.*
[11] *Rossi v. Hestdrive Ltd.* [1985] 1 E.G.L.R. 50.
[12] *British Bakeries, ibid.*
[12a] *Venetian Glass Gallery Ltd. v. Next Properties Ltd.* [1989] 30 E.G. 92.

Assignee company, part of a group

the court may very well take into account the position of any holding company of the proposed assignee. In *Re Greater London Properties Ltd.'s Lease*[13] the tenant sought consent for an assignment to a company which was a wholly owned subsidiary of a well-known combine, Allied Bakeries Ltd. The rent reserved was £225 p.a. The assignee company had a nominal capital of £50,000 of which £14,000 had been issued to a holding company whose capital, in turn, was wholly owned by Allied Bakeries Ltd. Its accounts showed liabilities of £257,153 of which £215,028 was payable to Allied Bakeries Ltd. The assignee company had used this latter sum to acquire fixed assets. It was carrying on business at a profit and a greater profit was expected in the next year. In view of the unfavourable ratio between the issued capital and the liabilities, the landlord refused consent unless Allied Bakeries Ltd. gave a guarantee for the rent (which it declined to do). Danckwerts J. held that consent had been unreasonably withheld. He found the landlord's objection absurd—"a point which might be taken by a pedantic chartered accountant." The figures, he pointed out, should not be taken "as a theoretical exercise without any regard to the probable facts." Although the assignee owed its holding company a large sum, it was not likely to be called in. Indeed the relationship between the holding company and the subsidiary was, he considered, a source of strength rather than weakness to the subsidiary. In any event even if the debt was called in, the subsidiary could sell its fixed assets and meet the debt.[14]

Changes in legal form

Where the assignment involves little more than a change in legal form, the landlord will not be justified in withholding consent. Thus in *Ideal Film Renting Co.* v. *Neilson*[15] the proposed assignee was a new company, formed by the tenant company which was to be wound up as part of a reconstruction. The new company had a larger issued capital than the tenant company and it was all paid up in cash. It would carry on the same business as before under the same directors. The landlord refused consent on the grounds that the new company had, as yet, done no business at all and the business in which it was engaged, film production, was "highly speculative." A new lease at a much increased rent was suggested as an alternative. Eve J. held that consent had been unreasonably withheld because the new company was well capitalised and the assignment involved no change in the type of business being carried on. The tenant company though initially just a film renting company, had gradually moved into film production and had been successful at it. In *Lam Kee Sdn Shd* v. *Lam Shes Tong*[16] the issue was whether the landlord could reasonably have withheld his consent to a parting with possession by the tenant (for the purposes of deciding whether the court should grant relief against forfeiture). The lease permitted the lessee to carry on business on the demised

[13] [1959] 1 W.L.R. 503.
[14] At p. 507.
[15] [1921] 1 Ch. 575.
[16] [1974] 3 All E.R. 137 P.C.

premises in partnership and this he did. Ultimately, together with his partners he formed a limited company and transferred the business to it. The tenant held the majority of the shares. Sir Harry Gibbs, while admitting that "a lessor is not bound blindly to give his consent . . . to any company which the lessee may form to carry on his business and although in some cases of that kind it may be prudent for the lessor to require guarantees from the lessees,"[17] in the present case consent had unreasonably been withheld.

Assignments involving a depreciation in the value of the landlord's reversionary interest

In more recent cases there has been a tendency to argue, from the financial and business status of the proposed assignee, not only that the landlord's right to future rent will be prejudiced but also that, consequentially, the value of his reversion, should he wish to sell it, will be depreciated. Clearly if a tenant is of

Poor financial standing and management poor financial standing or is not carrying on business profitably, the reversion will constitute a very poor investment to a prospective buyer. A landlord therefore has a legitimate interest in preventing such circumstances from arising. Where there is a rent review clause a more specific point can sometimes be made—namely that poor management will be reflected in the tenant's accounts and this may lead to a reduced rental on the next rent review and thus to a depreciation in the landlord's reversionary interest. This argument will be accepted in only limited circumstances though, because the rental value is usually fixed by reference to comparables rather than by reference to the tenant's accounts. This point was made in *City Hotels Group Ltd.* v. *Total Property Investments Ltd.*[18] which concerned a lease of an hotel. Judge Paul Baker Q.C. accepted[19] that in the case of a small retail shop "of which there were many comparables readily available" it would be "oppressive and quite improper" to look at a tenants accounts[20] but hotels were different because they varied in size, location, type and standard. Rental values in the case of hotels *may* be fixed by reference to the tenants accounts (as well as by means of comparables, if available). In the instant case therefore management quality could affect the landlord's relevant interests in the manner argued but, on the facts, the judge held that consent had been unreasonably withheld.

Is sale imminent? The success which a landlord can expect from arguing a depreciation in the value of his reversion may depend upon whether a sale of the reversion is in prospect. In *International Drilling Fluids Ltd.* v. *Louisville Investments (Uxbridge) Ltd.*,[21] where such a depreciation was argued to follow from the

---

[17] At p. 145.
[18] [1985] 1 E.G.L.R. 253.
[19] On the authority of *Barton Ltd.* v. *Longacre Securities Ltd.* [1982] 1 W.L.R. 398.
[20] At p. 253.
[21] [1986] 1 All E.R. 321.

intended user of the proposed assignee, Balcombe L.J. refused to interfere with the decision of the trial judge, Mr. Edward Nugee, Q.C., that although reasonable professional men could hold the view that the assignment could diminish the landlord's reversionary interest, "in the circumstances of this case, in which, so far as the evidence shows, there is no prospect of (the demised premises) being placed on the market or mortgaged to the fullest extent possible, that does not in my judgment constitute a ground for reasonable apprehension of damage to the (landlord's) property interest."[22] Balcombe L.J. also considered that the judges decision could be supported upon another ground, namely that if there *was* any diminution in the paper value of the reversion, it was in the circumstances a "minimum disadvantage" when compared to the disproportionate harm to the tenant if the landlord were entitled to refuse consent to the assignment.[22a] This may be contrasted with the decision in *Ponderosa International Developments Inc.* v. *Pengap Securities (Bristol) Ltd.*[23] which concerned a lease of a shop, in a new development, to a tenant, an American company with 650 restaurants in the United States and three in the United Kingdom. The tenant was aware when taking the lease that it was the landlord's intention, having let all the component units on the development, to sell the whole development to an investor. Shortly after the lease the tenant sought consent to an assignment to an English company with which it had entered into a franchise agreement. The landlord's refusal of consent was held to be reasonable by Warner J. *inter alia* because the landlord "wants and needs to sell. . . . There is evidence that, because of the nature of the arrangement that it made to finance the development, it will be in difficulties fairly soon."[24] In the circumstances the apprehended detriment to the landlord should consent be given outweighed that which would be visited on the tenant were it to be denied.[24a]

The last two cases addressed another issue of concern to landlords in preserving the value of their reversions—if the current tenant is of high financial and business calibre an assignment to a tenant of more modest status may occasion a reduction in investment value. However as was pertinently pointed out by counsel for the tenant in *Ponderosa*, there may be no *legal* justification for such a market reduction. If the

High status of current tenant

current tenant is the original tenant, then his covenants are not lost upon assignment but endure for the full duration of the lease.[25] If he is not the original tenant but nonetheless has himself made direct covenants with the landlord, the position will be the same. It is only where the current tenant is not the original tenant and has not made direct covenants with the landlord that his covenants are lost for the future and this was not the situation in *International Drilling* or in *Ponderosa*.

---

[22] *Ibid.*; quoted at p. 324 and see p. 326, *per* Balcombe L.J.
[22a] At p. 326.
[23] [1986] 1 E.G.L.R. 66.
[24] At p. 68.
[24a] See *infra*.
[25] Unless s.79 of the Law of Property Act is excluded.

Warner J. in *Ponderosa*, acknowledged the legal position but was not prepared to conclude that the market was necessarily acting unreasonably in writing down the value of the reversion—the point being that there may be administrative considerations which would justify it (a reference, perhaps, to the possible difficulty of suing those who are no longer concerned with the property). He went further and accepted that even if the market was reacting unreasonably, the landlord would be perfectly reasonable to take the market into account for he "has to live in the real world and to take the market as he finds it not as lawyers might wish it to be."[26]

It would appear therefore that a reduction in the status of the tenant is something which the courts are prepared to consider in connection with depreciation of reversionary interest but it is also true that the weight which will be accorded to it will vary. Paying too much regard to this factor could result in "gross unfairness" to the tenant as Balcombe L.J. recognised in *International Drilling*. He illustrated this by quoting an example from the judgment of the trial judge who had said:

> "It seems to me that, if counsel for the landlord is correct, the more substantial the lessee, the more easily the landlord would be able to justify a refusal of consent to an assignment, since unless the proposed assignee's covenant was as strong as the assignor's, a reasonable man might form the view that the market would consider the reversion less attractive if the lease were vested in the proposed assignee than if it were vested in the proposed assignor. To take the matter to extremes, if a lease were made in favour of a government department, it would be unassignable unless to another government department; for ... the market would prefer to have the government as a lessee ... rather than a company, however strong its covenant."[27]

He made it clear that the appropriate manner in which to proceed was to place the status objection in the balance with all other relevant matters and in the instant case it was easily outweighed by the "extreme and disproportionate" detriment which would be suffered by the tenant from a refusal.[28] The proposed assignees, modest though their status, were the only people who had expressed any serious interest in the property despite the best efforts of the agents, and a loss of that transaction would mean that the tenant, who had already moved out, would be faced with payment of a very considerable rent in relation to an empty property.

In *Ponderosa* the balance of interest was different because the landlord needed to sell in the near future and the tenant was not *in extremis* because the landlord was quite willing to grant consent to a sublease to the proposed disponee. The tenant was not particularly happy about granting a sublease

---

[26] At p. 68.
[27] At p. 326.
[28] At p. 326.

because he would still be involved with collecting rent, rent reviews and the like but Warner J. opined that these elements of detriment were "nothing like that faced by the tenant in *International Drilling*."[29]

Thus, it would seem from these cases that maintenance of the status of the tenant is not something which can certainly be achieved via the typical fully qualified covenant. The fact that the landlord had a "blue chip" tenant in the past will not necessarily guarantee such a tenant in the future. The best way to achieve this, as so much else, is by an absolute covenant which can be selectively waived.

Objections based on the disponee's legal status

Present legal status

The objection may be directed to the present or the future legal status of the disponee. The former is rather rare but *Parker* v. *Boggan*[30] is an example. The landlord refused consent to an underletting to a counsellor at the Turkish Embassy in London

Diplomatic immunity who had the benefit of diplomatic immunity. The tenant underlet anyway and the landlord brought proceedings for forfeiture. Counsel for the tenant argued that the subtenant's status was irrelevant because no circumstances could arise in which the landlord could sue the subtenant, there being no privity of contract or privity of estate between them. The landlord's counsel pointed out that if the tenant's tenancy was determined for any reason, he would be unable to get judgment for possession against the subtenant. Macnaghten J. held that consent had been unreasonably withheld but did not actually address these matters. He opined that the proposed subtenant's status was sufficient for most people to be certain that he would meet his obligations "not merely because of the responsibility of a gentleman in that position, but because the Turkish Republic could not afford to allow a man who was accepted by His Majesty as the Counsellor of the Embassy to disregard his contractual obligations with regard to the payment of rent or indeed, the observing of covenants which the lease imposed."[31] This sort of reasoning would seem to apply equally to a case where an assignment[32] to a person with a diplomatic immunity is proposed but one must question whether that would necessarily be correct. Such an assignment would involve depriving the landlord of the right of suit he would otherwise expect to enjoy by virtue of privity of estate. It is submitted that

7,18

[29] At p. 68.
[30] [1947] K.B. 346.
[31] At p. 349.
[32] The case under discussion is treated as one on assignment in *Woodfall, Landlord and Tenant*, 1, 1183.

this is a relevant interest which he is entitled to protect even if the assignee is backed up by a reliable foreign power because the landlord should not be expected to rely upon moral obligation. *A fortiori* he should be able to refuse his consent where there is any doubt about the reliability of the foreign power.

Future legal status

Comparison with Rent Acts

—under the Housing Act 1988.   Cases in the past have concerned proposed assignees who would in future qualify for protection under the Rent Acts, while the assignor would not have done so or would not have availed himself of that protection. Because of the security of tenure and rent control provisions of that Act, landlords understandably did not welcome a disposition which would bring the tenancy within its terms and could in certain circumstances[33] wit hold their consent. Dispositions in the future cannot have the consequence of triggering Rent Act protection because after the commencement of the Housing Act 1988, no more protected tenancies can come into existence.[34] It may be, however, that a similar situation could arise in relation to assured tenancies under the 1988 Act—for example it may be that the assignor is not entitled to protection under the Housing Act 1988, but the assignee would be. The Act, like its predecessor applies where "a dwellinghouse is let as a separate dwelling."[35] In order to qualify for an assured tenancy the tenant must be an individual[36] and must occupy the dwellinghouse as "his only or principal home."[37] The original letting may therefore have been to a company or to an individual who had a principal home elsewhere and thus not fall within the definition of an assured tenancy. A subsequent assignment or sublease to an individual as a principal home may[38] then result in protection under the 1988 Act. It must be understood however that the protection afforded to an assured tenant under the 1988 Act is more limited than under the Rent Acts, and therefore poses less of a threat to the landlord's interests. Where the disponee is potentially an assured tenant, he will be entitled to security of tenure but there is no control over the rent initially fixed, and subsequent variations are conditioned by the market: thus "there seems little point in conferring security of tenure if the landlord can increase the rent to a level beyond the tenant's means in order to remove the latter without recourse to possession proceedings."[39] It may also be noted that of the three grounds for possession which relate to non-payment of rent one is now in the mandatory list.[40] Despite these changes

[33] See below.
[34] See s.34(1) of the Housing Act 1988; save in the exceptional circumstances set out in s.1(1) which are not material in the present context.
[35] s.1(1).
[36] s.1(1)(*a*).
[37] s.1(1)(*b*).
[38] Note exclusions in s.1 and Sched. 1.
[39] C. P. Rogers, *Housing, the New Law*, (1989) p. 7.
[40] See Sched. 2, Ground 8: compare Grounds 10 and 11.

in the landlord's favour, it is likely that he can still argue that the potentially assured status of an assignee or sublessee interferes with his covenanted right to re-enter at the end of the
term and the Rent Act cases will continue to have some relevance should this objection be made.[41] Where the tenant is proposing to grant merely an assured *shorthold* tenancy under section 20 of the Housing Act 1988, because of the rather slight security of tenure conferred by such a lettings, it may be held not to damage the landlord's right of re-entry. In *Searle* v. *Burroughs*[42] the tenant sought permission to grant a furnished sublease at the time when furnished lettings carried little security (pre-1974 Rent Act) and the Court of Appeal decided that such a letting would not detract from the value of the landlord's reversion. It may be noted that the lease had 14 years still to run.

Principles derived from the Rent Act cases

(1) It is clear that the landlord will have a covenanted right to re-enter at the expiration of the term and this, having been in the contemplation of the parties when the lease was made, must be regarded as a relevant interest which he is entitled to protect when considering whether to grant his consent to a disposition.

Covenanted right to re-enter

(2) What may not have been in the contemplation of the parties at the time the lease was made was the precise nature of the danger which ultimately presented itself. Thus in *Leeward Securities Ltd.* v. *Lilyheath Properties Ltd.*[43] where the lease was made prior to the Rent Acts, the disposition provision was probably included to prevent the "introduction of unsuitable tenants who might possibly run the property down or give it a bad reputation, so that it was depreciated when it came back into the landlord's hands" rather than to ensure that the landlord was not left with a tenant entitled to security of tenure.[44] This will not matter. As long as the court can construe the general purpose of the disposition clause as being to protect the landlord's reversion, the fact that the particular danger was not known by the parties when the lease was made does not prevent it being a circumstance relevant to the question of the landlord's reasonableness.[45] The circumstances were slightly different in *West Layton* v. *Ford*[46] where the lease made it clear that the parties *did* contemplate the danger of a Rent Act tenancy and couched the disposition covenant in terms intended to avoid it, but, because of a change in the legislation, the chosen terms were ineffective for that purpose and in fact potentially counter-productive. The demised premises consisted of a butchers shop and flat above and the

Nature of the danger need not have been foreseen

---

[41] See *infra*.
[42] (1966) 110 S.J. 248.
[43] (1984) 271 E.G. 279.
[44] *Per* Oliver L.J. at p. 283.
[45] *Ibid.* a similar point arises in relation to the enactment of the Leasehold Reform Act 1967, see *infra*.
[46] [1979] Q.B. 593.

tenant covenanted not to sublet the flat except on a service tenancy to an employee or on a fully furnished tenancy, in the latter case, subject to the landlord's consent which was not to be unreasonably withheld. At the time the lease was made in 1971, the purpose of the disposition covenant was clear—in neither of the excepted cases would the subtenant be entitled to Rent Act protection. However, by the time the tenant sought permission to grant a furnished sublease in 1977, the law had been changed by the Rent Act 1974 and a furnished tenancy did come under the security of tenure provisions. The landlord refused consent and the tenant argued unsuccessfully that he was acting unreasonably because the tenant was only seeking to do what the lease contemplated. Roskill L.J. was of the opinion that the purpose of the covenant had to be judged as at the time when it was entered into: it was to preserve the commercial character of the letting so that at the end of the term it could again be let as a single business unit. This purpose would be frustrated if the flat was let on a furnished tenancy.

> "[T]he effect of the request which this landlord has had made to him by the tenant is to invite him to agree to alter the nature of the property which is being let from commercial property, namely a butcher's shop with residential accommodation above, to a property which would be let on a multiple tenancy."[47]

In recent years legislation has moved, not against the landlord, but in his favour, and this factor was noted in *Deverall* v. *Wyndham*[48] where it was found that the landlords' interests had not been depreciated from what originally they had expected.[49]

No possibility of protection for disponor

(3) If, disposition or no disposition, the landlord would still end up with a tenant entitled to security of tenure under the Housing Act 1988, the disposition occasions no detriment to his right of re-entry. The cases where the landlord has been held reasonable in objecting to the disponee's future legal status have been cases where the current tenant is either legally incapable of such protection[50] or, more usually, will not, as a fact, avail himself of it.[51] If there is no possibility of the disponor gaining protection, it is irrelevant whether this state of affairs arose as a matter of law or as a matter of fact. In contrast in *R. M. Cole* v. *Russells (Tulse Hill) Ltd.*[52] the landlord was going to end up with a protected tenant whether the proposed disposition went ahead or not: if the assignor could not assign, he would stay put and would therefore himself qualify for protection in seven years' time. It was held that consent had been unreasonably withheld.

---

[47] At p. 605.
[48] (1989) 01 E.G. 70.
[49] *Per* Paul Baker Q.C. at p. 77.
[50] *Lee* v. *K. Carter Ltd.* [1949] 1 K.B. 45 (company); *Brann* v. *Westminster Anglo-Continental Investment Co. Ltd.* (1976) 240 E.G. 927 (moved out of occupation having granted a legal sublease).
[51] *Swanson* v. *Forton* [1949] Ch. 143 (had previously moved out and sublet furnished); *Dollar* v. *Winston* [1950] Ch. 236 (did not want it).
[52] [1955] E.G. 133.

Harm to reversion insufficient per se

(4) Even where the proposed disposition may harm the reversion, the landlord's right of re-entry on expiration of the term in particular,[53] that, though very relevant, will not of itself justify a refusal of consent.[54] More has to be shown.

(5) The presence of the fully qualified disposition covenant is indicative that the tenant was to have some disposition rights[55] and, at least while the unexpired term has some commercial value, the court will be reluctant to put him in a position where he can by no means exploit it. In *Leeward*

Tenant's interest in exploiting the term

Securities Ltd. v. *Lilyheath Properties Ltd.*[56] the Court of Appeal was conscious that a decision in the landlord's favour, allowing him to refuse his consent to a sublease, would impose a serious restriction upon the tenant's user and, had consent been sought before the creation of shorthold tenure,[57] they would have held that any such refusal was unreasonable as preventing any effective exploitation of the premises by the tenant.[58] As it was, shorthold tenure was an available means whereby the tenant could exploit the value of the unexpired term without doing harm to the landlord's reversion and his failure to utilise it rendered the landlord's refusal of consent reasonable. The tenant was, in effect, told to utilise a form of letting which may limit the attractiveness of his asset. In the instant case the term, 38 years, had only four years to run and it remains therefore an open question at what point in a term the landlord will be able to begin dictating what sort of lettings his tenant grants. From his point of view it would obviously be preferable for the tenant to use an assured shorthold, thus limiting the disponee's security, rather than an assured tenancy. Or, in appropriate circumstances, he might suggest that the tenant serves a notice in writing upon the subtenant, prior to the grant, to render available one of the mandatory grounds for possession, for example Grounds three (Holiday Lettings), four (Student Lettings), five (Lettings to Ministers of Religion).[59] Use of a company let or a mere licence may also seem a good idea to him. Whether the tenant's failure to heed his advice renders his refusal reasonable will depend upon the facts.

(6) There seems to be a distinction between cases where the disponee will have secure status and *may* avail himself of it and cases where the whole purpose of the transaction was to

Intention to confer security

confer such security upon the disponee. In the latter case, the likelihood of the harm to the reversion actually materialising, is much greater and the landlord's apprehensions are therefore more likely to be reasonable. It has been said that in these

---

[53] The level of the rent may not be depressed by an assured tenancy cp. effect of rent restriction provisions of the Rent Act 1977.

[54] *Leeward Securities Ltd.* v. *Lilyheath Properties Ltd. ibid. per* O'Connor L.J. at p. 283; *Deverall* v. *Wyndham ibid.*

[55] Often, of course, other provisions in the lease re-inforce this see, *e.g. Deverall* v. *Wyndham ibid.*

[56] (1983) 271 E.G. 279.

[57] s.52 of the Housing Act 1980; now repealed and replaced by assured shorthold—see s.120, Sched. 18 and s.20 of the Housing Act 1988.

[58] At p. 283, *per* Oliver and O'Connor L.JJ.

[59] Sched. 2, Pt. 1.

circumstances the disposition is "abnormal" or "pregnant with future possibilities"[60] but such terminology is not really very helpful and has been criticised.[61] In *Lee* v. *K. Carter Ltd.*[62] the original lessee, being a limited company, would not qualify for protection under the Rent Restriction Acts and sought permission, in the last year of a seven year term, to assign to a resident director who would be entitled to such protection. The Court of Appeal held the landlord's refusal of consent reasonable within various tests laid down in *Re Gibbs and Houlder Bros. Ltd.*[63] and because the relationship between the landlord and the proposed assignee would be "pregnant with future possibilities." The purpose of the assignment was to secure statutory protection.[64] In *Swanson* v. *Forton*[65] consent was sought for the assignment of the last 12 days of a three-year term. The purpose of the assignment was not to enable the assignee to enjoy the remnant of the term, but to enable him to continue beyond the expiration of the term with the assistance of statutory protection and the landlord could reasonably refuse his consent.[66] By contrast in *Oriel Property Trust* v. *Kidd*[67] the landlord was held to have unreasonably withheld his consent. *Lee* and *Swanson* were distinguished upon the basis that in those cases "the sole object of the assignment was to enable the assignee to claim the protection of the Rent Acts. ... That end was not the object of the assignment in this case."[68] Another case where the purpose was lacking was *Thomas Bookman* v. *Nathan*.[69] Here the tenant, who would have qualified for protection at the end of the term had he remained in possession, had, in fact, bought a house and sought permission to assign the last seven-and-a-half months of a five year term. It was held that consent had been unreasonably withheld because the purpose of the assignment was to make accommodation available to a person who desperately needed it with a view to that person occupying for the remainder of the term and then trying to negotiate a new lease. In *Deverall* v. *Wyndham*[70] also, the court was satisfied that the proposed underlettings were not for the purpose of creating security of tenure—indeed such security was far from certain. The underlessees were in one case a relative and in another a friend of the tenant; they would

---

[60] *Lee* v. *K. Carter Ltd.* [1949] 1 K.B. 85, *per* Tucker L.J. at p. 96; *Swanson* v. *Forton* [1949] Ch. 143; *Dollar* v. *Winston* [1950] Ch. 236; *Thomas Bookman* v. *Nathan* [1955] 1 W.L.R. 815; *Watt* v. *Windler* (1975) C.L.Y. 2050; *Brann* v. *Westminster Anglo Continental Investment Co. Ltd.* (1976) 240 E.G. 927.

[61] *Per* Roskill L.J. in *West Layton* v. *Ford* [1979] Q.B. 593, 605 and the cases there referred to; *Leeward Securities* v. *Lilyheath Properties Ltd.* (1983) 271 E.G. 279, 280, *per* Oliver L.J.

[62] *Ibid.*

[63] [1925] Ch. 575.

[64] See also *Wallabrook Property Co. Ltd.* v. *Tubent (Iron and Steel) Ltd.* (1976) L.S. Gaz. 945.

[65] *Ibid.*

[66] See also *Dollar* v. *Winston* [1950] Ch. 236; *Watt* v. *Windler* (1975) C.L.Y. 2050; *Brann* v. *Westminster Anglo-Continental Investment Co. Ltd.* (1976) 240 E.G. 927.

[67] (1949) 100 L.J. 6.

[68] *Per* Devlin J. at p. 6.

[69] [1955] 1 W.L.R. 815.

[70] (1989) 01 E.G. 70.

not get security while he remained a resident landlord and if he left so, probably, would they.

The purpose of the disposition has been referred to as a "most important element" in cases of this type.[71] The difficulty of proving it has also been acknowledged.[72] It is submitted that if the unexpired term is too short to make occupation worthwhile, if it is a so-called "fag end," the court will be most likely to find the intention to confer security of tenure. The original length of the term and the circumstances of the disponee will also be relevant. It may be however, that where the intention *is* proven, consent can be reasonably withheld at any point in the term.[73]

Dispositions of "fag ends"

(7) Even in the absence of an intention to confer security, the landlord may still be able reasonably to withhold his consent if the disposition relates to the "fag end" of the term. This view was expressed by Denning L.J. in *Thomas Bookman* v. *Nathan*: "I can well imagine, that if there were an assignment of the last fortnight or three weeks of a term, a landlord could reasonably withhold his consent, even though the parties had no intention in fact of creating a statutory tenancy."[74]

Expectations of current landlord and tenant Refusals and the spirit of the legislation

(8) Where the landlord or the tenant acquired their interest by assignment it is not uncommon for the court to refer to the expectations they would have had at that time.[75]

(9) A refusal of consent upon the ground of the capacity of the disponee to claim an assured tenancy will not be contrary to the spirit of the Housing Act 1988. As Lord Greene M.R. states in *Swanson* v. *Forton*[76] in the context of the Rent Restriction Acts:

> "There is nothing in the Acts which restricts a lessor's right under the contract to withhold his consent. The lessee can only put his assignee in a position to become a statutory tenant if he can lawfully do so; whether he can or cannot lawfully do so depends upon the unreasonableness or reasonableness of the lessor's refusal. To say that it is unreasonable for the lessor to refuse his consent because it would prevent the lessee doing something which he can only do if the refusal is unreasonable, is to beg the question."

—under the Leasehold Reform Act 1967. Under the terms of this Act a qualified tenant[77] can acquire the freehold or an extended lease of the demised premises after three years[78] residence. It is obvious that the potential harm to the landlord's reversion from the operation of these provisions is altogether more radical than that which results from the application of the

[71] *Per* Denning L.J. in *Thomas Bookman* v. *Nathan, ibid.*
[72] *Per* Romer L.J. *ibid.* at p. 82.
[73] See Romer L.J. *ibid.* at p. 821.
[74] At p. 818.
[75] *West Layton* v. *Ford* [1979] Q.B. 593; *Wallabrook Property Co. Ltd.* v. *Tubent (Iron and Steel) Ltd.* (1976) L.S. Gaz. 945.
[76] [1949] Ch. 143, 148.
[77] See s.1.
[78] Or periods amounting to three years in the last 10 years, s.1(1)(b).

The gravity of the harm

Housing Act 1988. This was recognised by the Court of Appeal in *Norfolk Capital Group Ltd.* v. *Kitway*[79] where Geoffrey Lane L.J. opined that there is "a world of difference between an Act which simply protects a tenant's right to possess, and an Act which may remove from a landlord his freehold interest in the land altogether and vest it in the tenant."[80] The gravity of the potential harm seems to be the single most important factor in determining the reasonableness of the landlord's refusal in cases of this type. Thus Megaw L.J. in the above case could see no reason why "a landlord should be said to be acting unreasonably in refusing to give his consent to a transaction which would, or would be likely to, bring about for him that serious disadvantage, which is different in kind ... from that which the courts have had to consider in relation to the Rent Acts."[81] Similar sentiments were expressed by Browne L.J.: "having regard to the detriment to the proprietary and financial interests of the landlords which would in all probability result from the assignment, I find it quite impossible to say that the landlords have unreasonably withheld their consent"[82] and Geoffrey Lane L.J.: "Counsel for the tenant concedes that the value of the landlords' reversion is less if there is a possibility of any mews house being enfranchised. There is clearly such a possibility, and accordingly the value of the landlords' reversion is less. That being so, it would be a strange landlord indeed who gave his consent to the proposed assignment."[83]

Intention not necessary

It is clear from this case that it is not necessary for the landlord to show that the disponee intends to take advantage of the Act; he will be reasonable if it is "likely," "probable" or simply "possible"[84] that the disponee will do so. While the requisite likelihood, etc., is most manifest where there is an intention to use the Act or in the case of an assignment of the "fag end" of the term, in *Norfolk* neither of these elements were present.[85] On the matter of intention, Megaw referred for support to the 1st instance decision of Lawson J. in *Welch* v. *Birrane*.[86] This was a more straightforward case where the intention of the disposition *was* found to be to enable the disponee to qualify under the Act. The intention was inferred from the facts: the assignees, who were already, as subtenants, enjoying Rent Act protection in relation to the property, took an assignment of the last seven years of the lease, which included an onerous repairing covenant, with the assistance of a loan from the assignor, repayable five years hence by which time the assignee would have qualified to acquire the freehold[87]

[79] [1976] 3 All E.R. 787.
[80] At p. 793.
[81] At p. 791.
[82] At p. 793.
[83] At p. 794.
[84] See respectively above.
[85] The lease still had 35 years to run. Compare the Rent Act cases *supra* where it seems that intention can only be dispensed with in the case of a "fag end."
[86] (1975) 235 E.G. 501.
[87] Now three years, s.1(1)(*b*) of the Leasehold Reform Act 1967, as amended by Sched. 21 of the Housing Act 1980.

upon advantageous terms and could presumably, repay the assignor by raising a mortgage on the freehold.[88] It was held that the landlord had reasonably refused his consent.[89] It is probable that the same decision would have been reached even if it had been impossible to establish the intention. Lawson J. certainly purported to offer another ground for his decision namely that the proposed transaction was "pregnant with possibilities, possibilities of the landlord's proprietary or financial interest in the subject-matter of the proposed assignment being purchased in the future."[90] This clearly refers to the effect of the transaction rather than the intention with which it was made and was so interpreted by Megaw L.J. in *Norfolk* who understood it as meaning "that the very fact that there is this potential disadvantage to a landlord under the Leasehold Reform Act if the proposed assignment were to go through, is in itself sufficient to prevent that refusal from being unreasonable.[91]

Effect of the transaction

These two cases were not referred to in the judgments in the subsequent decision of the Court of Appeal in *Bickel* v. *Duke of Westminster*[92] but a similar decision was reached. Here too the landlord was held reasonably to have refused consent to an assignment, this time, of the last nine years of a 37 year term, to the current subtenant. The assignors could not qualify under the Act, though they held on a long tenancy under low rent, because they did not reside on the demised premises. The assignee did not qualify either because although she resided the sublease was not at a low rent. As Lord Denning commented:

> "In this situation the [assignors] and the lady put their heads together. Their plan is for the [assignors] to assign their headlease to the lady. If they do assign lawfully to her, then, after five years[93] have elapsed, the lady will have the right to buy up the freehold from the Grosvenor Estates; because she will then be a tenant of a leasehold house on a long tenancy at a low rent. ... She will get it at a very low price; because it is so ordered by the 1967 Act. So it is worth her while now to pay the [assignor] a good price for the headlease—because by so doing she is well placed to acquire the freehold in five years time."[94]

It is clear from this, that the purpose of the assignment was to gain qualification under the Act but that does not seem to have been the basis of the decision, rather it was the effect that any potential enfranchisement would have upon the landlords' interests. As Lord Denning M.R. pointed out: "They hold a large estate which they desire to keep in their hands so as to develop it in the best possible way. This would be much

---

[88] See Lawson J. at p. 507.
[89] And therefore that the tenant was in breach of covenant. The judge went on to hold that the breach had been waived by a subsequent demand for rent.
[90] At p. 505.
[91] At p. 791.
[92] [1976] 3 All E.R. 801.
[93] Now three years.
[94] At p. 803.

impeded if one house after another was bought up by sitting tenants. Further, if they are compelled to sell under the 1967 Act, they will suffer much financial loss, because the price is much less than the value of the house."[95] He also considered it important that, on the facts of the case, no injustice would be done to the parties to the prospective assignment by a decision in the landlords' favour.

> "Test it next by considering the position of the tenants.
> ... They hold the premises as an investment and want to sell it. It matters not to them whether they sell it to the landlords or to the subtenants, so long as they receive a fair price for it. They will give the [tenants] a sum equivalent to that offered by the subtenants. Test it next by considering the position of the subtenant herself. When she took her sublease she had no possible claim to enfranchisement. It was a high rent outside the 1967 Act. She is quite well protected by the Rent Acts. ... [96]"

Thus these cases indicate that if the disponee will qualify in due course to use the Act, the landlord will probably be reasonable in withholding his consent. One doubts whether it is going to be fruitful for the tenant to seek to establish that such use is "unlikely," "improbable" or "impossible" (and which?). It may be noted, however, that the three cases referred to, all concerned leases granted a long time before the Leasehold Reform Act. In relation to leases granted after the Act, it would, theoretically, be possible for the tenant to argue that the possibility of a tenant qualifying under the Act had been appreciated by the parties at the time of the lease, and the failure of the landlord to employ any sort of avoidance device[97] was indicative of his acquiescence in the risk.

Status of disponor

It is further submitted that whenever the lease was granted, the landlord will probably be held unreasonable in withholding his consent to an assignment if the assignor himself would also have qualified under the Act.[98] The Leasehold Reform cases[99] all concerned assignors who would *not*, as a matter of law or fact, have qualified under the Act.[1] In each of them the landlord was held to have reasonably refused his consent. In *Marsh* v. *Gilbert*[2] Nourse J., *obiter*, distinguished these cases as involving prejudice to the landlord's interest, whereas in the case before him the disponor would himself have qualified and the landlord could not therefore point to any additional detriment to his interests.[3] It was not necessary to decide the point because the disposition involved was a vesting order by the court and it was held that

---

[95] At p. 805; see also Orr and Waller L.JJ. at pp. 806 and 808.
[96] At p. 805.
[97] On such devices see Hague, *Leasehold Enfranchisement* (2nd ed.), p. 290.
[98] A similar point has been made in connection with the Rent Acts cases, *supra*.
[99] See *supra*.
[1] In *Welch* it was apparent that the property had been bought as an investment, in *Norfolk* and *Bickel* the landlords were respectively a company and a friendly society.
[2] (1980) 256 E.G. 715.
[3] At p. 717.

this did not amount to an assignment within the disposition covenant and therefore no consent was needed in any event.[4]

—under the Landlord and Tenant Act 1954. Under Part 11 of this Act a business tenant[5] can at the end of the tenancy claim security of tenure including the right to apply for a new tenancy.[6] This possibility formed the basis of the landlord's objection in *Re Cooper's Lease, Cowan* v. *Beaumont Property Trusts*.[7] The tenant wished to sublet part to an occulist. The lease was due to expire in three years time and the landlord feared that if the tenant did not then take a new lease, he would be left with the occulist who may well wish to continue in occupation of part and could take advantage of the 1954 Act. This would put the landlord in difficulty. They were quite prepared to allow the occulist to occupy upon terms which would exclude the operation of the Act.[8] It was held that consent had been reasonably withheld.

—under other protective legislation. In the unusual case where a tenancy of an agricultural holding includes a fully qualified disposition covenant,[9] it may be that a landlord can reasonably object to certain assignments which have the effect of sidestepping the current tenant's death, *e.g.* by an individual to a company or to a group of joint tenants, or by a father to a son.[10] Where the tenancy was created on or after July 12, 1984, with limited exceptions, there are no family succession rights,[11] just lifetime security, and therefore the landlord could expect to recover the property on the death of the current tenant by serving a notice to quit.[12] The introduction, by way of assignment, of another tenant or group of tenants with a longer life expectancy or, in the case of a company, with an almost infinite life expectancy, would have an adverse effect upon the value of the landlord's reversionary interest and may therefore constitute reasonable grounds for refusing consent. If the tenancy was created before July 12, 1984, the chance of the landlord recovering possession on the current tenant's death is substantially impaired by the family succession scheme, which could in any event delay recovery of the land for two generations. Even so an assignment could make the situation worse. This is because the landlord does have certain opportunities under section 43(1) of the Agricultural Holdings Act 1986 to recover possession on the current tenant's death in spite of family succession rights. His notice to quit can take effect in two circumstances: (a) where no application to become tenant of the holding is made within the requisite time or, (b) if one or more applications have been made and none of the

---

[4] See *supra*, Chap. 2, Types of Disposition Commonly Restricted.
[5] See s.23 and generally Tromans, *Commercial Leases*, Chap. 15.
[6] See s.24.
[7] (1968) 19 P. & C.R. 541.
[8] *e.g.*, as a licensee or employee of the tenant.
[9] See Chap. 7, p. 137.
[10] Gaunt, (1987) 284 L.S. Gaz. 1371, 1372.
[11] s.34(1) and Pt. VI of the Agricultural Holdings Act 1986.
[12] See s.26 and Sched. 3, Pt. 1, Case G.

applicants have been found suitable by the Tribunal or, if they have been found suitable, the Tribunal nonetheless consents to the operation of the notice to quit.[13] If it could be shown that the removal of this *spes* devalued the reversion, there is a chance that consent could be reasonably withheld.

Objections based upon other aspects of the assignee's personality

The relevance of the assignees personality in assessing the reasonableness of the landlord's refusal has long been accepted. A. L. Smith L.J. in *Bates* v. *Donaldson*[14] referred to the purpose of the disposition covenant as including the exclusion of "an undesirable tenant" and Warrington L.J. in *Re Gibbs & Houlder Bros. & Co. Ltd.'s Lease*[15] made it clear that an objection connected with the personality of the intended assignee would be reasonable.[16] The vagueness of these statements is regrettable.[17] It cannot be reasonable for a landlord to object to an assignee merely because he does not like the look of him. In many cases it is possible to link the personality objection to damage to one of the landlord's covenanted rights and some such cases have been previously dealt with.[18] If it is not possible to point to harm to the landlord's covenanted rights, it is submitted that the refusal is unreasonable. In *Mills* v. *Cannon Brewery Co. Ltd.*[19] which concerned an assignment of an under lease of a pub,[20] the immediate landlords objected to three facets of the assignee's personality:

Personality & covenanted rights

> (1) That he was of German origin and that this would affect business, (2) that he did not intend to reside upon the demised premises and (3) that he had other business interests which would prevent him giving sufficient time to the pub.

The landlord pointed out that the lease contained a covenant by the lessee to purchase all intoxicating liquor from him and damage to the business through having a non-resident, part-time German tenant would lower consumption and also that the licensing justices in London were taking into account the residence and other business interests of those applying for new licences and that as a result of this, they, the landlords, now used tenancy agreements which stipulated for the tenant's residence and also bound him to devote his whole time to the

---

[13] See s.44(2) and s.27 for the grounds upon which the Tribunal's consent can be sought, *e.g.* greater hardship, C. P. Rogers, pp. 139–142.

[14] [1892] 2 Q.B. 241.

[15] [1925] All E.R. 128, 133.

[16] At p. 133.

[17] See *supra* p. 72 *et seq.*

[18] See Objections based upon anticipated user, Objections based upon harm to other property, Objections based upon the financial or business status of the assignee, Objections based on the legal status of the assignee.

[19] [1920] 2 Ch. 38.

[20] The *head* landlord had given his consent.

business. The landlords dropped the nationality objection[21] and Lawrence J. found the others to be unreasonable. As the underlease contained no covenant relating to residence or full-time devotion to the business, such objections amounted to an attempt to extract a collateral advantage. The court was being invited "to ignore entirely the nature of the underlease which has 20 years still to run and for the grant of which the defendant company received the sum of £3,070. ... The defendant company admits that it cannot impose the conditions upon an assignee of the underlease, yet it states its determination to refuse its consent because the proposed assignee says that he is not going to conform to two of the said conditions."[22] Thus, it is submitted, the harm alleged must be related to covenanted rights. It must also be substantiated. Lawrence J. doubted in the instant case whether grounds (2) & (3) constituted the real reasons for the landlords' refusal, regarding the damage alleged as "far fetched"; in view of the very limited residential accommodation which the premises afforded, it was extremely unlikely that anyone of greater financial status and proved business acumen than the proposed assignee could be found to take the lease. Another case where, it is submitted, the objection to the assignee's personality bore no relation to the landlords' covenanted rights and were therefore unreasonable is *Pimms Ltd.* v. *Tallow Chandlers in the City of London.*[23] The Court of Appeal held otherwise. The case concerned a proposed assignment of the last 13 years of a 34-year lease. The landlords refused consent because the proposed assignee was a development company (of which the chairman was Charles Clore) and would, unlike the assignors, exploit the nuisance value of the remaining period of the term to force the landlords into allowing them to participate in a comprehensive redevelopment scheme affecting the demised property and the profits derived therefrom. The tenants maintained that as the redevelopment proposed could not take place during the currency of the lease, the objection "had no relation to the lease or to the relationship of landlord and tenant in respect of it"[24] Danckwerts L.J. considered that point effectively covered by the Rent Act cases and in particular by the approach of Tucker L.J. *Lee* v. *K. Carter*[25]: that though the contractual relationship after the assignment may be the same as before, the landlord could still reasonably object if it was pregnant with future possibilities which would not have resulted from the previously existing relationship between the landlord and tenant. It is submitted that he was wrong to import this approach into a case with such very

---

[21] Which did not prevent the judge opining that it was unreasonable; see also *infra* Objections based upon race, sex, etc.

[22] At p. 50; The landlords' admittedly covenanted right under the provision concerning purchase of intoxicating liquor did not help him because it was so weak. It only applied so long as the premises were used as a public house and the tenant was under no obligation to continue to use them for that purpose.

[23] [1964] 2 Q.B. 547.

[24] See p. 571.

[25] [1949] 1 K.B. 8.

different facts. It was not alleged that the proposed assignment
would enable the assignee to claim a new tenancy at the
expiration of the term under the Landlord and Tenant Act
1954, perhaps because it was realised that any such claim could
be successfully resisted by the landlord on the grounds of the
projected redevelopment,[26] thus ruling out any direct analogy
with the Rent Act cases. An indirect analogy based merely
upon the proposition that something unpleasant may happen in
the future is very unconvincing: in the Rent Act cases, the
assignee would have the right to bring about the harmful
situation whereas in the instant case, even if the lease was
assigned as proposed, the assignee would still have no right to
participate in the redevelopment. Such participation would
remain subject to the landlords' agreement. It is submitted that
though the objection related to the assignees personality, it was
not linked to any covenanted right of the landlord and should
have been held unreasonable. It may also be noted that the
tenant, on receiving the Clore offer, had written to the
landlords as alternative purchasers and the landlords had
delayed making an offer until after the tenants were
contractually bound to the Clore company.

Objections based on the continuance of the term

To secure a surrender of the term

A refusal based upon an objection to the term running its full
course and intended to precipitate a surrender[27] is
unreasonable. It clearly precludes any assignment at all of the
demised premises contrary to the tenant's rights under the
qualified covenant. In *Lehmann* v. *McArthur*[28] the tenant bowed
to the pressure of the landlord, who wished to redevelop, and,
despite having contracted to assign the lease to the plaintiff
subject only to the landlord's consent, he surrendered the lease
to the landlord for an equivalent consideration. The plaintiff
sought a decree of specific performance, coupled with an order
that the landlord concur in the assignment, on the ground that
the landlord had unreasonably withheld his consent and that
therefore the tenant had been free to assign to him without it.
Sir John Stuart V.C. granted the relief sought saying:

> "The question . . . is whether or not there was any power
> in the lessor, who has contracted to allow his lessee to
> assign where he might reasonably assign, to refuse to allow
> the lessee to assign at all, because he wishes him to give up

---

[26] See s.30.
[27] Compare an objection based upon the failure of the tenant to accord to the
landlord a covenanted right to be offered a surrender prior to a request for a
licence, as to which see *supra* Chap. 4, p. 36.
[28] (1867) 3 L.R. Eq. 746.

the lease, and himself make a new bargain with the lessee. In my opinion no lessor has a right to use a stipulation in a covenant of this kind so as to defeat the right of the lessee to assign, where the assignment or agreement for an assignment has been honestly made."[28a]

In *Bates* v. *Donaldson*[29] the tenant was in negotiation with the landlord for a surrender but on a delay occurring on the landlord's part, she contracted to assign it to Donaldson for £400. The landlord then refused his consent to the assignment. He maintained that he had been willing to pay the tenant £400 before she contracted with Donaldson, and that it was immaterial to her whether she sold to Donaldson or to him. The lease was assigned to Donaldson, after a decree of specific performance had been obtained in his favour and in the present action the landlord was seeking possession on the basis that his consent had been reasonably withheld. He was unsuccessful. The Court of Appeal held that he had acted unreasonably, A. L. Smith L.J. opined "It is not . . . the true reading of this clause that permission can be withheld in order to enable the lessor to regain possession before the termination of the term . . . " or " . . . to enable the lessor to, if possible, coerce a tenant to surrender the lease so that the lessor might obtain possession of the premises. . . . "[30] He rejected the suggestion that a willingness to pay whatever the tenant wanted rendered the landlord reasonable. Kay L.J. thought that it may have made a difference had the landlord made a definite offer when he was refusing his consent: "The plaintiff must show strong reasons for withholding his consent. Clearly it is not sufficient for him to say,

Relevance of an equivalent offer

> "I want to oblige the lessee to sell to me. He must at least be able to show that at the time when consent was refused . . . that the refusal did no harm to the lessee. I cannot find that before or at the time when the plaintiff refused his consent, he had offered to buy the lessee's interest for £400 or for any sum. He does not allege in his pleadings that he did so. He does not offer to do so in his pleadings."[31]

In *Re Winfrey Chatterton*[32] Sargant J. preferred the view of A. L. Smith L.J. that it is never reasonable to refuse consent with a view to coercing the tenant to surrender however fair the terms. Here the reversion passed to the defendant who wished to occupy the premises herself. Negotiations took place between the defendant and the tenant but no enforceable agreement was reached. The tenant then assigned to another, despite the defendant having refused his consent. Sargant J. considered that "the defendant is really asserting her right as lessor in order to strengthen her position as purchaser of the premises. In my opinion the landlord is not entitled so to use

---

[28a] At p. 75.
[29] [1892] 2 Q.B. 241 C.A.
[30] At p. 247.
[31] At p. 245.
[32] [1921] 2 Ch. 7.

her power to withhold her assent, but can use that power only to secure herself her proper right not to have an undesirable assignee."[33] In *Pimms Ltd.* v. *Tallow Chandlers in the City of London*[34] the tenant on receiving an offer from a third party, wrote to his landlord as an alternative purchaser. Before any offer was forthcoming from the landlord, the tenant entered into a formal contract to assign to the third party and then sought the landlord's consent. The Court of Appeal in fact held

Too late? that consent had been reasonably withheld[35] but the fact that the pleadings stated that the landlords were now willing to purchase for the sum offered by the third party was not an effective factor in that decision because the tenant "has already bound himself to sell to someone else and so would have to commit a breach of contract to sell to the landlord."[36] Danckwerts L.J. further opined that "It may well be that the situation is the same if he is only morally bound as where the sale is 'subject to contract.' "[37] The suggestion by Kay L.J. in *Bates* v. *Donaldson* that the landlord may be reasonable if, when refusing his consent, he made an equivalent offer had to be qualified accordingly.[38] While this does carry with it the possibility that a landlord could be held reasonable if he made his equivalent offer before the tenant had reached even an informal agreement with a third party, and there was no reason, *e.g.* connected with the other terms of the agreement or the relationship between the tenant and the third party, why the tenant should have preferred the third party, it is unlikely

Never that a court would so hold. A refusal in these circumstances
reasonable still amounts to an attempt to obtain an uncovenanted advantage; the landlord has no right to a surrender of the term, gratuitous or otherwise. While it may be thought that the tenant was acting unreasonably in spurning the landlord's offer in such circumstances, it must be remembered that the question is not whether the tenant has acted reasonably in his dealings with the landlord, but whether the landlord has reasonably refused his consent to assign to the third party and the fact that he, the landlord, would have liked the lease himself is irrelevant. There are provisions which can be included in leases giving the landlord a right to a surrender[39] but if he has not employed them, he cannot subsequently extract equivalent rights on the occasion of request for licence to assign.

The cases consistently indicate that it makes no difference that the landlord is pursuing a policy which conforms to the
Good estate principles of "good estate management." Indeed, landlords are
management commonly motivated by factors which could fall within that description, such as the desire to redevelop,[40] or to select the

---

[33] At p. 10.
[34] [1964] 2 Q.B. 547 C.A.
[35] Criticised *supra* Objections based upon other aspects of the assignee's personality.
[36] At p. 565.
[37] *Ibid.*
[38] *Ibid.*
[39] See *supra* Chap. 4, p. 36.
[40] *Lehmann* v. *McArthur, ibid.*

next tenant themselves rather than leave it to the current tenant.[41] It was in *Bromley Park* v. *Moss*[42] that the most concerted effort was made to legitimise the landlord's desire for a surrender by reference to the principles of "good estate management." It was unsuccessful. In many cases, and certainly here, those principles correspond to the interests of the landlord and not at all to those of the tenant. They cannot be allowed to operate at the tenant's expense. In *Bromley* the refusal had as its aim the surrender of the lease[43] so that the premises could be let as a whole to the existing business tenant of the ground floor. Cumming-Bruce L.J. pointed out that:

> "It may well enhance the financial interests of the plaintiff to obtain a single tenant holding the whole building on a full repairing covenant with long term capital advantage when they put the building on the market, but that intention and policy is entirely outside the intention to be imputed to the parties at the time of the granting of the lease."[44]

Hidden surrender motive

It need hardly be said that if the landlord relies upon other reasons to justify his refusal, the court will be astute to recognise any indication that the true ground is to achieve a surrender. In *Farr* v. *Ginnings*[45] the grounds put forward— non-compliance with the repairing covenant by the tenant— were in any event too trivial to justify a refusal of consent but Clauson J. regarded the fact that the landlord had suggested that the tenant negotiate a surrender as "significant." If on the other hand the offer by the landlord to accept a surrender is not the reason for his refusal but is merely made to make that refusal more palatable, no adverse consequences will flow from it, and if the other reasons justify the refusal the court may even be impressed by such an offer. Thus in *Bickel* v. *Duke of Westminster*[46] the court considered that the landlord was reasonable in withholding his consent because the proposed assignee would qualify under the Leasehold Reform Act 1967 and Lord Denning M.R. was prepared to test the justice of this by reference to the effect that it had on the tenant and in view of an offer made by the landlord, was satisfied that he had no cause for complaint.[47]

To pursue a claim for forfeiture

Occasionally when considering an application for a licence to assign, the landlord may discover that events have occurred which consitute grounds for forfeiture. This does not justify an outright refusal of consent. In *Pakwood Transport Ltd.* v. *15,*

[41] *Oriel Property Trust* v. *Kidd* (1950) 100 L.J. 6; *Bromley Park Garden Estates Ltd.* v. *Moss* [1982] 2 All E.R. 890. Compare *Bates* v. *Donaldson, ibid.* and *Re Winfrey & Chatterton, ibid.* where the motive was occupation.
[42] *Ibid.*
[43] No consideration was offered, see p. 893.
[44] At p. 899.
[45] (1924) 44 T.L.R. 249.
[46] [1976] 3 All E.R. 801.
[47] At p. 806.

Beauchamp Place Ltd.[48] in the course of considering an application, the lessors became aware that the tenant had passed a resolution to wind-up and had appointed a liquidator. They immediately lost interest in the financial and other information which they had solicited from the tenant and sent a notice of forfeiture under section 146 of the Law of Property Act 1925 to the liquidator commenting that "the question of a licence to assign will not now arise." The liquidator sought relief against forfeiture and a declaration that consent had been unreasonably withheld. Relief was granted as was the declaration, Goff L.J. taking the view that the existence of grounds for forfeiture would justify the landlord in deferring a

Justifies deferral of decision decision but not in declining even to consider the application. He went on to say that he was not satisfied in this case that the grounds for forfeiture—the liquidation—were the real reason for the refusal of consent to the assignment. This was merely seized upon in an attempt to be rid of what had become a burdensome lease:

> "it saw what it had been seeking for some time, namely an opportunity to destroy the lease to escape the consequences of its failure to operate the rent review clause[49] and that cannot be a good ground for refusing a licence."[50]

Objections based upon assignor's breach of covenant

The landlord has no automatic right to refuse consent to assign because the tenant is in breach of one of the covenants or conditions in the lease. He is entitled to sufficient time to consider the legal position and may defer a decision accordingly so long as he complies with the duty under section 2(3)(*b*) of the Landlord and Tenant Act 1988 to communicate his decision within a reasonable time. If he goes on to serve a forfeiture notice, he is entitled to defer a decision pending the outcome of

Trivial breaches those proceedings.[51] Where the breach turns out not to be serious, the landlord should give his consent. In *Farr* v. *Ginnings*[52] the landlord refused consent because of a continuing breach of the repairing covenant. Repairs amounted to £100 and the assignee, who was respectable and responsible, intended to complete them. Clauson J. held the consent had been unreasonably refused:

> "the effect of the assignment would be that the [landlord] would not only retain her right to damages for breach of covenant against the Plaintiff, but would also have a right

[48] (1978) 36 P. & C.R. 112 C.A.
[49] Three years previously.
[50] At p. 120.
[51] *Pakwood Transport Ltd.* v. *Beauchamp Place Ltd.* (1978) 36 P. & C.R. 112 C.A.
[52] (1928) 44 T.L.R. 249; and see *Midland Bank p.l.c.* v. *Chart Enterprises Inc.* [10] 44 E.G. 68.

against the proposed assignee to compel him to put the premises in repair under pain of forfeiture. The position of the [landlord] would be made better by the assignment."[53]

Serious breaches

Similarly in *Cosh* v. *Fraser*[54] minor breaches of a covenant against alterations which were easily remediable were held not to constitute reasonable grounds for refusal. However, where the breach is serious, the court will not be so impressed with the argument that the assignment increases the landlord's remedies and will allow a pause to enable the landlord to pursue his existing remedies. In *Goldstein* v. *Sanders*[55] the plaintiff took an assignment of a 99-year lease which contained covenants restricting certain trades and prohibited building on the demised premises. It was subject to a 21-year underlease which contained fully qualified covenants restricting dispositions and business user. On inspecting the premises, the plaintiff discovered breaches of covenant relating to user and repair, as well as what was described as "gross waste." The owner of the neighbouring property, Sanders, had demolished that property making it necessary to shore up the demised premises and he had incorporated part of the demised premises into his own and built lavatories on it—all with the consent of the underlessee, Hill. When challenged, Hill wrote that he was planning to assign the underlease to Sanders. The plaintiff refused consent pending counsel's opinion but Hill assigned anyway. Eve J. held that consent had been reasonably refused:

> "no reasonable person could have advised her to take any other course, nor can I imagine any prudent man, discovering what the plaintiff had discovered, being willing to consent to the assignment, and to defer to a subsequent date the questions of his remedies against the assignor and his own position with the ground landlord. On the facts, the action on this point is in my view an undefended one."[56]

While the plaintiff's position as a lessee, "bound by covenants of which the existing state of things would seem to evidence more than one flagrant breach," was undoubtedly relevant to the reasonableness of her refusal, Eve J. opined that his decision would have been the same had she been the fee simple owner.[57] Accordingly she was granted a declaration that the underlease was at an end, and possession. These cases were cited with approval in *Orlando Investments Ltd.* v. *Grosvenor Estates Belgravia*[58] where there were serious breaches of a repair covenant and the proposed assignee had broken several promises to at least initiate work to make the premises wind and water tight. In the light of this, the landlord offered his licence, subject to the assignee agreeing to a strict timetable for the execution of the works and providing security for their due

[53] At p. 249.
[54] (1964) 108 S.J. 116.
[55] [1915] 1 Ch. 549.
[56] At p. 556.
[57] At p. 555.
[58] [1989] 43 E.G. 175 C.A.

completion. The tenant sought a declaration that this amounted to an unreasonable withholding of consent. Nourse J. refused the declaration, opining that

> "if there are breaches of the covenant to repair which are anything more than minimal, more especially if they are extensive and of long-standing, it is not in general unreasonable of a landlord to refuse his consent unless he can be reasonably satisfied that the proposed assignee will remedy them."[59]

Objections unlawful under the Sex Discrimination Act 1975 and the Race Relations Act 1976

Both of these Acts, as well as making discrimination on grounds of sex or race in the disposal of property unlawful,[60] also make unlawful such discrimination on the part of anyone who has power to consent to a disposal. The relevant sections are section 31 of the Sex Discrimination Act 1975 and section 24 of the Race Relations Act 1976. Section 31 of the Sex Discrimination Act 1975 provides as follows:

> "(1) Where the licence or consent of the landlord or of any other person is required for the disposal[61] to any person of premises in Great Britain comprised in a tenancy, it is unlawful[62] for the landlord or other person to discriminate[63] against a woman[64] by withholding the licence or consent for disposal of the premises to her.
> (2) Subsection (1) does not apply if:
> > (*a*) the person withholding the licence or consent, or a near relative[65] of his ('the relevant occupier') resides, and intends to continue to reside, on the premises, and
> > (*b*) there is on the premises, in addition to the accommodation occupied by the relevant occupier, accommodation (not being storage accommodation or means of access) shared by the relevant occupier with other persons residing on the premises who are not members of his household, and

---

[59] At p. 181; see *infra* "Conditional Consents," for cases where consent is granted on condition.
[60] s.30 Sex Discrimination Act 1975; s.21 Race Relations Act 1976. Also they both provide that a term, *e.g.* an absolute covenant, in a contract, prohibiting the disposal of property on grounds of sex or race is void: s.77 Sex Discrimination Act 1975 and s.72 Race Relations Act 1976.
[61] See s.82(1).
[62] See ss.66 and 67 for enforcement.
[63] See s.82(1) and s.5(1).
[64] See s.82(1) and s.2 the latter providing that s.31 is to be read as applying equally to the treatment of men.
[65] See s.82(1) and (5).

    (c)   the premises are small premises as defined in section 32(2).

(3) In this section 'tenancy' means a tenancy created by a lease agreement or in pursuance of any enactment; and 'disposal,' in relation to premises comprised in a tenancy, includes assignment or assignation of the tenancy and subletting or parting with possession of the premises or any part of the premises.

(4) This section applies to tenancies created before the passing of this Act, as well as to others.

Section 24 of the Race Relations Act 1976 is drafted in identical terms but subsection (1) refers to discrimination which is further defined as racial discrimination,[66] i.e. on grounds of colour, race, nationality or ethnic or national origins.[67]

Unreasonable

In both sections the relevant conduct is made unlawful. There is no provision that it is to amount to an unreasonable withholding of consent[68] but there can be little doubt that it would be so held.[69] Even before the Race Relations legislation, in *Mills* v. *Cannon Brewery Co. Ltd.*,[70] racial discrimination seems to have been considered unreasonable. In that case the landlord objected *inter alia* to the name and nationality of the proposed assignee because he considered that people might boycott the demised premises, a pub, resulting in a fall in consumption of liquor which he had the right to supply. This objection was not proceeded with at the trial, but the fact that it had not been formally abandoned by the landlord provoked Lawrence J. to hold that neither the name or nationality of the proposed assignee could constitute reasonable grounds for withholding consent.[71]

Finally, it should be noted that where the "small premises" exclusion applies, the discriminatory conduct will be lawful; it does not necessarily follow that it will be reasonable[72] though the court may be expected to adopt the same policy as the Act towards such premises and find it to be so.[73]

---

[66] s.1.

[67] s.3(1); "near relative" is defined in s.78(5) and "small premises" in s.22(2).

[68] Compare s.5(1) of the Race Relations Act 1965 which s.24 of the Race Relations Act 1976 replaced.

[69] Compare Woodfall, *Landlord & Tenant*, Vol. 1, 1–1184.

[70] [1920] 2 Ch. 38.

[71] At p. 46; he gave no reasons and it *may* be that rather than finding the conduct intrinsically objectionable, he took the view that any reduction in consumption, for whatever cause, would not justify a refusal of consent because the clause relating to the purchase of liquor was so badly drafted as to enable the tenant to disregard it anyway. However it is surely preferable to take his words at face value.

[72] See D. J. Walker and M. J. Redman, *Racial Discrimination*, 1977, p. 73.

[73] See, *e.g. Schlegel* v. *Corcoran* [1942] I.R. 19 where Gavan Duffy J. found that a widow had reasonably withheld her consent to an assignment to a Jewish dentist because anti-Semitism goes back 2,000 years and is "too prevalent to be dismissed out of hand ... without regard to the actual conditions under which consent was withheld" (p. 25) namely that the widow, a Christian, lived on the premises and that the proposed assignee was "from her standpoint, a most undesirable participator in the narrow shelter of her roof. Amenities are the salt of life, and, though they may defy definition, they may fairly be taken to comprise all the factors that go to make ones home a happy and pleasant refuge ... " (p. 26).

Conditional consents

Under the general law, a grant of consent subject to a condition which is unreasonable amounts to an unreasonable withholding of consent entitling the tenant to assign, etc., without consent or to apply for a declaration of unreasonableness.[74] Where, as will commonly be the case, the Landlord and Tenant Act 1988 applies,[75] the unreasonable condition will result in the landlord failing to fulfil his duty under section 1(3)(a) "to give consent, except in a case where it is reasonable not to give consent"[76] and thus expose him to a claim under section 4 for breach of statutory duty.[77]

It is submitted that a condition will be unreasonable if the landlord is attempting to exploit the necessity for a licence in order to extract from the tenant a collateral advantage.[78] The advantage sought often takes the form of a variation of the

Variation of the lease

terms of the lease. A number of cases illustrate this point. In *Young* v. *Ashley Gardens Properties Ltd.*[79] the lease contained a covenant on the part of the lessor to pay all existing and future rates. Consent to assign was offered upon condition that the tenant and assignee assumed liability for any increase in the rates consequent upon the assignment. The condition was held to be unreasonable. The landlord was attempting to transfer his express liability under the lease on to the shoulders of the other parties. In *Premier Rinks Ltd.* v. *Amalgamated Cinematograph Theatres Ltd.*[80] the landlords were trying to impose a new restrictive covenant. The landlords held the leases on two premises, one of which they used as a cinema. The other they sublet but the sublease contained no covenant preventing the sublessee from using it as a cinema. The sublessee sought permission to assign and the landlords sent a licence which required the sublessee to covenant not to use the premises as a cinema, such covenant to be construed as if it had been contained in the original sublease. Joyce J. held the condition to be unreasonable and was reported to have said:

> "the defendants thought the application for their consent was a good opportunity for, in effect, inserting a new clause in the underlease, to all intents and purposes as if it had originally been there. They were in fact seeking to alter the terms of the underlease for the remainder of the term. The simple question was, was that reasonable? He thought not. It was an attempt to extort a fresh term which, by restricting the use of the premises during the residue of the underlease, would diminish the value of the . . . underlease."[81]

---

[74] *Young* v. *Ashley Gardens Properties Ltd.* [1903] 2 Ch. 112 C.A.
[75] See *supra* Chap. 5.
[76] See s.1(4).
[77] See Chap. 5.
[78] See generally *Bromley Park Garden Estates Ltd.* v. *Moss* [1982] 2 All E.R. 890; *supra* p. 73.
[79] *Ibid.*
[80] (1912) W.N. 157.
[81] At p. 158.

This case was cited with approval in *Mills* v. *Cannon Brewery Co. Ltd.*[82] where Lawrence J. opined *obiter* that the landlord in that case would not have been entitled to impose conditions on his licence requiring the assignee to personally reside on the premises and carry on the business of licensed victualler (the lease containing no such covenants) because this "would in effect be introducing into the underlease a new term which would be inconsistent with the provisions of the underlease and would change its character."[83]

Direct covenants

Sometimes the advantage sought does not alter the terms of the lease so much as the legal relationships, so important for the enforcement of covenants, which flow from it. In particular, though the contractual relationship between the original landlord and tenant subsists throughout the term,[84] the relationship between the landlord and an assignee, based upon privity of estate, lasts only while the term is vested in that assignee and between the landlord and a subtenant there is no relationship at all.[85] In normal circumstances[86] these consequences must be taken to have been contemplated by the parties when the lease was entered into, and therefore one would suppose that the landlord could not seek to change them on the occasion of an application for a licence. The cases are less clear cut. *Waite* v. *Jennings*[87] is consistent with the

Covenants by assignees

suggested approach. It concerned an assignee who had, in fact, acceded to the landlord's condition and covenanted by deed to be responsible for the rent and covenants for the remainder of the term. Having done so, the Court of Appeal held that he was bound by the deed and had to pay up upon a subsequent assignee's default but Vaughan-Williams L.J. opined *obiter* that it "may well be that as between the parties to the lease the lessee could have disregarded the absence of a licence if the lessor refused to grant one, unless and except upon the condition of a covenant for payment of rent during the term."[88] A different view was taken in *Re Spark's Lease, Verger* v. *Johnson*[89] where the landlord sought a direct contractual relationship with a subtenant as a condition of a licence. The

Covenants by sub-lessees

lease, in addition to the qualified disposition covenant, contained a covenant restricting user. The tenant proposed to underlet, the underlease containing identical covenants by the subtenant with the tenant. The landlord refused his consent unless the subtenant entered into a covenant directly with him in relation to these two matters. Swinfen-Eady J. held that the condition was reasonable. It is clear that his decision was heavily influenced by the fact that the landlord remained in

---

[82] [1920] 2 Ch. 38.
[83] At p. 47.
[84] Unless s.79 of the Law of Property Act 1925 has been excluded.
[85] Save perhaps in connection with restrictive covenants which may be enforceable between them under the rules relating to benefit and burden.
[86] But see *infra*.
[87] [1906] 2 K.B. 11.
[88] At p. 16; compare *Balfour* v. *Kensington Gardens* [1932] 49 T.L.R. 29 *contra* where it was suggested, again *obiter*, that to require an assignee to enter direct covenants with the landlord might well be reasonable—*per* MacNaghten J. at p. 31.
[89] [1905] 1 Ch. 456.

occupation of a part of the same building and that in these circumstances the underlease would deprive him of direct control over the remainder. But, on the evidence of the lease, direct control over the remainder was not in the contemplation of the parties when the lease was granted—or they would have drafted it differently[90] and therefore, it is submitted, the landlord secured a collateral advantage as the price for his consent and the condition should have been held unreasonable. In *Balfour* v. *Kensington Gardens*[91] *Spark's* was distinguished upon the basis that the landlord was in occupation and MacNaghten J. held that a condition requiring a subtenant to covenant directly with the landlord was unreasonable. In this case the tenant wished to sublet to a respectable and responsible person at a rent of £450 per annum. The lease reserved a rent of £700 per annum and the landlord made his consent conditional upon the subtenant covenanting directly with him for the payment of the higher rent. However

> "it was not reasonable to ask a sublessee who was already bound by the sublease to pay rent to his immediate lessor also to pay rent to the head lessor. It was inconsistent with the sublease, and, even if both rents had been the same, it would have been an unreasonable requirement. But where, as here, the rent payable under the sublease was less than that payable under the head-lease, it was idle to expect any sublessee to enter into the covenant demanded by the defendants and in the existing circumstances—namely where the rental value of the property had decreased since the granting of the head-lease—such a demand would in effect be a refusal to consent at all."[92]

It is submitted that in relation to requirements for sublessees to enter into direct covenants with the head landlord *Balfour* is to be preferred. Indeed the decision of Wynn Parry J. in *Vienit Ltd.* v. *W. Williams & Sons (Bread Street) Ltd.*[93] would tend to support this, being based upon the proposition that a head landlord who imposes such a requirement[94] acts unreasonably.[95] The reason given was that the objection had no reference to the personality of the proposed disponee, his user of the property or the terms of the lease[96] but since *Bromley Park Garden Estates Ltd.* v. *Moss*[97] the conclusion could as easily be justified upon the ground that the head landlord was seeking a collateral advantage in the form of an alteration of the network of legal relationships contemplated by the parties when the head lease was granted.

Thus far it has been assumed that there is nothing in the lease according the landlord a right to direct relations with

[90] For example direct control could have been secured by using an absolute disposition covenant.
[91] (1932) 49 T.L.R. 29.
[92] At p. 31.
[93] [1958] 3 All E.R. 621.
[94] In this case upon an assignee of a subtenant.
[95] And the tenant cannot therefore plead that refusal as justifying his own refusal to consent to the assignment by his subtenant, see *infra*.
[96] See *Re Gibbs & Houlder Bros. & Co. Ltd.'s Lease* [1925] Ch. 575.
[97] [1982] 2 All E.R. 890.

assignees and sublessees. It is, in fact, common to find provisions designed to secure such a right.[98] If the assignee or sublessee obliges the landlord and enters into the direct covenant, it is clear that he will be bound no matter how many others may subsequently have assumed a similar liability—the court will not construe such covenants as only intended to last until the next person assumes a contractual liability nor will they be ready to imply a release on the occasion of the next disposition.[99] If the assignee or sublessee refuses to enter direct covenants, and the landlord withholds his consent, whether he is acting unreasonably will depend on the way in which the provision designed to give him this right has been drafted. If, as in *Balfour* v. *Kensington Gardens* it is drafted as an agreed gloss upon the meaning of "unreasonably" ("Provided always that the lessors may as a condition of such consent to any assignment or underlease require the proposed assignee or underlessee to enter into direct covenants with the lessors to perform and observe all the covenants on the tenants part herein contained, and non-compliance with such condition shall be deemed to be a reasonable ground for refusing such consent") it will be ineffective under section 19(1)(*a*) of the Landlord and Tenant Act 1927.[1] If, on the other hand, it is expressed to be a condition precedent to any right to dispose[2] it will be effective[3] to confer upon the landlord the right to direct covenants and his insistence upon his right as a condition of granting consent cannot be construed as unreasonable.

Sometimes the suggested condition has nothing to do with varying the terms of the lease or the enforcement relationships between the respective parties—the landlord is seeking some other sort of price for his consent. Thus, in *Greater London Properties Ltd.'s Lease* v. *Covent Garden Properties Co. Ltd.*[4] permission was sought to assign to a company which was the wholly owned subsidiary of a large and well-known combine. The landlord refused consent unless the holding company guaranteed the rent. Danckwerts J. found that the assignee company was financially sound in its own right and that the condition was unreasonable: "No doubt, it would be very nice for the defendants to have the additional support for their rent of a guarantee ... but in my view they are not entitled to demand anything of the sort."[5] Had the assignee company been

Guarantors and sureties

---

[98] See, *e.g.* R. W. Ramage Kelly's *Draftsman* (15th ed.), p. 370; *The Encyclopedia of Forms and Precedents*, (5th ed.), Vol. 22, p. 287, 5.9:4 (assignees) and p. 288, 5.9:7 (sublessees).

[99] *J. Lyons & Co. Ltd.* v. *Knowles* [1943] 1 K.B. 366 C.A.

[1] See *supra* Chap. 4, p. 35. It is submitted the proviso suggested in Kelly's *Draftsman*, *ibid.* is also questionable—although the Court of Appeal in *J. Lyons* v. *Knowles* passed no adverse comment upon a very similar clause. As the assignee in that case had obligingly entered into direct covenants, the question of whether the landlord had any right to require it never arose.

[2] Consider *Encyclopedia of Forms & Precedents* (5th ed.), Vol. 22, pp. 287, 288, paras. 5.9:4, 5.9:7.

[3] See *Adler* v. *Upper Grosvenor Street Properties Ltd.* [1957] 1 All E.R. 229; *S. A. Bocardo* v. *S. & M. Hotels Ltd.* [1979] 3 All E.R. 737; discussed in Chap. 4, at pp. 36–41.

[4] [1959] 1 All E.R. 728.

[5] At p. 733.

of doubtful financial status, the landlord could clearly have refused his consent altogether[6] and would therefore be entitled to take the lesser course and to consent subject to a reasonable guarantee.

However, here again the position may be influenced by the terms of the lease. It is not unusual for leases to provide, for example, that in the case of an assignment to a limited company, its directors must act as sureties. Where the relevant provision is drafted as a condition precedent to any right to assign[7] it may be effective to give the landlord the right to insist upon such sureties regardless of the financial status of the company assignee; where it takes the form of an agreed gloss upon the meaning of "unreasonably" it will not be.[8]

Landlords fees

The advantage sought in *City Hotels Group Ltd.* v. *Total Property Investments Ltd.*[9] was also financial—the landlords were claiming to be paid their fees in respect of a *previous* abortive application for consent. Paul Baker Q.C. considered this an extraneous matter saying:

> "If, for example, there was a bona fide dispute as to the fees of a previous abortive application, the landlords have their rights under the relevant covenant and the lease, and the grant or refusal of a licence cannot be made dependent upon a satisfactory outcome in the landlords' eyes of their claim for their fees."[10]

If the landlord is requiring payment of a "reasonable sum in respect of his legal or other expenses" incurred in connection with the licence currently being sought, his conduct is expressly sanctioned by section 19(1)(*a*) of the Landlord and Tenant Act 1927.[11]

Objections based upon the terms of a proposed sublease

Rent too low

In both *Re Town Investment's Underlease*[12] and *Duckworth* v. *Witting (Liverpool) Ltd.*[13] the landlord was objecting that the rent reserved by the proposed sublease was too low. In the former, the defendants held a 63-year term and had underlet it to the plaintiff for 21 years. The plaintiff wished to sub-underlet to *R* at a rent well below both the market value and the rent reserved in the underlease and in consideration of a premium. Danckwerts J. held that the defendants had reasonably withheld their consent. The low rent would not

---

[6] See *supra* "Objections based upon the financial or business status of the assignee."
[7] It is tentatively suggested that the clause in *Encyclopedia of Forms & Precedents* (4th ed.), Vol. 11, p. 320 is so drafted: compare Kelly's *Draftsman*, (15th ed.), p. 370.
[8] See Chap. 4, p. 35.
[9] [1985] 1 E.G.L.R. 253.
[10] At p. 255.
[11] See Chap. 4, where demands in the nature of a fine are also considered.
[12] [1954] Ch. 301.
[13] (1970) 213 E.G. 69.

prejudice the defendant if the undertenant suffered a forfeiture or went bankrupt because in those circumstances R may become liable to pay the higher rent reserved in the underlease, however if the undertenant simply defaulted on his obligations, the rent payable by R would be insufficient to satisfy the defendant's right under the Law of Distress Amendment Act 1908[14] to serve notice on R to pay rent directly to him until the debt is discharged. Furthermore if the defendants wanted to sell the lease or use it as security for a loan, the purchaser or mortgagee may conclude from the disparity between the rentals that the higher one was inflated and the lower represented the true letting value of the property and would consequently be deterred. In *Duckworth* the tenant held two leases and sought the landlord's consent to underlet both. Here the rent reserved by the proposed underleases was more than that reserved by the leases but the landlord objected because the rent was lower than the current letting value of the property. The tenant unsuccessfully challenged the landlord's valuation, His Honour Judge Ruttle taking the view that the landlord was entitled to take his own expert's valuation so long as it was not excessive. On the basis that the rent *was* low, he considered that the landlord could be prejudiced if he wished to sell or mortgage and also because the low rent could be used as a comparator against him in relation to negotiating rents for lettings of his other properties.[15]

It seems clear from these cases that the landlord can reasonably refuse his consent if the rent under the sublease is less than the current letting value. If the rent is equal to the current letting value, it would appear that the landlord cannot reasonably object although that letting value may be less than the rent reserved in the lease because to allow him to do so would be, in effect, to deprive the tenant of any right to sublet at all.[16] The case would probably be different if the lease required the tenant, as a condition precedent to any right to sublet at all, to procure the payment of a rent at least equal to that reserved in the lease.[17]

Objections based upon the refusal of a superior landlord to give a necessary consent

Sometimes a disposition requires the consent not only of the immediate landlord but of one or more superior landlord. It

---

[14] s.1; see Hill & Redman's *Law of Landlord and Tenant* (18th ed.), Vol. 1, para. 1816.

[15] And see *Kaye* v. *Shop Investments Ltd.* (1966) 198 E.G. 1091 where in the case of a lease at a premium subject to a ground rent, the landlord was held reasonable in refusing his consent to four sublettings because the aggregate rents reserved were not equal to three times the ground rent.

[16] Consider *Balfour* v. *Kensington Gardens* (1932) 49 T.L.R. 29, *per* MacNaghten J. at p. 31; *supra* p. 117.

[17] See *supra* Chap. 4, pp. 36–41 and consider *Encyclopedia of Forms and Precedents* (5th ed.), Vol. 22, p. 287, 5.9:6.

could also be that before the immediate landlord consents, *he* needs the approval of a superior landlord before doing so. The duties of the superior landlord in relation to such consents and approvals, have been considered in Chapter 5. A further issue arises here: if the superior landlord refuses his consent or approval, can this fact, in itself, justify a refusal of consent by the immediate landlord? This was considered in *Vienit Ltd.* v. *W. Williams & Sons (Bread Street) Ltd.*[18] where Wynn Parry J. made a preliminary finding that, in the circumstances of the case, the superior landlord had unreasonably refused his consent to the disposition. He held therefore that the refusal of the immediate landlords to consent to the disposition, in reliance upon it, was also unreasonable. The immediate landlords also attempted to justify their action on the basis that they themselves had covenanted with the superior landlord not to grant a licence without the superior landlord's approval (not to be unreasonably refused) and that as such approval was not forthcoming, they would, by granting the licence, be exposing themselves to liability. This justification also failed—as the superior landlord's refusal to approve the licence would be unreasonable, the immediate landlord was free to grant the licence without consent and without any risk. Thus, where the refusal of the superior landlord to give a necessary consent is unreasonable, it cannot provide others with the basis of a reasonable refusal.

Arbitrary objections

It is implicit in the nature of a fully qualified covenant (and now also in the duty imposed upon the landlord to give reasons for his refusal under section 1(3)(*b*)(ii) of the Landlord and Tenant Act 1988)[19] that the landlord will at least *consider* the tenant's application for a licence. Any indication that he has not done so will necessarily make his refusal of consent unreasonable. In *Shanley* v. *Ward*[20] the landlord initially refused consent without even taking up the proposed assignee's references. Cozens-Hardy M.R. described this as unwise and went on to opine that

> "if the matter had rested there, there would plainly have been an unreasonable refusal which would have released the lessee . . . at least until it had been withdrawn and standing by itself would have justified an action and entitled the plaintiff to costs at any rate up to a certain stage in the action."[21]

In fact the landlord subsequently took up references and, with notice of this, the tenant instituted his action for a declaration. It was held that the subsequent refusal was reasonable because the references were unsatisfactory and that because the tenant

[18] [1958] 3 All E.R. 621.
[19] See *supra* Chap. 5.
[20] (1913) 29 T.L.R. 714 C.A.
[21] At p. 715.

had not waited for the outcome of the landlord's belated consideration before commencing his action, he was liable for costs from the date of the issue of the writ and not merely from the date of the landlord's reasonable refusal. Even where the landlord has discovered grounds for forfeiture, he is not entitled to refuse to consider an application for a licence to assign. In *Pakwood Transport Ltd.* v. *15, Beauchamp Place Ltd.*[22] upon finding out that the tenant company had gone into liquidation, the landlord rejected information (as to the proposed assignee's guarantor and user of the property) which he had earlier requested, because "having regard to the notice [of forfeiture] which has now been served, the question of a licence to assign will not now fall for consideration." The Court of Appeal held that there was no justification for declining, outright, even to consider the application, though the landlord could have deferred. In the event the tenant was granted relief against forfeiture and a declaration that consent had been unreasonably withheld.

Since the Landlord & Tenant Act 1988[23] the landlord can no longer disguise an arbitrary refusal as merely a failure to give reasons, as this will give rise to liability for breach of statutory duty under section 4.[24]

(3) Reasonable apprehension of harm

The landlord does not have to prove that the apprehension of harm to his relevant interest was *in fact* well-founded; it is sufficient if he can satisfy the court that it was an apprehension which could be entertained by a reasonable landlord. Typically the landlord's fears relate to possible future events and are therefore inherently incapable of absolute proof. Thus as Danckwerts L.J. expressed it in *Pimms Ltd.* v. *Tallow Chandlers in the City of London*[25] "it is not necessary for the landlords to prove that the conclusions which led them to refuse consent were justified, if they were conclusions which might be reached by a reasonable man in the circumstances."[26] The matter was equally well put in *Re Town Investments Underlease*[27]

> "The question is, have the landlords dealt with the matter in the way a reasonably prudent man of business would have dealt with it? That is the correct test; it is not a question of finding as a fact whether the landlords *will* be prejudiced by the proposed transaction ... what the court has to determine is (a) whether the [landlords] believe that the [disposition] will adversely affect their interest in the

---

[22] (1978) 36 P. & C.R. 112 C.A.; see *supra* Objections based on the assignor's breach of covenant.

[23] s.1(3)(*b*)(ii).

[24] See Chap. 5.

[25] [1964] 2 All E.R. 145, 151.

[26] A statement approved by Balcombe L.J. in *International Drilling Fluids Ltd.* v. *Louisville Investments (Uxbridge) Ltd.* [1986] 1 All E.R. 321, 325.

[27] [1954] Ch. 301.

property; and (b) whether that opinion can be entertained by a reasonable man."[28]

(4) Balancing the parties' interests

As Balcombe L.J. pointed out in *International Drilling Fluids Ltd.* v. *Louisville Investments (Uxbridge) Ltd.*[29]

"[t]here is a divergence of authority on the question, in considering whether the landlord's refusal is reasonable, whether it is permissible to have regard to the consequences to the tenant if consent to the proposed assignment is withheld."[30]

In *Viscount Tredegar* v. *Harwood*[31] Viscount Dunedin "was not inclined to adhere to the pronouncement of the C.A. in *Re Gibbs & Houlder Bros. & Co.*[32] that reasonableness was only to be referred to something which touched both parties to the lease"[33] and Lord Phillimore had similar doubts: "If it be a question whether a man is acting reasonably, as distinguished from justly, fairly or kindly, you are to take into consideration the motives of convenience and interest which affect him, not those which affect somebody else."[34] Support for this view may also be derived from the comments of Roskill L.J. in *West Layton* v. *Ford*[35] that the "landlord has not got to consider anybody else's interests except his own. He is the person who has, in all the circumstances, to decide whether or not he will grant consent," those of Cumming-Bruce L.J. in *Bromley Park Garden Estates Ltd.* v. *Moss*[36] and those of Oliver L.J. in *Leeward Securities Ltd.* v. *Lilyheath Properties Ltd.*[37] It is certainly true that the landlord is in a better position to consider his own interests than those of anyone else, however it may perhaps be remembered that though the purpose of the restraint is to protect the landlord's interests, the purpose of the fully qualifying provision, as Warrington L.J. pointed out in *Re Gibbs & Houlder Bros. & Co. Ltd.'s Lease*[38] is to prevent the lessor making an unreasonable use of that protection. It is hard to see how the latter judgment could be made without

---

[28] L. A. Blundell, counsel for the landlords at p. 305, with whose analysis Dankwerts J. was in apparent agreement; other similar statements may be found in *Shanley* v. *Ward* [1913] 29 T.L.R. 714, 715; *Premier Confectionary London Co. Ltd.* v. *London Commercial Salerooms Ltd.* [1933] Ch. 904, 913; *Searle* v. *Burroughs* [1966] 110 S.J. 248 "the test ... was not subjective. The test was what a reasonable person in the landlord's position would think," *per* Denning M.R. at p. 248; *City Hotels Group Ltd.* v. *Total Property Investments Ltd.* (1985) 1 E.G.L.R. 253, 254; *Rayburn* v. *Wolf* (1986) 18 H.L.R. 1 C.A.
[29] *Ibid.*
[30] At p. 325.
[31] [1929] A.C. 72.
[32] [1925] All E.R. 128.
[33] At p. 78.
[34] At p. 82.
[35] [1979] Q.B. 593, 605.
[36] [1982] 1 W.L.R. 1019, 1027.
[37] (1984) 271 E.G. 279, 282.
[38] *Ibid.* at p. 133.

account being taken of the tenant's position. It is not suggested that the landlord should conduct an investigation into the tenant's circumstances, merely that he pay regard to such information as is made available to him. If the landlord's interest in refusing consent and the tenant's interest in securing it are evenly balanced, he may well be entitled to prefer his own interests; but if the benefit he would derive from withholding consent is slight, as compared to the harm which it would inflict upon the tenant, the result may differ. There are authorities for the more balanced view going back to *Re Gibbs & Houlder Bros.* where Warrington L.J. commented that "the outstanding circumstances to be considered [in determining whether a refusal is unreasonable] are the nature of the contract to be construed and *the relations between the parties resulting from it.*"[39] This also stresses that the interests to be considered, on both sides, are relevant interests[39a] and one is not determining in a general way which of them will suffer the greater hardship. Any hardship falls for consideration only in so far as it can be shown to be consequent upon loss of, or prejudice to, a relevant interest.[40] Two more recent statements perhaps sum the matter up: "in my judgment a proper reconciliation of those two streams of authority can be achieved by saying that while a landlord need usually only consider his own relevant interests, there may be cases where there is such a disproportion between the benefit to the landlord and the detriment to the tenant if the landlord withholds his consent to an assignment, that it is unreasonable for the landlord to refuse consent."[41] "He [Balcombe L.J.] is saying that while the landlord's interests are of great importance and usually all the landlord need consider, he cannot just ignore the tenant's interests but has to consider those."[42]

---

[39] Author's italics.

[39a] See *supra*.

[40] See also *F.W. Woolworth plc* v. *Charlwood Alliance Properties Ltd.* [1987] 282 E.G. 585, 593.

[41] *Per* Balcombe L.J. in *International Drilling Fluids, ibid.* at p. 326.

[42] *Per* Judge Paul Baker Q.C. in *Deverall* v. *Wyndham & Ors.* (1989) 247 E.G. 70 at p. 76; the court had regard to the balance of interests in *Ponderosa International Developments Inc.* v. *Pengap Securities (Bristol) Ltd.* [1986] 1 E.G.L.R. 66, 68 and *Orlando Investments Ltd.* v. *Grosvenor Estate Belgravia* [1989] 43 E.G. 175, 182.

7 SPECIAL CATEGORIES OF TENANT

It was mentioned in Chapter 1 that a tenant's disposition rights may be restricted by statute. The scope of such restrictions and the tenants to whom they apply are considered here.

Tenancies subject to the Rent Act 1977

The Rent Act 1977 will now only apply to tenancies entered into prior to the coming into force of the Housing Act 1988: *i.e.* before January 15, 1989.[1] Where it applies, under section 98, the court has a discretion to order possession of a dwellinghouse which is let on a protected tenancy or subject to a statutory tenancy[2] where it considers it reasonable to make such order and the circumstances are as specified in any of the cases in Part 1 of Schedule 15 of the Act. Case 6 refers to the tenant having[3] without the consent[4] of the landlord assigned or sublet the whole of the dwellinghouse or sublet part of the dwellinghouse, the remainder being already sublet. Thus, while the Act does not directly restrict the Case 6 dispositions, it attaches to them consequences adverse to the tenant and thus operates as a restraint.

Case 6 Pt. I Sched. 15 Rent Act 1977

Assignments

An assignment during the contractual term may allow the landlord to recover possession of the land under Case 6 at the

---

[1] See s.1(2) & Sched. 1, Pt. I, para. 1 of the Housing Act 1988.

[2] Defined in ss. 1 and 2 of the Rent Act 1977. See J. T. Farrand, *Current Law Statutes Annotated*, (1977). The majority of housing association tenancies are excluded from protected status (see ss. 15 & 16) and are most likely to come under the secure tenancy regime: see *infra* & Alder & Handy, *Housing Association Law* (1987). The Rent Act 1977 does not apply to Scotland or Northern Ireland: s.156(3).

[3] After the relevant date there specified.

[4] Although consent may be express or implied, there can be no implication unless the landlord knew of the disposition. Thus consent will not be implied merely from the fact that the landlord neglected to restrict dispositions in the lease. See *Dalrymple's Trustees* v. *Brown* [1945] S.C. 190, followed in *Regional Properties Co. Ltd.* v. *Frankenschwerth* [1951] 1 All E.R. 178 C.A. Consent can be given at any time before the issue of proceedings; it does not have to be given at or before the time of the disposition. The fact that the disposition was a breach of covenant which the landlord had waived by acceptance of rent, did not necessarily give rise to the implication that the landlord had consented for the purposes of Case 6. "Consent to an act is not the same thing as a waiver of its consequences" *per* Evershed M.R., *Hyde* v. *Pimley* [1952] 2 All E.R. 102, 105, C.A. The waiver in this particular case was sufficient to amount to consent to the act.

During the contract of tenancy

end of the term. It can have this effect even if there was no restriction on dispositions in the contract of tenancy. *Regional Properties Co. Ltd.* v. *Frankenschwerth and Chapman*[5] concerned an assignment while the contractual term, a monthly tenancy imposing no restrictions on disposition, was still running. The landlord served notice to quit whereupon the assignee became a statutory tenant and could only be removed on one of the grounds set out in the Act. Although there had been an assignment without consent here, when it took place the tenant was free to make it. It was held that this did not prevent the landlord from recovering possession at the end of the term.

Relevance of terms of contractual tenancy

> "It is plain that during the term of the contract, if there is no prohibition against assigning or underletting, the tenant can assign or underlet without asking the landlords consent or leave, but what Parliament has said is, whether or not consent is necessary, if in fact there has been an assignment without the landlords consent then it is fair that the court should have power to make an order for possession against the assignee who *ex concessis* is somebody unknown to and not approved by the landlord."[6]

Nor apparently can the claim for possession be resisted by the assignee arguing that Case 6 refers to the "*tenant*" having assigned etc. and he as the new tenant has not done so. In *Leith Properties* v. *Springer*[7] it was held that "tenant" referred to the last immediate tenant of the landlord "excluding an assignee of the tenancy or a subtenant who has not yet been accepted by the landlord as a tenant."[8] While Case 6 can be made out regardless of whether the assignment was a breach of covenant on the part of the tenant, the court has to be satisfied that it would be reasonable to make an order for possession. The fact that an assignment *was* a breach of covenant can be very material at this stage. In *Pazgate Ltd.* v. *McGrath*[9] there was an assignment of the lease (an assent to a non-beneficiary by the executors of the deceased tenant) during the contractual term in breach of a qualified covenant against assignment. It was held to have vested the term in the assignee who on the termination of the lease became a statutory tenant. The original tenant would not have had such protection because he did not live there but had taken the lease to provide a home for his daughter in law, the assignee. A possession order was granted to the landlord on the basis of Case 6. The assignment was without the landlord's consent and it was reasonable to make the order. As Fox L.J. pointed out

> " . . . the execution of the assent totally destroyed, in breach of covenant, the nicely balanced situation created by the lease. It converted [the assignee] into a statutory tenant. Really the position was this, that, in breach of

---

[5] See n. 4.
[6] *Per* Evershed M.R. at p. 181.
[7] [1982] 3 All E.R. 731 C.A.
[8] *Per* Slade L.J. at p. 737.
[9] [1984] 272 E.G. 1069 C.A.

covenant, the executors were choosing the next tenant without the consent of the landlord and greatly against the landlord's interests."[10]

Assignments by statutory tenants

Thus far consideration has been given to assignments while the contractual tenancy subsists. What of assignments after the termination of the contractual term, by those qualifying as statutory tenants? The curious nature of a statutory tenancy imposes its own limitations on disposition, as Bankes, L.J. opined in *Keeves* v. *Dean*,[11] a case concerning an assignment for valuable consideration,

Personal nature of statutory tenancy

"I think that it is a pity that that expression [statutory tenant] was ever introduced. It is really a misnomer, for he is not a tenant at all; although he cannot be turned out of possession so long as he complies with the provisions of the statute, he has no estate or interest in the premises as a tenant has. His right is a purely personal one, and as such, unless statute expressly authorises him to pass it on to another person, must cease the moment he parts with possession or dies."

Lush J. made remarks to a similar effect, adding that

"the difficulty in the way of a statutory tenant which seems to me insuperable is that it is essential to the validity of an assignment that the assignee should have a right of entry. But the moment the assignor gives up possession, his right of entry ceases and the assignee cannot possibly claim a right which the assignor did not himself possess."[12]

Relevance of terms of contracts of tenancy

It was argued that the express statutory authorisation to pass the tenancy on, referred to by Bankes, L.J. above, could be found in section 15(1) of the Increase of Rent and Mortgage Interest (Restrictions) Act 1920[13] which provided that the statutory tenant was entitled to the benefit and must observe "the terms and conditions of the original contract of tenancy so far as the same are consistent with the provisions of the Act." Where, as in the instant case the original contract of tenancy imposed no restrictions on disposition the statutory tenancy was it was argued, similarly free of restrictions. Neither Bankes L.J. nor Lush J. were willing to characterise a tenant's common law freedom to assign, where there was no provision in the tenancy restraining him, as "a term" or "condition" of the tenancy, rather it was a right incident to the estate and thus outside the provision. Scrutton L.J. was not prepared to draw this distinction between a term or condition of the tenancy on the one hand and a right incident to the estate on the other. He considered that the common law freedom to assign would pass, as a "term" of the original tenancy, to the statutory tenant under section 15(1) *but only* if "consistent with the provisions

---

[10] At p. 1072.
[11] [1924] 1 K.B. 685 C.A.
[12] At p. 698.
[13] Now s.3(1) of the Rent Act 1977.

of the Act." One provision of the Act with which a general power to assign did not sit well was section 15(2)[14] which expressly prohibited assignments for valuable consideration by the statutory tenant to anyone other than his landlord. He too concluded therefore that there was no general power to assign a statutory tenancy. No *general* power because section 15(2) did

Voluntary assignments not prohibit voluntary assignments and was therefore consistent with the transfer of such a power to a statutory tenant. Even if the transfer of such a limited power could take place, the statutory tenant could only exercise it by deed: if it was not exercised by deed the common law would not help the assignee and neither would equity because of the voluntary nature of the transaction. In the later case of *Roe* v. *Russell*[15] the same judge doubted whether even this limited power could survive the introduction, in the 1923 Increase of Rent and Mortgage Interest (Restrictions) Act, of the ground of possession now referred to as Case 6 which encompasses all assignments without the landlords consent, a ground which was introduced because "presumably in the opinion of the legislature his interest as statutory tenant was not one that he could assign in that by assigning he ceased to be a statutory tenant."[16] Furthermore as Lush J. pointed out in *Keeves*[17] the provisions relating to transmission on death are not consistent with the tenant being able to assign to someone of his choice.

In a case where, unlike *Keeves*, the original contractual tenancy was subject to a restriction on assignment, it would of course be clear that such restriction was a "term" or "condition" of the original contract of tenancy which the statutory tenant would be bound to observe.[18]

Thus, it appears from the foregoing, and is in fact generally accepted, that a statutory tenant has no power to assign. The effect of him doing so, and thus relinquishing residence, would be the loss of statutory protection for himself and the failure to validly confer any protection upon the assignee. In such circumstances the landlord does not need to have recourse to Case 6 in order to regain possession: whether Case 6 is available to him depends upon whether it covers ineffective attempts to perform the acts to which it refers.[19]

Finally it should be noted that the court can effect a transfer of a statutory tenancy under section 7 & Schedule 1 of the Matrimonial Homes Act 1983[20] but apparently not under

---

[14] Now para. 12–(1) Sched. 1, Part II, of the Rent Act 1977.

[15] [1928] 2 K.B. 117 C.A.

[16] At p. 126.

[17] At p. 697.

[18] And in respect of a breach of which the landlord would be able to rely on Case 1.

[19] See Halsbury's *Laws of England*, (4th ed.), Vol. 27, para. 691; R. E. Megarry, *The Rent Acts*, (10th ed.), Vol. 1, p. 275; Pettit, *Landlord and Tenant under the Rent Act*, 1977 p. 200.

[20] See paras. 1 & 3, Schedule 1. See also *infra* "Change of Statutory Tenant by Agreement."

section 24 of the Matrimonial Causes Act 1973 (Property Adjustment Orders) because of the non-proprietary status of the statutory tenancy.

Subleases

During the contract of tenancy

The position in relation to subleases is similar in some respects to that relating to assignments. Considering first subleases during the contractual term, once that term has terminated, Case 6 applies to *subleases* of the whole or subleases of part, the remainder being already let,[21] *regardless* of whether the particular sublease was a breach of the contractual tenancy.[22] However if it was not, it may be regarded as "lawful" for the purposes of section 137(2) of the Rent Act 1977 which provides that:

> "Where a statutorily protected tenancy is determined either as a result of an order for possession or for any other reason, any subtenant to whom the dwellinghouse or any part of it has been lawfully sublet, shall subject to this Act, be deemed to become the tenant of the landlord on the same terms as if the tenant's statutorily protected tenancy had continued."

"Lawful"

This protection may be illusory as shown by *Leith Properties* v. *Springer*.[23] Here the tenant sublet the whole while the contractual term was still subsisting. Because there was no restriction on dispositions, the sublease was "lawful" within section 137(2) but the protection which that conferred upon the subtenant was "subject to this Act." It was thus subject to the landlord's right to recover possession under section 98(1) and Schedule 15 of the Rent Act 1977, if he could bring his action within its terms. In this case it was held that he could bring himself within Case 6 as the *tenant* had sublet the whole without consent. An argument that by virtue of section 137(2) the subtenant was now the tenant and he had not sublet within the terms of Case 6, failed to impress the court which remitted the case to the county court simply on the question of whether it would be reasonable to make an order.

Case 6 does not of course apply to *subleases* of part where the remainder is *unlet*. Where such a sublease was a breach of the terms of the contractual tenancy, the landlord would be able to rely upon Case 1; where it was not, it would be a lawful[24] sublease conferring upon the tenant the protection of section 137(2) which in these circumstances may be real.[25]

---

[21] Assuming that these circumstances have existed, it does not matter that they have ceased to exist at the date when proceedings are commenced, see *Finkler* v. *Strzelczyk* [1961] 3 All E.R. 409 ("if the tenant has done that thing at any time after the date specified [in Case 6] then assuming reasonableness, the court is empowered to make the order" *per* Evershed, M.R. at p. 410).

[22] See *Leith supra*, n. 7.

[23] See n. 7.

[24] *Roe* v. *Russell supra* n. 15.

[25] Case 6 not being available.

Subleases by Statutory Tenants

Turning to subleases by statutory tenants, a sublease of the whole or part, the remainder being already let, usually involves the tenant in giving up residence[26] and, as with assignments, thus relinquishing his rights under the Act. He would therefore have no rights to confer on the sublessee unless there was a statutory provision to the contrary[27] and, as with assignments, such a provision is absent. The landlord should therefore be able to recover possession off either of them in reliance on his common law rights. Again whether Case 6 could be invoked against them depends upon whether it covers ineffective transactions.[28]

However a sublease of part where the remainder is *unlet* is not at all inconsistent with the continuance of a statutory tenancy. The tenant does not give up residence by virtue of such a disposition and can in some circumstances make a valid sublease. This would be so if there was no restriction on subleases of part in the original contract of tenancy.[29] If there was such a restriction the statutory tenant would be bound to observe it by virtue of section 3(1) of the Rent Act 1977, and liable to proceedings under Case 1 if he failed to do so. On re-entry by the landlord the subtenant would not be a lawful subtenant and would therefore not gain any assistance from section 137(2).

Change of statutory tenant by agreement

It is provided by section 3(5) and Schedule 1, Part II, paragraph 13 of the Rent Act 1977 that a statutory tenant can transfer his status to another by an agreement in writing with the incoming tenant to which the landlord (and any superior landlord whose consent would have been required to an assignment of the previous contractual tenancy) has been made party. It is an offence for any person to exact a pecuniary consideration in connection with such an agreement.[30] It has been stated, with some justification, that this "represents in substance a direct contradiction of the proposition that a statutory tenancy cannot be assigned."[31]

---

[26] The notion of residence *can* comprehend temporary absence accompanied by subletting, see J. T. Farrand, *Current Law Statutes Annotated* 1977, 42/2.

[27] It was argued in *Trustees of Henry Smith's Charity* v. *Willson* [1982–1983] 6 H.L.R. 55 that s.137(2) contained an indication that a statutory tenant *could* sublet the whole because it conferred protection upon lawful subleases of "the dwellinghouse or any part" but Slade J. refused to "grapple any further with these conceptual problems" (p. 66). Perhaps the response to this argument should be that s.137(2) clearly applies to lawful subleases of the whole *during the contractual term* and it is to these circumstances which it is referring. It was held that even if there could be a sublease of the whole by a statutory tenant, in this case it was not a lawful one because it was in breach of a qualified disposition covenant imported into the statutory tenancy by virtue of s.3(1).

[28] *Quaere* whether the sublease could ever be regarded as lawful for the purposes of s.137(2)?

[29] Or even if there was, if it had been waived. See *Oak Property Ltd.* v. *Chapman* [1947] 2 All E.R. 1 C.A.

[30] Para. 14.

[31] J. T. Farrand, Current Law Statutes Annotated 1977, 42/Sched. 2.

Tenancies subject to the Housing Act 1985: Secure Tenancies[32]

Assignment

Not assignable By section 91 of the Housing Act 1985, in general, secure tenancies[33] are not capable of being assigned.[34] This applies whether the tenancy is a periodic tenancy or a term certain granted on or after November 5, 1982.[35] In the case of a term certain granted before that date, an assignment leads to permanent loss of secure status[36] but the assignment is valid to pass the tenancy to the assignee and this is so regardless of whether the assignment was a breach of the terms of the agreement.[37] Both the prohibition, and the loss of secure status where applicable, are subject to the exceptions set out in subsection (3) which refers to:

Exceptions

(a) an assignment by way of exchange under section 92
(b) an assignment in pursuance of a property[38] adjustment order under section 24 of the Matrimonial Causes Act 1973
(c) an assignment to a person who would be qualified to succeed if the tenant died immediately before the assignment.

Property adjustment orders The freedom which these exceptions confer may of course, exist alongside a covenant restricting disposition. In relation to assignments by way of exchange this would be irrelevant as any consent necessitated by such a covenant would be supplied in the course of complying with section 92.[39] This would not be so in relation to a property adjustment order, and there is some dispute as to whether the court can order an assignment of a secure tenancy under section 24 in the face of a provision restricting dispositions, and as to the effect of such an order if it was made. In *Hale* v. *Hale*[40] Megaw, L.J. opined that there would be no jurisdiction, stating that

---

[32] The Act applies to England & Wales: see s.625.
[33] See s.79 of the Housing Act 1985 and Arden, Current Law Statutes Annotated 1985, 68/79.
[34] Sections 91–95 do not apply when the interest of the landlord belongs to a "co-operative housing association": see s.109. This term is defined in s.5. See also s.80 which specifies to which housing associations the secure regime applies and, generally, *Housing Association Law* (1987) Alder & Handy.
[35] Subs. (1).
[36] Subs. (2).
[37] See *Governors of the Peabody Donation Fund* v. *Higgins* [1983] 3 All E.R. 122 C.A. concerning an analogous provision of the Housing Act 1980 (s.37(1)—now repealed).
[38] Includes tenancies, fixed term and periodic, (*Hale* v. *Hale* [1975] 2 All E.R. 1090—weekly) and whether of a private or a local authority landlord. *Thompson* v. *Thompson* [1975] 2 All E.R. 208 C.A.
[39] See *infra*.
[40] See *supra* n. 38 at p. 1094 (*obiter*). By implication Stephenson L.J. would similarly have considered a tenancy incapable of assignment without the landlord's consent in the face of a covenant against assignment.

"if there is no contractual or statutory provision which prevents it being transferred by the tenant himself, the court has power ... to make an order for that transfer, which the tenant himself could have made without consulting or obtaining the consent of the landlord ... if there be some contractual condition, then a different situation arises."

However, Ormrod L.J. in *Thompson* v. *Thompson* took a slightly different view commenting that

" ... a council tenancy is undoubtedly 'property' within the meaning of section 24 of the Matrimonial Causes Act 1973, and therefore can be dealt with under the powers of the court to make property adjustment orders, although whether such an order is effective may well depend upon the precise terms of the tenancy. ... "[41]

This he repeated, in effect, in *Hutchings* v. *Hutchings*[42] expressing the opinion that the court would have jurisdiction but would not make the order if it would be ineffective because the council could thereupon recover possession.

Though not referred to in section 91 the court also has jurisdiction to order the transfer of a secure tenancy under section 7 and Schedule 1 of the Matrimonial Homes Act 1983.

Matrimonial Homes Act 1983

The court making the decree of divorce, nullity or judicial separation can make the transfer order on or at any time after the decree, so long as the applicant has not remarried. Some commentators express the view that this jurisdiction (in contrast to the section 24 jurisdiction) exists regardless of the presence of a contractual restriction on assignment.[43] The view seems to be based on the fact that under the Matrimonial Homes Act the court order itself effects the transfer ("by virtue of the order and without further assurance") whereas under section 24 of the Matrimonial Causes Act the court orders the tenant spouse to effect the transfer. This clearly has a bearing upon whether an assignment could constitute a breach of covenant on the part of the tenant, giving the landlord grounds to recover possession—presumably the tenant is not liable for the orders of the court. Thus an order under the Matrimonial Homes Act would be more effective from this point of view. However if the problem in relation to section 24 is not simply one of making an effective order but of jurisdiction to make the order at all, that would seem to beset the Matrimonial Homes Act jurisdiction too. The better view would seem to be that the court has no jurisdiction under either Act where there is an absolute covenant against assignment or, indeed, where there is a qualified covenant in respect of which the landlord has

---

[41] *Supra* n. 38 at p. 212 and see Sir John Pennycuick at p. 213. Compare Buckley L.J. at p. 211 who seems to doubt the jurisdiction where there is a restrictive covenant.

[42] (1975) E.G. 57 C.A.; discussed in (1979) 129 N.L.J. 1069 (Radevsky); see also *Regan* v. *Regan* [1977] 1 W.L.R. 84, 85.

[43] Arden (*supra* n. 33) and Hand (*Current Law Statutes Annotated* (1983), 19/Sched 1).

reasonably withheld his consent.[44] The policy of these Acts surely does not require the court to direct or effect a transfer which disregards the covenanted rights of the landlord.[45]

Assignments to successors

The third situation in which a secure tenancy can be assigned, is where an assignment is to a person who would be qualified to succeed if the tenant died immediately before the assignment. No question of the court's jurisdiction arises here. It has been established that if such an assignment is in breach of covenant, it will nonetheless be valid to pass the tenancy to the assignee who may thus have secure status. Because of the breach of covenant however, the landlord will be able to recover possession in reliance upon section 84 and Ground 1 of Schedule 2 of the 1985 Act if the court considers it reasonable.[46]

Exchanges between secure tenants

The provisions of section 92, facilitate exchanges between secure tenants, even where they hold of different landlords. The section incorporates a term into a secure tenancy that the tenant may, with the written consent of the landlord, assign the tenancy to another secure tenant who also has the written consent of his landlord.[47] The drafting of the section permits not only two-way but also multiple exchanges. Where a party to the exchange was a secure tenant by succession that status is retained despite the exchange.[48] The landlord can only withhold consent on one or more of the grounds set out in

Grounds for withholding consent

Schedule 3 of the Act[49] and he can only rely upon these if he has within 42 days of the tenant's application for consent served upon the tenant a notice specifying the ground and giving particulars of it.[50] If it is withheld on any other ground it is to be treated as given.[51] A positive withholding outside the 42 day period will of necessity be outside the Schedule 3 grounds, and will therefore be treated as a consent. A silence on the part of the landlord extending beyond this period may not amount to "withholding"[52] for the purposes of subsection (3) with the consequence that it cannot be treated as a consent. Thus unless the tenant can by some means force a response, any exchange will fall under the general prohibition in section 91.

It is only in exceptional circumstances that the landlord has the option of giving his consent conditionally.[53] The

---

[44] See Radevsky *supra* n. 42.

[45] Another problem with the Matrimonial Homes Act jurisdiction is the possibility that the court will not make an order, upon an application made after decree absolute, for a transfer by a sole secure tenant who has ceased to occupy the premises, because the very existence of the secure tenancy under s.79 of the Housing Act is dependant upon the maintenance of the "tenant condition" (occupation) under s.81. Until decree absolute the condition can probably be maintained through the residence of the applicant spouse. See Arden *supra*, n. 33 and comments in *Lewis* v. *Lewis* [1985] 2 All E.R. 449 H.L.

[46] *Governors of the Peabody Donation Fund* v. *Higgins supra* n. 37.

[47] Subs. (1) & (2).

[48] S.88(3).

[49] Subs. (3).

[50] Subs. (4).

[51] Subs. (3).

[52] Compare s.94(6)(*b*) infra.

[53] Subs (6).

Conditions

exception applies where the tenant has not paid rent lawfully due or has broken or not performed an obligation of the tenancy. The landlord can in these circumstances impose conditions as to payment, remedying the breach or performance of the obligation respectively. Furthermore as he is consenting, rather than "withholding," he can presumably issue such a conditional consent during or after the 42 day period. His other option would appear to be the service of notice of proceedings for possession against the tenant applicant upon Ground 1 of Part 1 of Schedule 2 of the Act which proceedings constitute a valid ground, under Schedule 3,[54] to withhold consent to the exchange. Attempts to impose conditions other than those just referred to, result in an unconditional consent.[55]

Subleases

Subleases of part: written consent necessary

By section 93(1)(*b*) it is a term of every secure tenancy that the tenant will not without the written consent of the landlord, sublet or part with possession of part[56] of the dwellinghouse. Non-compliance with this term will not affect the validity of the sublease between the tenant and the sublessee[57] but the landlord can recover possession under section 84 and Ground 1, Part 1 of Schedule 2. In this event there is no statutory provision shielding the sublessee from the effects of such a possession order and therefore the sublease will terminate upon the determination of the superior term.[58]

Not to be unreasonably withheld

Section 94(2) introduces the well-known qualification that consent shall not be unreasonably withheld. It further provides, in contrast to the position under section 19(1) of the Landlord and Tenant Act 1927,[59] that the burden of proof is upon the *landlord* to show that the withholding was *not* unreasonable. In discharging this burden he can use arguments similar to those relevant for the purposes of section 19(1) but in addition subsection (3) requires two other matters to be taken into account if they can be demonstrated by the landlord, *vis*, (a) the consent would lead to overcrowding within the meaning of Part X of the Act and (b) that the landlord proposes to carry out works on that dwellinghouse, or a building of which it forms part, and that the proposed works will affect the accommodation likely to be used by the subtenant who would reside in the dwellinghouse as a result of the consent. Where the tenant has applied in writing for the consent, subsection (6) comes into operation. It provides that (a) a landlord refusing consent shall give a written statement of his reasons and (b) a

---

[54] Ground 1.
[55] Subs. (6)—rather than being construed as a withholding.
[56] This does not preclude taking in lodgers—which is expressly permitted by s.93(1)(a); for subleases of the whole, see *infra*.
[57] Though such a subtenant would probably not have full Rent Act protection because of the presence of a resident landlord. See Arden *supra* n. 33, 68/93.
[58] Compare where the determination results from a surrender or tenant's notice to quit. *Parker* v. *Jones* [1910] 2 K.B. 32; Arden *ibid*.
[59] *Shanley* v. *Ward* [1913] 29 T.L.R. 714; but see s.1 of the Landlord & Tenant Act 1988, *infra* Chap. 5.

landlord neither giving nor refusing consent within a reasonable time, shall be taken to have withheld it. If consent is withheld, whether the withholding results from a declared refusal or a failure to reach a decision within a reasonable time, and the withholding is unreasonable, it is provided by subsection (1)

Effect of unreasonable withholding

that consent shall be treated as given. The County Court has jurisdiction to determine whether consent was unreasonably withheld[60] and before proceeding without consent, a tenant should consider seeking a declaration rather than run the risk of providing the landlord with grounds to recover possession. If he does enter the sublease first, and possession proceedings are brought against him, he can, of course, defend them on the basis that the withholding was unreasonable and could therefore be treated as consent under section 94(2).

Consent after sublease

Where the sublease has been made before the tenant has even sought consent, he can still seek it[61] and should do so, however futile he feels it to be, because until he does, he is in breach of the statutory term and cannot rely upon section 94 as there will have been no withholding of consent on the landlord's part.

No conditional consents

It is provided by subsection (5) that consent cannot be given subject to a condition and if the consent purports to be conditional it shall be treated as given unconditionally.[62]

Sublease of the whole, etc.

Section 93(2) deals with subleases of the whole of the dwellinghouse. The effect of such a sublease (and of a sublease of first part and then the remainder) is that the tenancy ceases, permanently, to be secure.[63] It is therefore possible to grant such a sublease, but the tenancy will lose its secure status and will therefore come to end at the expiration of the term or upon service by the landlord upon the tenant of a notice to quit. Section 93(2) does not import into the tenancy any restrictive term[64] in relation to subletting the whole, *etc.* but presumably if there happened to be one non-compliance by the tenant would form the basis of forfeiture proceedings. Here again there is no provision saving the subtenancy which would thus also terminate.

Assignment and subletting where the tenant condition is not satisfied

Section 95 addresses the situation where the secure tenant ceases to occupy the premises as required by section 81 and

---

[60] s.110.

[61] Subs. (4).

[62] It has been asserted (Arden, *ibid.* 68/94) that this provision pre-empts use of the device whereby a tenant must offer to surrender the lease to the landlord before applying for consent to sublet. Compare *Adler* v. *Upper Grosvenor Street Investments* [1957] 1 W.L.R. 227. This would seem to be unsound, as a surrender back proviso does not in any way condition the consent. If the tenant complies with the proviso and offers the surrender the landlord can accept or reject it. If he accepts it, the tenant has not even the opportunity to apply for consent. If he rejects it, the proviso has exhausted its force and in no way operates upon any consent which may subsequently issue.

[63] See also s.81 which defines the tenant condition as occupying premises as the only or principal home.

[64] Compare s.93(1), *supra*—"it is a term of every secure tenancy" etc.

thereupon loses security, it ensures that he does not lose the restrictions on assignment and subletting which previously affected him.

Protected shorthold tenancies

This type of tenancy was introduced in the Housing Act 1980 which, by sections 51–55, modified the operation of the Rent Act 1977 in relation to protected tenancies[65] which were granted for a term certain of not less than one year nor more than five years and satisfied the conditions in section 52.[66] One such modification affects disposition rights. In relation to subletting, section 54(1) provides that if the landlord has become entitled to possession as against the tenant he shall also be entitled to possession against the sub-tenant and section 137,[67] which can protect subtenants, shall not apply. Under section 54(2) a protected shorthold tenancy is not capable of being assigned except in pursuance of an order under section 24 of the Matrimonial Causes Act 1973.[68]

Tenancies subject to Part II of the Landlord and Tenant Act 1954

Business tenancies subject to the 1954 Act may contain any or none of the usual provisions restricting dispositions. Where a restriction is in qualified form, it becomes subject to full qualification under section 19(1)(a) of the Landlord & Tenant Act 1927. That apart, the disposition rights of business tenants are not generally subject to statutory intervention. However, when granting a new tenancy under section 35 of the 1954 Act, the court must have regard to the terms of the current tenancy, whatever they may be, and to all relevant circumstances. Thus if there was freedom to assign, that freedom will continue under the terms of the new tenancy unless there is evidence to justify its restraint. In considering such evidence the court will be mindful of the effect of the proposed restriction upon the tenant's goodwill, and may be reluctant to sanction a surrender-back provision where previously there was but a fully qualified covenant.[69]

---

[65] See *supra*.

[66] These provisions only apply to tenancies granted after November 28, 1980 and before January 15, 1989; they have now been succeeded by the assured shorthold tenure introduced by the Housing Act 1988.

[67] Rent Act 1977; see *supra*.

[68] Whether the court would order such an assignment in the face of a provision restricting disposition is doubtful: *supra*.

[69] *FitzPatrick Bros.* v. *Bradford Corporation* [1960] 110 L.J. 208; *Cardshops* v. *Davies* [1971] 1 W.L.R. 591; and see *supra* pp. 36–41.

Tenancies subject to the Agricultural Holdings Act 1986

In so far as an agricultural tenancy[70] makes provision as to the tenant's disposition rights, it may do so by use of any of the usual types of covenant—absolute, qualified or fully qualified. If an absolute covenant is used the landlord can, of course, refuse to waive it regardless of his grounds. This is also the position if a qualified covenant is used: in relation to agricultural tenancies, there is no implication under section 19(1) of the Landlord and Tenant Act 1927 that "such consent shall not be unreasonably withheld."[71] If a fully qualified covenant is expressly included, the disapplication of section 19(1) by section 19(4) is irrelevant and the covenant will take effect as intended by the parties and thus consent must not be unreasonably withheld

If the agreement is silent as to disposition rights, the position at common law would be that the tenant is free to dispose. Up to a point this is so with agricultural tenancies but such freedom is liable to be terminated if the landlord refers the terms of the tenancy to arbitration under section 6 of the Agricultural Holdings Act 1986. He may do this to prevent the tenant circumventing the notice to quit provisions of the Act, *i.e.*, on receipt of a notice to quit, a tenant who is free to do so, may assign to a successor.[72] Under section 6, where the tenancy is oral, or where it is written but does not make provision for one or more of the matters specified in Schedule 1, the landlord can serve notice on the tenant requesting the preparation of a written agreement which provides for the Schedule 1 matters,[73] one of which, in paragraph 9, relates to powers of disposition. If this request is not fruitful, the landlord can refer the terms of the tenancy to arbitration. It is the duty of the arbitrator to make an order specifying the existing terms of the tenancy.[74] If those terms make some provision, albeit provision inconsistent with paragraph 9, as to rights of disposition, those terms cannot be overruled.[75] However if the terms do not include any provision as to rights of disposition, the arbitrator must, if it appears reasonable and just between the parties,[76] make the provision specified in paragraph 9, namely the incorporation of a qualified covenant "not to assign, sublet or part with possession of the holding or any part of it without the landlord's consent in writing." In these cases therefore, the tenant's position is changed from one of freedom to one of considerable restraint bearing in mind the inapplicability of section 19(1) of the Landlord and Tenant Act 1927 to tenancies of this type. Although by section 6(4) the change in terms is from the date of the award, by virtue of

[70] See s.1 of the Agricultural Holdings Act 1986.
[71] See s.19(4) of the 1927 Act.
[72] See C.P. Rodgers, *Agricultural Tenancies, Law and Practice*, p. 42.
[73] See subs. (1).
[74] Subs. (2)(*a*).
[75] Subs. (2)(*b*).
[76] Subs. (5).

subsections (5) & (6), the tenant is effectively restrained from the date of the initial notice requesting a written agreement. This is to prevent him assigning, *etc.*, while the arbitration is pending. An assignment in breach of this pre-emptive restraint is void.[77]

Assured Tenancies[78]

Assured tenancies were first introduced by the Housing Act 1980 as an incentive to build for rent. They were exempted from the provisions of the Rent Act 1977[79] and subjected instead to the business tenancy regime in Part II of the Landlord and Tenant Act 1954 as modified[80] so as to make it applicable to residential tenancies. The Housing Act 1988 introduced a new form of assured tenancy.[81] Existing assured tenancies, under the Housing Act 1980, are converted to the new form[82] and "old style" assured tenancies can no longer be created.[83]

Tenancies protected under the Rent Act 1977 and entered into before the Housing Act 1988 came into operation, are unaffected[84] by the new assured tenancy regime but, generally, no new protected tenancies can be granted.[85]

Though the new form of assured tenancy is residential in nature (business tenancies and tenancies of agricultural holdings are excluded[86]), like the old protected tenancy, it does not cover all residential lettings.[87] In particular, secure tenancies are excluded.[88] As far as security of tenure is concerned a *periodic* assured tenancy can only be brought to an end by an order of the court; a *fixed term* assured tenancy can be brought to an end without such order if it contains a power for the landlord to determine.[89] The effect of the landlord exercising this power is, however, to create a statutory periodic tenancy[90] which again, can only be determined by an order of the court.[91] The grounds upon which such an order can be made are set out in Schedule 2.[92] Unlike under the Rent Act, they do not include any ground specifically based upon the tenant

---

[77] This modifies the position at Common law. See Chap. 1.
[78] The relevant provisions extend only to England and Wales: s.127(5) & (6).
[79] S.56(2) of the Housing Act 1980.
[80] See ss.56–58 & Sched. 5 of the Housing Act 1980.
[81] And variants of it in the form of the assured shorthold tenancy and the assured agricultural occupancy: see Chaps. II & III of the Act.
[82] S.1(3).
[83] S.37.
[84] S.1(2) & Sched. 1, Pt. I, para. 1.
[85] s.34.
[86] Sched. 1, Pt. I, paras. 4 & 7.
[87] See *ibid*. for categories of residential tenancies excluded.
[88] *Ibid*. para. 12.
[89] S.5(1); it is considered that this refers to the exercise of a "break clause" rather than a proviso for re-entry: see C. P. Rodgers, *Housing—The New Law*, (1989), 2, 9.
[90] Which, unlike its counterpart under the Rent Act 1977 (see *supra*), seems to have proprietary, rather than merely personal, status: see *ibid*. 1, 5 *et seq.*
[91] S.5(2).
[92] And see s.7.

having assigned or sublet. They do, however, include the familiar discretionary ground[93] referring to an obligation of the tenancy having been broken or not performed.[94] The availability of this ground, in the event of a disposition of the term, depends upon the terms of the tenancy, which may or may not contain a provision restricting disposition—a matter upon which section 15 may have a bearing.

Section 15(1) applies to assured *periodic* tenancies and provides in relation to such tenancies that "it shall be an implied term . . . that, except with the consent of the landlord, the tenant shall not—(a) assign the tenancy (in whole or in part); or (b) sublet or part with possession of the whole or any part of the dwellinghouse let on the tenancy." It is further provided that the term so implied is not subject to section 19 of the Landlord and Tenant Act 1927 with the consequence that consent can be withheld upon any ground whether reasonable or not. The operation of section 15(1) however is limited by subsection (3) which provides that if the periodic tenancy is not a *statutory* periodic tenancy[95] and

> "(a) there is a provision (whether contained in the tenancy or not) under which the tenant is prohibited (whether absolutely or conditionally) from assigning or subletting or parting with possession or is permitted (whether absolutely or conditionally) to assign, sublet or part with possession; or
>
> (b) a premium is required to be paid on the grant or renewal of the tenancy"

subsection (1) shall not apply. Thus the statutory restriction is not implied in the case of a contractual periodic tenancy which either contains its own disposition provision (albeit different from the statutory restriction) or which provides for the payment of a premium upon the grant or renewal of the tenancy. Nor will it be implied into a fixed term assured tenancy. In these cases, disposition rights are determined by the presence or absence of contractual provision; in so far as such a provision is qualified, it will be subject to full qualification under the Landlord & Tenant Act 1927, section 19(1)(a).[96]

---

[93] See Rent Act 1977, s.98 & Sched. 15, Pt. I, Case 1.
[94] Sched. 2, Pt. II, Case 12.
[95] See s.5(2).
[96] See generally, Rodgers, Housing: The New Law, 2, 11.

PART 2

8 RESTRICTIONS ON ALTERATIONS AND IMPROVEMENTS

Freedom at Common Law

At Common Law, a tenant is free to alter the demised premises unless the lease contains a term, express or implied,[1] which imposes some restriction.[2] Such freedom, where it exists, must be exercised with due regard to the extent of the demise and the law of waste. In relation to the former, the tenant may not execute alterations which involve a trespass upon parts of the premises not demised to him.[3]

Effect of the law of waste

Waste has been defined generally as "any act which alters the nature of the land, whether for better or for worse"[4] and exists to protect those with interests in remainder or reversion from the actions of the limited owner in possession. Developed originally in connection with freehold estates, it has long since been applied to the relationship of landlord and tenant. There are four types of waste: permissive, ameliorating, voluntary and equitable. Liability for permissive waste—"failure to do that which ought to be done"[5]—attaches only to certain types of tenant, in particular tenants for a fixed term of years.[6] In the context of alterations to the premises, which by definition involve positive action rather than inaction on the part of the tenant, it has no role to play. The other types of waste, which are capable of applying to tenants of all sorts, involve positive action on the part of the tenant, and are therefore relevant in the present context.

Ameliorating waste

Ameliorating waste, which changes the nature of the land for the better, presents little risk to the tenant bent on improvements. Though giving rise to an action for damages at law, it will not give rise to any damages in fact because no

[1] *E.g.*, in relation to secure tenancies, under ss.97–101 of the Housing Act 1985, *infra*.
[2] See *infra*.
[3] See *Commercial Leases—the Implications of Alterations*, Tromans, (1987) L.S.G. 716 and the cases there referred to; compare *Davies* v. *Yadegar* [1990] 09 E.G. 67 see *infra*. p. 165; *Haines* v. *Florensa* [1990] 09 E.G. 70 (alterations held not to amount to a trespass or an actionable nuisance).
[4] Megarry and Wade, *The Law of Real Property*, (5th ed.) p. 96.
[5] *Ibid.*
[6] Statute of Marlbridge 1267; yearly and other periodic tenants are liable in varying degrees for inaction, tenants at will or sufferance not at all, *ibid.* pp. 702–3.

damage will have been suffered and equity will be reluctant to grant the landlord an injunction to restrain a technical waste at Common Law. In *Doherty* v. *Allman*[7] the tenant under two very long leases proposed to convert the demised premises, dilapidated barns, into houses. An injunction was refused because what was proposed was ameliorating waste "which so far from doing any injury to the inheritance, improves the inheritance"[8] and to prevent it by injunction would occasion harm to the tenant out of all proportion to the benefit which would accrue to the landlord. Other examples of ameliorating waste may be found in *Jones* v. *Chappell*[9] (erection of a steam engine) and *Meux* v. *Cobley*[10] (conversion of farm into market garden with glass houses etc.). Whether the inheritance has been improved, or not, is largely, but perhaps not totally,[11] a question of its value as a result of the alterations.

Voluntary waste
Voluntary waste, by contrast, is a form of injurious action, "the committing of any spoil or destruction."[12] In *Hyman* v. *Rose*[13] the assignee of a 99 year lease of a chapel converted it into a cinema, opening up a doorway in the wall, removing the iron railings which separated it from the street and making certain internal changes. It was held that there was no liability for waste because the acts of the tenant did not "change the nature of the thing demised."[14] It was relevant to the decision that although the lease contained restrictions on user, it did not prohibit use as a cinema. The premises were therefore always potentially a cinema. By contrast in *Marsden* v. *Edward Heyes Ltd.*[15] where the tenant of a shop and house removed the partition wall, staircase and fireplaces and converted the premises into just a shop, there was held to have been a change in the nature of the thing demised. "The defendants became tenants of premises which included a dwellinghouse. They have made alterations to such an extent that there is no longer any dwellinghouse. That is voluntary waste."[16] It is clear that the alterations in this case were of a very radical nature—the premises had been gutted leaving only the four walls standing. In *Mancetter Developments Ltd.* v. *Garmanston Ltd.*[17] the removal of tenant's fixtures at the end of the term without making good the inevitable damage was held to be voluntary waste—unless the damage was *de minimis* like decorating or filling screw and nail holes. The reasoning was that originally all fixtures became part of the realty and therefore belonged to the landlord. A tenant who removed

---

[7] (1878) 3 App Cas. 709.
[8] *Per* Lord Cairns at p. 723.
[9] (1875) L.R. 20 Eq. 539.
[10] (1892) 2 Ch. 253.
[11] See *Jones* v. *Chappell ibid. per* Jessel M.R. at p. 541.
[12] Bacon's *Abridgement* (7th ed.), viii 379.
[13] [1912] A.C. 623.
[14] *Per* Lord Loreburn L.C. at p. 682; the question arose in a forfeiture action, which was based upon admitted breaches of covenant, wherein the tenant claimed relief. The landlord challenged the claim for relief *inter alia* because of the alleged waste.
[15] [1927] 2 K.B. 1 C.A.
[16] *Per* Scrutton L.J. at p. 7.
[17] [1986] 1 All E.R. 449 C.A.

them was in excess of his rights and therefore liable in waste.[18] Ultimately the Common Law modified this principle by allowing the tenant to remove his fixtures but this right, at least in its developed form, was conditional upon an obligation on the tenant to make good any damage. If the tenant removed the fixtures without making good, he was therefore again in excess of his rights and liable for waste.[19] The case concerned the removal of extractor fans and pipes from a metal clad building without filling the holes left thereby and it was held that the assignee or licensee (it was not established which) of the tenant who had originally lawfully installed the fixtures, was liable for voluntary waste for not filling the holes. The holes could not be regarded as *de minimis* because they left the property open to

Tortious v. Contractual liability

the wind and weather. This tortious liability of a tenant for voluntary waste is often co-extensive with a contractual liability arising from an implied duty to use the premises in a tenant-like manner and to deliver them up at the end of the term.[20] Where there is such a contractual liability, it is usual for the landlord to rely upon it[21] and in *Mancetter* Kerr L.J. opined that he must do so.[22] *Mancetter* was unusual because the party being sued was not subject to any contractual liability. The assignee/licensee who effected the removal *was* liable contractually but was, in fact, in liquidation and for practical purposes the action was against its controller, an individual. He was found liable upon the basis that a tortious waste had been committed by the company which he had directed and procured.

Equitable waste

When perpetrated in a very heinous form, *i.e.* maliciously or without regard to ordinary prudence, voluntary waste takes on the cloak of "equitable" waste.[23] In *Vane* v. *Lord Barnard*[24] the defendant, who had previously settled Raby Castle upon himself for life, remainder to his son "having taken some displeasure against his son, got 200 workmen together and of a sudden, in a few days, stript the castle of the lead, iron, glass, doors, boards etc. to the value of £3000." He was restrained and ordered to repair the property. In *Turner* v. *Wright*[25] it became clear that equity would intervene even where there was no malice, if the person in possession fails to measure up to the "dictates of prudence and reason."[26] It was held to be equitable waste to cut down timber intended for ornament and shelter. Lord Campbell L.C. opined that a bona fide belief that an improvement was being effected would not prevent the act

[18] Conversely a tenant who refused to remove them was within his rights, unless they had been erected in contravention of some stipulation in the lease: *Never-Stop Railway (Wembley) Ltd.* v. *British Empire Exhibition (1924) Inc.* [1926] 1 Ch. 877.
[19] *Per* Dillon L.J. p. 454.
[20] The content of this duty is discussed in *Warren* v. *Keen* [1954] 1 Q.B. 15, 20 *per* Denning L.J.
[21] And there may be some advantage in so doing from the point of view of the Limitation Acts: *Marsden* v. *Edward Heyes Ltd.* [1927] 2 K.B. 1.
[22] At p. 456.
[23] The significance of which is considered below.
[24] (1716) 2 Ver. 738.
[25] (1860) 2 De G.F. & J. 234.
[26] *Per* Lord Campbell L.C.

being classified as equitable waste if it was destructive of the subject matter of the grant—as *e.g.* where a medieval castle is destroyed out of a sincere dislike for turrets and moats, thought by the perpetrator to be entertained by all other sensible men, in order to make a garden of roses, lilies and gravel paths. The significance of classifying certain degrees of voluntary waste as "equitable" is that it is possible for the lease to negative liability for voluntary waste *simpliciter* by providing that the tenant is to be "unimpeachable for waste," but liability for equitable waste can only be excluded where the lease makes it clear that the tenant is to be allowed to commit the "wanton acts of destruction"[27] by which that type of waste is characterised.[28]

Restrictions implied into the lease

Public sector residential tenancies

The most likely source of restriction upon a tenant's right to alter the premises is the lease itself. Certain types of tenancy are subject to an implied restriction. Thus section 97(1) of the Housing Act 1985 provides that it is a term of every secure tenancy[29] that the tenant will not make any *improvement* without the written consent of the landlord. This implied qualified covenant is not subject to section 19(2) of the Landlord and Tenant Act,[30] which provides that such consent is not to be unreasonably withheld, rather the section itself, in subsection (3), makes identical provision with the important addition that if consent is unreasonably withheld, it is to be treated as given. "Improvement" is defined is section 97(2) as "any alteration in, or addition to, a dwellinghouse." It includes additions and alterations to landlord's fixtures, those relating to the provision of services,[31] the erection of a wireless or television aerial and the carrying out of external decoration.[32] The inclusion of "*any*" alteration or addition within the definition of "improvement" makes it clear that the implied term operates without proof that the property would be improved and without regard to the possibly differing points of view of the parties.[33] There is no provision that the tenant must apply for consent in writing, but there are advantages in

---

[27] Megarry and Wade, *ibid.* p. 97.

[28] Thus in *Vane* v. *Lord Barnard ibid.*, *Turner* v. *Wright ibid.*, and *Williams* v. *Day* (1680) 2 De G.F. & J. 234 equity intervened despite the grant expressing the tenant to be unimpeachable for waste.

[29] Except where the interest of the landlord belongs to a co-operative housing association, see s.109; "secure tenancy" is defined in s.79.

[30] s.97(4).

[31] *e.g.* installation of central heating as in *Pearlman* v. *Governors and Keepers of Harrow School* [1979] Q.B. 56 C.A., see Arden, *Current Law Statutes Annotated* 1985—note to s.97.

[32] *Ibid.*

[33] Compare s.19(2) which has been held to apply only where there has been an improvement, that being judged from the tenant's point of view—*Ball Bros.* v. *Sinclair* [1931] 2 Ch. 325; *F.W. Woolworth* v. *Lambert* [1937] Ch. 37 C.A.; see *infra*.

his so doing, namely,[34] if the landlord refuses, the tenant is entitled to a written statement of the reasons; if the landlord neither gives nor refuses consent within a reasonable time, consent will be taken to have been withheld.[35] Where consent is withheld, or taken to have been withheld, the burden of proof is upon the landlord to show that he was not acting unreasonably.[36] In determining this question, the court is to have particular regard to the likely impact of the improvement upon the safety of occupiers of the premises or any other premises, upon the level of the landlord's expenditure and upon the selling or rental value of the premises.[37] It is likely that it will also consider case law dealing with the question of unreasonableness in the context of fully qualified improvement covenants generally.[38] By virtue of section 99, the landlord may give his consent subject to conditions, but the imposition of an unreasonable condition in response to a written request by the tenant for consent will be deemed an unreasonable withholding of consent. The consequence of an unreasonable withholding of consent is, as has been mentioned, that consent will be deemed to have been given[39] and the tenant will not therefore be in breach of his obligations under the secure tenancy. A declaration that consent has been unreasonably withheld can be sought under section 110(2)(b). Where a tenant has failed to apply for consent prior to effecting the improvement, he should do so afterwards: section 98(3) provides that a consent given after the action requiring it may be validly given. Whether an unreasonable refusal given at this stage gives rise to a deemed consent is not clear.

Private sector residential tenancies

In the case of private sector residential tenancies, section 81 of the Housing Act 1980 remains in force.[40] It applies only to protected and statutory tenancies under the Rent Act 1977: for the future, these have been replaced by the assured tenancy under the Housing Act 1988 and that Act contains no implied restriction on improvements. Not all protected and statutory tenancies fall within the ambit of section 81. Subsection (4) excludes tenancies where the tenant has been given notice on any of the mandatory grounds for possession in the Rent Act 1977, including shorthold lettings and lettings by servicemen,[41] "unless the tenant proves that at the time the landlord gave the notice[42] it was unreasonable for the landlord to expect to recover possession under that Case." Where section 81 does apply, it implies into the tenancy a term that the tenant will not make any improvement without the landlord's written consent.[43] Section 19(2) of the Landlord and

---

[34] See also s.99(2) *infra*.
[35] s.98(4); compare Landlord and Tenant Act 1988 s.1(3) in relation to disposition covenants.
[36] s.98(1).
[37] s.98(2).
[38] See *infra* pp. 168–174.
[39] s.97(3).
[40] It used to cover secure tenancies too.
[41] Cases 11 to 20 of Schedule 15 of the Rent Act 1977: see Arden, *Manual of Housing Law* (4th ed.) para. 12.69.
[42] Referred to in the relevant Case.
[43] Subs. (2).

Tenant Act 1927 does not apply,[44] rather the section itself expressly provides that consent is not to be unreasonably withheld and, as in section 97 of the Housing Act 1985[45] it is additionally provided that if unreasonably withheld, consent shall be treated as given.[46] The definition of "improvement" is substantially the same as under s.97 of the Housing Act 1985[47] save that where the landlord is under an obligation to carry out external decoration or to keep the exterior in repair, it does not include the carrying out of external decoration.[48] S.82 makes provision for the burden of proof, the matters to be considered in relation to reasonableness, etc. in all respects similar to those applying under s.97 of the 1985 Act.[49]

Restrictions expressed in the lease

Terms indirectly restricting alterations

In many cases the lease will contain express terms[50] which operate as a restraint upon alterations. Such terms, to be effective, need not necessarily address directly the question of alterations, for example, if the works proposed by the tenant will result in a change of use, the presence of a restrictive user clause may operate as a sufficient brake[51] and, in appropriate circumstances, covenants not cause a nuisance, annoyance or injury to the landlord or adjoining occupiers may also come into play.[52] It has been argued that a covenant to maintain the walls of a building is broken by making a doorway through[53] and it has been held that affixing an advertisement to the end wall of premises, was contrary to a repair covenant on the ground that it injured the wall.[54]

Tenancy directly restricting alterations

Where the provision does directly restrict alterations (the term "improvements" though featuring in the legislation[55] is scarcely ever used when drafting leases), it may do so in varying degrees of particularity depending upon the length of the term and the type of premises. In the case of a residential letting at a nominal rent to a relative, a total restriction may be

---

[44] Subs. (1).
[45] *Supra.*
[46] s.81(2).
[47] *Supra.*
[48] Subs. (5).
[49] See *supra.*
[50] The distinction between a covenant, a condition and an agreement is dealt with in Chapter 1.
[51] See *e.g. Day* v. *Waldron* [1919] 88 L.J. K.B. 937 and *Westminster (Duke)* v. *Swinton* [1948] 1 K.B. 524 both of which concerned the conversion into flats of premises subject, *inter alia*, to a covenant to use only as a private dwellinghouse. In *Barton* v. *Reed* [1932] 1 Ch. 362 a similar conversion and letting fell foul of a covenant not to use for business purposes. See now s.165 of the Housing Act 1957, *infra.*
[52] *E.g. Day* v. *Waldron ibid.; Heard* v. *Stuart* [1907] 24 T.L.R. 104.
[53] *Hyman* v. *Rose* [1912] A.C. 623.
[54] *Heard* v. *Stuart ibid.*, where Joyce J. also tendered the suggestion that the erection and letting out of the hoarding was contrary to a covenant to use the premises only for the trade of tailor.
[55] See *e.g.* s.97 of the Housing Act 1985, s.81 of the Housing Act 1980 and s.19(2) of the Landlord and Tenant Act 1927.

appropriate, whereas in the case of a commercial lease the ability to adapt the premises to the changing needs of the tenant's business will have to be built in.[56] Covenants commonly refer to alterations and additions to the demised premises and to cutting or maiming the walls or timbers. In this context, as in many others, the restriction is liable to be construed against the landlord[57] and in construing its extent,

Intention of the parties the court will have regard to what the parties would have contemplated when the lease was granted. In *British Empire Mutual Life Assurance Co.* v. *Cooper*[58] Kay J. had to decide whether making two openings to link the demised premises with those adjoining, constituted an alteration of the type permitted by a provision in the lease. As the adjoining premises belonged to a third party, and at the time the lease was granted the landlord had no idea that the tenant was in negotiation for a lease in respect of them, he regarded the suggestion that such an alteration could be within the contemplation of the parties as "absolutely preposterous."[59] An important element in what the parties can be expected to have contemplated, is the purpose for which the lease was granted and there is a strong tendency to construe the lease so as to enable the tenant to carry on the business for which the lease was granted.[60] *Bickmore* v. *Dimmer*[61] concerned a covenant not to make any alterations to the demised premises, which were let to a watchmaker. The latter attached a large clock to the outside of the building, using iron bolts which penetrated six inches into the wall. This did not amount to a breach of covenant because, amongst other things, it would be wrong to construe the covenant so as "to prevent a tenant doing those acts which are convenient and usual for a tradesman to do in the ordinary conduct of his business."[62] The landlord had argued unsuccessfully, that the only alterations which the tenant was entitled to make were those absolutely necessary to the carrying on of the business. If the alteration is not in the ordinary conduct of the tenant's business, this may lead the court to conclude that it was intended to be restricted. *London County Council* v. *Hutter*[63] concerned the erection of an "advertising station" on the curved wall of a building at the junction of Shaftesbury Avenue and Piccadilly Circus. This was not incidental to the purposes for which the building was let, and this was relevant to the decision that it was within the terms of a covenant restricting alterations. If the covenant refers to an alteration "of the

"Of the premises" premises" it may be held, as in *Bickmore* v. *Dimmer*,[64] that it applies only to alterations "which would affect the form and

[56] See Hill & Redman's *Law of Landlord and Tenant* (18th ed.) Vol. 1, para. 1242.
[57] *Per* Lindley M.R. in *Gresham Life Assurance Society Ltd.* v. *Ranger* [1899] 15 T.L.R. 454 C.A.
[58] [1888] 4 T.L.R. 362.
[59] At p. 362.
[60] See *e.g. Gresham Life Assurance Society* v. *Ranger ibid.*
[61] [1903] 1 Ch. 158.
[62] Vaughan Williams L.J. at p. 167.
[63] [1925] Ch. 626.
[64] *Ibid.*

structure of the premises."[65] The holes in the wall in that case did not amount to a change in form or structure, but on the other hand in *Westminster* v. *Swinton*,[66] the work involved in converting a house into six flats, with kitchens, bathrooms, partitions, etc. did amount to an alteration in the structure. In *Joseph* v. *London County Council*[67] the covenant was rather different, referring to alterations "in the elevation or in the architectural decoration thereof" but this too was held to refer only to alterations in the fabric, and did not therefore apply to the erection of a frame, which was easily removable without damage, to hold an illuminated advertisement. There was a similar covenant in *London County Council* v. *Hutter*[68] but because the means by which the advertisement was attached to the building were very much more intrusive,[69] there was held to have been a structural alteration within the terms of the restriction. Where the covenant refers to "external" alterations, it has been held that this refers not only to the outside of the building let, but also to everything "out of doors"[70] and it

Alterations in appearance

therefore covered raising the sea wall and wharf by 3 feet, The scope of the covenant can be extended beyond structural alterations by making clear that it covers changes in the appearance of the building[71] but even so it may not restrict some appearances which the landlord finds objectionable. In *Gresham Life Assurance Society Ltd.* v. *Ranger*[72] the landlord argued (unsuccessfully) that a covenant not to do anything to change or affect the external appearance of the premises was broken by virtue of the tenant keeping the canvas sun awning, which was retained by the landlord but which the tenant had a right to use, permanently down in order to enhance an illuminated display of jewels. A covenant against cutting or

"Cutting or maiming"

maiming any of the walls or timbers often accompanies one restricting alterations to the premises. In *London County Council* v. *Hutter*[73] the holes in the wall were found to contravene both covenants. In *Lily & Skinner* v. *Crump*[74] and *Ball Bros.* v. *Sinclair*[75] the works fell within the clause restricting alterations but outside that concerned with cutting and maiming. In the former case the tenant proposed to make two openings in the party wall between the two premises let to him by the landlord and Rowlatt J. "could not think that the mere fact that an apperture was made in the main wall made the operation *ipso facto*" a cutting as against an alteration."[76] In the latter a removal of the staircase was in the issue and this too was but an alteration. It may be that where, as in these two cases, the

[65] *Ibid. per* Vaughan Williams L.J. at p. 167 and see Cozens Hardy L.J.
[66] [1948] 1 K.B. 524.
[67] (1914) 111 L.T. 276.
[68] *Ibid.*
[69] Involving 23 holes, two and a half inches square and six inches deep.
[70] *Per* Williams J. in *Perry* v. *Davies* (1858) 3 CBNS 769.
[71] As in *Heard* v. *Stuart* (1907) 24 T.L.R. 104.
[72] [1899] 15 T.L.R. 454.
[73] *Ibid.*
[74] (1929) 73 S.J. 366.
[75] [1931] 2 Ch. 325.
[76] At p. 366.

covenant against cutting, etc. is absolute and that against alterations is fully qualified,[77] the court will construe the cutting covenant to refer only to a very radical form of structural interference.

Covenants restricting alterations, of all sorts, have a bearing on the physical condition of the demised property during the term. It has therefore never been disputed that they touch and concern the land demised and pass under the doctrine of privity of estate thus binding successors of the tenant.

Statutory regulation of terms

The operation of express restrictions upon alterations may be affected by statute in a number of ways. Section 610 of the Housing Act 1985, section 84 of the Law of Property Act 1925 (and certain others)[78] allow the variation or discharge of alteration restrictions, while section 3 of the Landlord and Tenant Act 1927 may result in such a restriction being overridden.[79] Section 96 of the Telecommunications Act 1984 turns absolute covenants into fully qualified ones, while section 19(2) of the Landlord and Tenant Act 1927 turns qualified covenants into fully qualified covenants.[80] The scope of these provisions is considered below.[81]

Section 610 of the Housing Act 1985[82]

Conversion of large houses

This deals with the very specific situation where a house is too large for single occupation but cannot be converted into flats because of restrictions in the grant. It originated in the Housing Town Planning etc. Act 1919, which was passed to deal with an acute shortage of housing. The situation of a tenant is well exemplifed in *Day* v. *Waldron*[83] where the tenant was bound by various restrictions which put him in breach of covenant in converting a house into three flats. The landlord was at liberty to enforce his rights even though the tenant had, for two years prior to conversion, been unable to let the house as it stood, and other owners in the area had found it necessary to convert. The section applies to freehold property as well as leasehold and provides as follows:

    (1)   The local authority or a person interested in a house may apply to the county court where:

[77] See Chaps. 1 & 4 *supra*.
[78] See "Miscellaneous Statutory Provisions" *infra*.
[79] If the landlord is willing to consent, it is unnecessary to rely upon these provisions.
[80] These terms are explained in Chap. 1.
[81] See also chart at pp. 152–153.
[82] Previously s.165 of the Housing Act 1957, the substance, though not form, of which it repeats.
[83] (1919) 88 L.J. K.B. 937.

STATUTORY REGULATION OF ALTERATION TERMS

Provision	Application	Effect
Section 610 Housing Act 1985	Any lease containing restrictions which prevent the conversion of houses into flats.	Court may vary the terms of the lease.
Section 84 Law of Property Act 1925	Leases granted for more than 40 years, of which at least 25 years have already expired, containing restrictions which are obsolete, impede reasonable user or restrictions which have been agreed to be varied or if varied would cause no injury.	Power to discharge or modify the restriction and order compensation.
Section 169 Factories Act 1961	Leases of factories containing restrictions preventing alterations necessary in order to comply with the Act.	Power to set aside or modify the terms of the lease, apportion the cost of the alterations, determine the lease.
Section 73 Offices, Shops and Railway Premises Act 1963	Leases of offices, shops or railway premises containing restrictions preventing alterations necessary to comply with the Act.	Power to set aside or modify the terms of the lease and adjust the rent.

Section 28 Fire Precautions Act 1971	Leases of premises in relation to which the Fire Authority has served a notice that a fire certificate is compulsory and which contain restrictions preventing alterations necessary to comply with the Act.	Power to set aside or modify the terms of the lease and adjust the rent.
Section 3 Landlord and Tenant Act 1927	Leases, other than mining leases, leases of agricultural holdings and service lettings, of premises used wholly or partly for any trade or business.	Court may authorise the improvement regardless of any restriction in the lease.
Section 96 Telecommunications Act 1984	Leases for a term of a year or more granted on or after August 5, 1984, containing restrictions which have the effect of imposing on the lessee restraints in relation to telecommunications.	The restriction becomes fully qualified (if not so qualified already) and in considering whether consent has been unreasonably withheld the court must consider all the circumstances including the principle that no person should be unreasonably denied access to the telecommunications system.
Section 19(2) Landlord and Tenant Act 1927	All leases, save mining leases and leases of agricultural holdings, containing a covenant, etc., restricting the making of improvements without consent.	The restriction becomes subject to a proviso that such consent is not to be unreasonably withheld.

> (a) owing to changes in the character of the
>   neighbourhood in which the house is situated,
>   it cannot readily be let as a single tenement
>   but could readily be let for occupation if
>   converted into two or more tenements, or
> (b) planning permission has been granted under
>   Part III of the Town and Country Planning
>   Act 1971 (general planning control) for the use
>   of the house as converted into two or more
>   separate dwellinghouses instead of as a single
>   dwellinghouse,
>
> and the conversion is prohibited or restricted by the
> provisions of the lease of the house, or by a restrictive
> covenant affecting the house, or otherwise.
>
> (2) The court may, after giving any person interested an
>   opportunity of being heard, vary the terms of the lease
>   or other instrument imposing the prohibition or
>   restriction, subject to such conditions and upon such
>   terms as the court may think just.

"House"   Section 623 makes it clear that the "house," mentioned in both (a) and (b) of subsection (1), includes "any yard, garden, outhouses and appurtenances belonging to the house or usually enjoyed with it." It appears that the requirement that there be a house is not to be too strictly interpreted. In *Johnston* v. *Maconochie*[84] Atkin L.J. opined that the house need not be a dwellinghouse (though it was in that case)—"It might include a block of offices suitable for conversion into dwellinghouses"[85] and the dictionary would seem to confirm this.[86] It was held in this case that although the Act of 1919 was concerned with housing the working classes, the operation of the section was not confined to conversions which would provide accommodation for that class.

Where the tenant proceeds under subsection (1)(*a*) there is no need for him to engage in any structural alterations. In *Stack* v. *Church Commissioners for England*[87] the tenant wished to convert the house into one room flatlets with shared bathroom facilities. The landlord argued that the section did not apply because what the tenant proposed involved no conversion, a term, he argued, which implied structural alterations. Somervell L.J. considered that *some* structural alteration would be involved in the work the tenant proposed, but even if the changes were purely functional, such as a change of use, they could nevertheless amount to a conversion. The argument that the legislation could not have intended to facilitate a lowering in the character of the neighbourhood, which could result from bedsits, was met with the riposte that, to a certain extent, that was what the legislation did intend. However the fact that the section could be used, did not mean

---

[84] [1921] 1 K.B. 239.
[85] At p. 424.
[86] See *Concise Oxford Dictionary*.
[87] [1952] 1 All E.R. 136; It has been recommended that the section be amended to make this clear, see Law Com. No. 141 *Covenants Restricting Dispositions, Alterations and Changes of User*, para. 9.14.

that the tenant would get an order and the effect of the conversion upon the neighbourhood could be considered by the court when exercising its discretion. Under subsection (1)(*a*), the court must be satisfied (1) that the house is not readily lettable as a single unit (2) that it would be readily lettable in more than one unit and (3) that this is due to changes in the character of the neighbourhood. It is clear from *Alliance Economic Investment Co.* v. *Berton*[88] that the court will require both the neighbourhood and the changes in it alleged to have brought about the difficulty in letting, to be quite closely defined. The view expressed in that case that the character of the neighbourhood would remain unchanged if, though the houses have largely been converted into flats, the occupants remain of the same class as before, has however been criticised by the Law Commission.[89]

Where the tenant proceeds under subsection (1)(*b*), he does not need to show (1), (2) & (3), above. He relies upon a planning permission. If the planning permission which he has obtained involves changes which incorporate property other than the "house" into the units created, he cannot succeed. In *Josephine Trust* v. *Champagne*[90] planning permission had been obtained for the conversion of two four-storey houses, held of the same landlord, into four flats each extending to an entire floor of the joint property. It was held that the court had no jurisdiction in such a case.[91] The section presupposed the conversion of a single house into complete and self-contained dwellinghouses whereas as a result of this conversion, one house would consist entirely of bedrooms and the other of kitchens and bathrooms and this would amount to a destruction of the subject matter.[92] It seems clear that where the conversion is limited to the demised premises, it can involve the incorporation of garages and gardens and out-buildings.[93] Finally, securing a planning permission sufficient to give the court jurisdiction under (1)(*b*) does not entitle the tenant to an order—the court still retains a discretion whether to grant the application or not, and as to the terms and conditions.

The Law Commission[94] has recommended, in paragraph 9.16, that the court should have power (if such power cannot presently be implied from the policy of the Act of facilitating housing), when making an order under section 610 varying an alteration covenant, to order consequential amendments in a disposition covenant which would otherwise prevent the converted property from being the let and, in paragraph 9.17,[95]

---

[88] [1923] 92 L.J. K.B. 750 C.A.
[89] Law Com. No. 141, para. 9.11.
[90] [1963] 2 Q.B. 160.
[91] Nor, it is submitted would it have jurisdiction where the application was brought under (1)(*a*).
[92] See Law Com. No. 141, *supra*, para. 9.15 where it is recommended that the jurisdiction be extended; it is pointed out however, that the court might not make an order unless the houses were held on the same terms from the same landlord.
[93] See s.623 *supra*.
[94] See generally Law Com. No. 141 paras. 9.5–9.19.
[95] See also paras. 9.34–9.35.

that the court (if it does not already have it, by virtue its general discretion under subsection (2)) be given power to award compensation to the party with the benefit of the covenant where his rights are varied, and also to sanction an increase in the rent for the future to reflect the fact that the lease is subject to less restrictions than previously.

Section 84 of the Law of Property Act 1925,[96]

Modification or discharge of restrictions

This section also provides a means whereby a tenant may seek a variation of restrictions upon alterations.[97] It was primarily intended for use by the owner of a freehold estate but subsection (12) permitted its use by holders of long leases. Since 1954[98] such leaseholders have been defined as those holding under a lease granted for more than 40 years, of which at least 25 years have already expired.[99] The requirement of a minimum 40 year term was to ensure that the leaseholders who used the section were roughly equivalent in status to the freeholders for whom the section was designed, and the expired period of 25 years, was to ensure that tenants did not apply for a variation of the terms of the lease soon after it was granted.[1]

Affecting "user" or "building"

The section applies to restrictions affecting the user[2] of the demised property "or the building thereon,"[3] the latter phrase being interpreted as bringing within the section covenants restricting the erection or alteration of buildings. The jurisdiction of the Lands Tribunal under section 84(1) to discharge or modify the restriction exists where it is satisfied[4]

(a) that by reason of changes in the character of the property or the neighbourhood or other circumstances which the Lands Tribunal may deem material, the restriction ought to

Obsolete

be deemed obsolete, or

Impedes reasonable user

(b) the continued existence of the restriction would impede some reasonable user[5] of the land for public or private purposes and, (see subsection (1A)) either it does not secure to the persons who are entitled to the benefit of it any practical benefits of substantial value or advantage to them or, it is contrary to the public interest and (in either case) that money will be adequate compensation for any loss or disadvantage

---

[96] Set out in appendix 4; see generally Preston & Newsom, *Restrictive Covenants Affecting Freehold Land* (7th Ed.) Chap. 7.

[97] It also allows him to apply for a declaration, whether or not the property is affected by a restriction and as to the nature, extent and enforceability of the restriction: subsection (2).

[98] Landlord & Tenant Act.

[99] The 25 years must be reckoned from the date of the lease, even where the term is expressed to have begun earlier: *Earl of Cadogan* v. *Guinness* [1936] Ch. 515.

[1] See Law Com. No. 141 paras. 9.27–9.30 where it is recommended that the 40 year period be reduced to 14 or abandoned altogether and that tenants, like freeholders, be enabled to use the section immediately (albeit that the Lands Tribunal would be more reluctant to grant a variation of such a fresh lease).

[2] See Chap. 9.

[3] Subs. (1).

[4] See subs. (1).

[5] If the proposed use is not contrary to the public interest, it is reasonable: *Memvale Securities Ltd.'s Application* (1975) 233 E.G. 689, 716.

which any such person may suffer as a result of the modification, or,

Agreement
(c) that those interested in the benefit of the restriction have expressly or impliedly agreed,[6] to the modification of their rights, or,

No injury
(d) that the modification will not injure the persons entitled to the benefit of the restriction.

In determining the issues referred to above, the Lands Tribunal has to take into account "the development plan and any declared or ascertainable pattern for the grant or refusal of planning permission in the relevant areas, as well as the period at which and the context in which the restriction was created or imposed, and any other relevant circumstances."[7] An order discharging or modifying the restriction may direct the

Compensation
applicant to pay compensation to the landlord either to make up for any loss sustained in consequence of the discharge or, alternatively, to make up for the effect that the restriction would have had in reducing the consideration received at the time the lease was granted.[8] In some cases it may be that the *content* of the restriction has little significance from the landlord's point of view, and that therefore a modification occasions him no loss for which he should be compensated. But what if, in these circumstances, it is argued that the very *existence* of the restriction was a potential source of profit to him—that the covenant was absolute and that he could have demanded a fine for waiving it?[9] The legitimacy of such an argument has been recognised in two cases, *Re Phillips' Application*[10] and *Ridley* v. *Taylor*.[11] In the latter Russell L.J.

Loss of bargaining power
found it "unnecessary to decide whether in every case, it can be said that a deprivation in bargaining power will cause injury"[12] but he was satisfied that there was loss in the case before him. The landlord had waived an absolute covenant restricting use to a single private dwellinghouse, and in the licence he permitted the conversion of the house into five flats as a temporary measure until the tenant obtained planning permission to convert the premises into three maisonettes. While he was using it as five flats the tenant agreed to pay an extra £200 per annum rent and once he had planning permission for the maisonettes the additional rent was reduced to £35 to reflect the reduction in the rents he would receive. He applied to have the restriction modified so as to allow permanent conversion to five flats. The injury to the landlord lay in the fact that the desired modification would allow the tenant to enjoy the benefit of using the premises as five flats without paying the increased rent which had been the subject

---

[6] Agreement can be implied from a failure to terminate the prohibited use but knowledge of the breach must be shown; furthermore it does not suffice to show that the landlord has been guilty of laches and is therefore precluded from objecting to the change; *Memvale ibid.*
[7] Subs. (1B).
[8] Subs. (1).
[9] For qualified covenants see s.19(2) *infra.*
[10] [1957] 7 P. & C.R. 182.
[11] [1965] 1 W.L.R. 611 C.A.
[12] At p. 622.

of the bargain between the parties—the tenant could get planning permission for the maisonettes, not use it and pay just the £35 increase provided for in the lease. In the last two cases the loss of bargaining power provided sufficient justification for refusing to grant the modification at all. In *Re E.M.I. Social Centres Ltd.'s Application*[13] the landlord sought to build upon this foundation by conceding the grounds for a variation (allowing the sale of alcohol) and then seeking £3000 compensation for the loss, as being the amount it could have demanded for a waiver, V. G. Wellings, Q.C. rejected the compensation claim and distinguished *Ridley* on its special facts. The loss arose not from the content of the modification ordered, but from the fact that the Tribunal had power to modify at all, and "had Parliament intended such a loss to be compensated for, it would have said so expressly in the Statute but it had not done so."[14] At present there is no power to order an increase in the rent by way of compensation.[15] There is power, though only with the applicant's consent, to add further restrictive provisions to the lease to take account of the relaxation of the existing provisions.[16] If the applicant does not consent the Tribunal may refuse the modification.

Exclusions   Section 84 does not apply to mining leases or to restrictions imposed on the occasion of a disposition made gratuitously or for a nominal consideration for public purposes.[17]

Miscellaneous statutory provisions

Works which are necessary in order to comply with certain statutory requirements relating to health and safety, cannot be prevented by leasehold restrictions. Accordingly, the measures referred to below, empower the court to set aside or modify the terms of the lease.

Factories Act 1961 section 169   This applies to premises the whole, or any part, of which have been let as a factory[18] and it enables an owner or occupier prevented, by the terms of their agreement, from carrying out any structural or other alterations necessary to comply with the Act, to apply to the county court which may set aside or modify the agreement as it considers just and equitable. The applicant can also seek an order apportioning the expenses of such alterations between the owner and occupier and in this connection the court must have

---

[13] (1980) 39 P. & C.R. 421.
[14] At p. 426; the Law Commission, *ibid.* para. 9.40, endorse the view that there should be no compensation for mere loss of bargaining power.
[15] But see Law Com. No. 141 paras. 9.34–9.40.
[16] Subs. (1C).
[17] Subss. (12) & (7) nor does it apply in the circumstances mentioned in subs. (11).
[18] Defined in s.175.

regard to the terms of the agreement between the respective parties.[19] Instead of apportioning of the expenses, the court can, at the request of either party, determine the lease.[20]

Offices, Shops and Railway Premises Act, 1963, section 73 The premises to which this Act applies are defined in detail in section 1 of the Act. In relation to modifying or setting aside the terms of agreements, the drafting of section 73(1) follows the pattern set in section 169 of the Factories Act 1961 (*supra*). As in that section the court has power to apportion expenses[21] but it has no power to determine the agreement; there is however jurisdiction to adjust the rent.

Fire Precautions Act 1971, section 28 This applies to premises in relation to which the fire authority has served a notice (under section 3) that a fire certificate is compulsory. Here again the court has power to set aside or modify any terms of an agreement or lease which prevents any person from complying with the requirements of the Act.[22] Subsection (3) allows apportionment of expenses and adjustment of the rent analogous to section 73(2) of the Offices, Shops and Railway Premises Act 1963.[23]

Section 3 Landlord and Tenant Act 1927.[24]

The primary purpose of this provision is to enable tenants of business premises to secure compensation at the end of the term for improvements which they have carried out. This involves the tenant in complying with a procedure, the end result of which, he hopes, will be the certification of the improvement as a "proper improvement." He may then execute the improvement "anything in any lease of the premises to the contrary not withstanding." Certification therefore provides a means for overriding[25] any restrictions upon improvements contained in a lease to which the section applies. In some cases this will be the main purpose of seeking certification rather than any future intention of claiming compensation, and the section thus provides a useful addition to the provisions previously considered.

Application   The section applies to premises used wholly or partly for carrying on any trade or business,[26] excluding those held under a mining lease or a lease of an agricultural holding within the meaning of the Agricultural Holdings Act 1986.[27] It does

---

[19] s.170.
[20] *Ibid.*
[21] s.73(2).
[22] Subs. (2).
[23] *Supra.*
[24] See appendix 4.
[25] Rather than varying—compare s.610 of the Housing Act 1985 & s.84 of the Law of Property Act 1925, *supra*.
[26] Other than the business of subletting the premises as residential flats, whether or not the provision of meals or any other service is provided: s.17(3)(*b*).
[27] s.17(1): for improvements to agricultural holdings see the Agricultural Holdings Act 1986, ss.64–70.

not apply to any holding let, in writing and expressing the purpose of the letting, to a tenant as the holder of any office appointment or employment from the landlord and continuing for as long as the tenant holds such office, appointment or employment.[28] Where the premises are used partly for business purposes, the act only covers improvements relating to the business.[29] Premises regularly used for the carrying on of a profession are deemed to be used for business purposes.[30]

Improvements   While the term "improvement" is not defined in the Act, certain operations do not qualify, *viz.* the installation of fixtures which the tenant is entitled to remove,[31] work done prior to March 25, 1928, work done prior to October 1, 1954 pursuant to statutory obligation, and work done pursuant to a contractual obligation for valuable consideration.[32] In *Owen Owen Estate Ltd.* v. *Livett*[33] the tenant unsuccessfully sought certification in relation to the provision of a lavatory which he had obliged himself to install under the terms of a sublease; it was held that the contractual obligation was sufficient to disqualify the works although it existed, not between the landlord and tenant, but merely between the tenant and a third party *i.e.* the sub-tenant. It was decided in *National Electric Theatres Ltd.* v. *Hudgell*[34] that the demolition of a cinema, which the local authority had refused to certify for such use in the future, and its replacement with a row of shops with flats above, was an improvement within the section and that there was no need for any of the original building to remain.

Procedure   The tenant is required to serve on the landlord notice of his intention to make the improvement, together with a specification and plan. The landlord has three months to serve a notice of objection on the tenant and, if he does so, the tenant may apply to the Lands Tribunal to certify the improvement.[35] The Tribunal must be satisfied that it is calculated to add to the letting value of the holding at the end of the term, that it is reasonable and suitable to the character thereof[36] and that it will not diminish the value of any other property of the landlord or a superior landlord. The Tribunal cannot certify the improvement if the landlord can prove that he has himself offered to execute the improvement "in consideration of a reasonable increase in rent, or such increase of rent as the tribunal may determine."[37] Where the improvement is certified, or where the landlord has not objected within the prescribed time, the tenant can execute the improvement in accordance with the plan and specification

---

[28] s.17(2).
[29] s.17(4).
[30] s.17(3), proviso.
[31] s.1(1).
[32] s.2.
[33] [1956] 1 Ch. 1.
[34] [1939] 1 All E.R. 567.
[35] s.3(1).
[36] In this connection the court must have regard to any evidence from the landlord or a superior landlord (only) that the improvement is calculated to injure the amenity or convenience of the area: subs. (2).
[37] s.3(1).

served on the landlord, where appropriate, as modified by the Tribunal.[38]

Following the procedure in section 3 is thus a method of authorising improvements which would be forbidden by the lease. The type of improvement for which it can be used is circumscribed by the requirements set out above. In particular, it should be noted that the landlord can avoid a certification under the section by offering to do the improvement himself.

Absolute covenants However, unlike section 19(2) of the same act, which applies only to qualified covenants,[39] it can be used even where there is an absolute covenant against alterations.

Reform While the section has been found useful for the purpose of authorising improvements, it has been under used for its primary purpose of enabling tenants to claim compensation for improvements at the end of the term. The reasons for this were considered by the Law Commission.[40] They include the impact of Part II of the Landlord and Tenant 1954 in enabling tenants to apply for a new lease when the original lease expires, and thus to continue to enjoy the benefit of the improvement and the prevalence of contractual arrangements which would exclude compensation.[41] The Law Commission recommended that the compensation scheme be abolished[42] but that section 3 should remain in place for the purpose of authorising improvements,[43] subject to a redefinition of the tenancies to which it applies, in order, in the interests of simplification, to bring it into line with those covered by Part II of the Landlord and Tenant Act 1954[44] (except, unlike that Act, it would apply to certain on-licensed premises and short tenancies[45]).

Section 96 of the Telecommunications Act, 1984[46]

Application This section applies to any lease for a term of a year or more granted on or after August 5, 1984.[47] It operates upon provisions in a lease which have the effect of imposing upon the lessee any restriction or prohibition in relation to[48] (a) the running of relevant[49] telecommunication systems, (b) the connection of any telecommunications apparatus to such systems or the connection of such systems to each other or (c) the installation, maintenance, adjustment, repair, alteration or

---

[38] s.3(4): which subsection also provides that the procedure cannot be used to authorise improvements which would contravene a restriction imposed for naval, military or air force purposes, for civil aviation purposes under the Air Navigation Act 1920 or for securing any rights of the public over the foreshore or bed of the sea.

[39] See *infra*.

[40] Law Com. 178, *Landlord and Tenant: Compensation for Tenant's Improvements 1989* at paras. 3.5–3.14.

[41] See s.2 *supra*.

[42] Para. 3.23: subject to transitional arrangements.

[43] Para. 4.6.

[44] See s.23 Landlord and Tenant Act 1954.

[45] compare ss.43(1)(*d*) & 43(3) *ibid*.

[46] See appendix 4.

[47] Subs. (5)—which also gives power to the Secretary of State by order to apply it to leases granted before that date.

[48] See subs. (3).

[49] See subs. (7).

use of any telecommunications apparatus for purposes connected with the running of a relevant telecommunication system. Unless the Secretary of State has ordered otherwise[50] the restriction etc., in relation to the works specified in section 96(1)(a) & (b),[51] has effect as if it were subject to the landlord's consent, such consent not to be unreasonably withheld.[52] In determining whether consent has been unreasonably withheld (whether that issue arises by virtue of the section or otherwise[53]) regard should be had to all the circumstances and to the principle that no person should unreasonably be denied access to a telecommunication system.

Full qualification

Section 19(2) Landlord and Tenant Act, 1927

The section provides:

(2) In all leases[54] whether made before or after the commencement of this Act containing a covenant condition or agreement against the making of improvements without licence or consent, such covenant condition or agreement shall be deemed, notwithstanding any express provision to the contrary, to be subject to a proviso that such licence or consent is not to be unreasonably withheld; but this proviso does not preclude the right to require as a condition of such licence or consent the payment of a reasonable sum in respect of any damage to or diminution in the value of the premises or any neighbouring premises belonging to the landlord, and of any legal or other expenses properly incurred in connection with such licence or consent nor, in the case of an improvement which does not add to the letting value of the holding, does it preclude the right to require as a condition of such licence or consent, where such a requirement would be reasonable, an undertaking on the part of the tenant to reinstate the premises in the condition in which they were before the improvement was executed.

General issues A number of preliminary points may be made about the section.

Exclusions

(i) It does not apply to leases of agricultural holdings or mining leases[55] though the Law Commission have recommended that it should so apply in the future.[56]

(ii) It does not operate upon absolute covenants; in the case of an absolute covenant, unless the tenant can use one of the provisions referred to earlier in this chapter, he will have to seek a waiver to effect the prohibited improvements and will be at the mercy of the landlord in respect of its terms. There must

---

[50] See subs. (4).
[51] Namely things which are done (a) inside a building, or part of a building occupied by the lessee under the lease; or (b) for purposes connected with the provision to the lessee by any telecommunications operator of any telecommunications services.
[52] Subs. (1).
[53] This presumably refers to restrictions which are fully qualified without the assistance this Act, *i.e.* by virtue of their express terms or as a result of s.19(2) of the Landlord and Tenant Act 1927, see *infra*.
[54] See s.25 & *supra* Chap. 4.
[55] See s.19(4).
[56] Law Com. 178, (1989) paras. 4.11, 5.3.

be a covenant against the making of improvements "without licence or consent" before the section will operate to restrict the grounds upon which the landlord can withhold the consent; in *F.W. Woolworth* v. *Lambert*[57] the Court of Appeal refused to regard an absolute covenant which was susceptible to waiver as such a covenant.[58] Leases often differentiate between radical alterations, which are made subject to an absolute covenant, and less radical ones which are subject to the landlord's consent; in such a case it may be necessary for the court to determine in to which category the alteration falls.[59]

"Notwithstanding express provision to the contrary"

(iii) The main effect of the section is felt in relation to clauses which, while referring to the landlord's consent, do not go on to express the fully qualifying phrase "such consent not to be unreasonably withheld"; however, as is the case with disposition covenants, the section can still operate even where the fully qualifying phrase is expressed, if in fact the effect of the express clause as a whole is not identical to that provided for in the section, and is therefore an attempt to expressly provide "to the contrary"[60]

No covenant by landlord

(iv) Unless the fully qualified alteration covenant is drafted in the form of a covenant by the landlord not to unreasonably withhold his consent, the tenant will have no remedy in damages for an unreasonable refusal. In the usual form of covenant the fully qualifying phrase simple limits the scope of the restriction accepted by the tenant[61]—if the landlord does unreasonably withhold his consent, the tenant is free to act without it or to seek a declaration—it does not amount to a covenant on the landlord's part.[62]

Covenants having the effect of restricting improvements

Application to *alteration* covenants Section 19(2) applies to qualified restrictions upon "improvements." It is clear that this encompasses terms which have the *effect* of restricting improvements, and that it is unnecessary for there to be any express reference to improvements as such. In *Ball Bros.* v. *Sinclair*[63] the tenant covenanted not, without consent, to make any alteration or addition to the premises. He wanted to move a staircase in order to sublet to an optician and the landlord refused his consent. It was held that section 19(2) operated upon the covenant and thus the landlord could not unreasonably refuse his consent. Luxmore J. pointed out that, although the section nominally applies to improvement covenants, in practice there was no such thing and

> "what is being dealt with ... is a particular class of covenants which were in existence at the time of the passing of the Act and which would in fact restrict the

---

[57] [1937] 1 Ch. 37.
[58] *Per* Romer L.J. at p. 58; also discussed in Chap. 4 in relation to disposition covenants, at p. 44.
[59] *Ibid.* see Romer L.J. at p. 60.
[60] See *supra* Chap. 4, at p. 35.
[61] See Chap. 4 at p. 33.
[62] See *F. W. Woolworth* v. *Lambert* [1937] Ch. 37 *per* Romer L.J. at p. 53. The duties and remedy introduced by the Landlord and Tenant Act 1988, ss.1 & 4 do not extend to alteration covenants. See *supra* Chap. 5.
[63] [1931] 2 Ch. 325.

making of improvements. An alteration or addition may be an improvement or the reverse, if the alteration or addition sought to be made in fact effects an improvement it comes within the section."[64]

This was followed by the Court of Appeal in *F.W. Woolworth* v. *Lambert*[65] where Lord Wright M.R. made it clear that the word "improvement" did not generally appear in covenants and that it was unnecessary for it to do so. "The sub-section refers to any covenant against alterations without licence or consent. If you have such a clause, in whatever terms, and the proposed alterations are in fact capable of being deemed to be improvements, then the section would apply."[66]

Application to positive covenants

There is some doubt about the application of the section to a provision which is drafted, not restrictively, but positively,— *e.g.*, a covenant to effect certain building work subject to the plans etc. being approved by the landlord. One could argue that the effect of this is to restrict the intended improvement, and that therefore the section applies and approval should not be unreasonably withheld. In *Commissioner for Railways* v. *Avrom Investments Proprietary Ltd.*[67] the covenant was to spend not less than £150,000 in erecting an hotel on the demised premises, the new building at all times to be in accordance with such design plan and specification as the lessor may in his absolute discretion approve and "notwithstanding anything hereinbefore contained, the building design plan and specification of the said building shall be subject to the reasonable requirements of the lessor." As a matter of construction it was held that the lastly quoted words modified the earlier words of the covenant and meant that the lessor could not unreasonably refuse his approval and it was thus unnecessary for the court to decide whether section 133 Conveyancing Act 1919—1943[68] would have implied words to the same effect. Lord Somervell of Harrow referred to it as a matter of "difficulty and importance."[69]

Definition of "improvement" The tenant can only rely upon the section 19(2) implication to the extent that he can establish that the works proposed constitute an improvement to the demised premises. It has been clear since *Ball Bros.* v. *Sinclair*[70] that, as a matter of statutory construction, this has to viewed largely from the tenant's point of view. The point was

Improvement from the tenant's point of view

well put by Romer L.J. in *F.W. Woolworth* v. *Lambert*[71]:

"It has been held, and quite plainly rightly held, that the improvement may be an improvement within the meaning of the subsection even though it does not improve the premises from the point of view of the landlord. That is

---

[64] At p. 330.
[65] [1937] Ch. 37.
[66] At p. 49.
[67] [1959] 1 W.L.R. J.C. 389.
[68] The equivalent of s.19(2).
[69] At p. 402.
[70] *Ibid. per* Luxmore L.J. at p. 331.
[71] [1937] Ch. 37.

plain ... from the fact that the subsection itself contemplates that the landlord's property may be damaged by the improvements, and that in respect of that damage he may reasonably ask for a sum to be paid to him as a condition of giving his consent."[72]

Strictly this was *obiter*, the basis of the decision being that even if the works were improvements within section 19(2), the tenant had failed to show that the landlord had been unreasonable in refusing his consent.[73] However the matter was put beyond doubt in *Lambert* v. *F.W. Woolworth No. 2*[74] where for example MacKinnon L.J. opined that it sufficed that the works were regarded as improvements by the tenant and "desired as such by him," it being unnecessary that they should be improvements "from the point of view of even the most altruistic landlord."[75] Important though the tenant's view may be, it should not be thought that all works which he **Alterations** desires to carry out are capable of being improvements. Even **involving trespass** from his point of view, works which involve trespass will not be regarded as improvements. In *Tideway Investment & Property Holdings Ltd.* v. *Wellwood*[76] the lease prohibited alterations without the landlord's written consent. The tenants, being without hot water, installed gas geysers without such consent. The landlords brought an action for possession based upon breach of covenant. The tenants argued that section 19(2) applied and that the landlords had unreasonably withheld their consent. Harman J. held that section 19(2) did not apply because although a flat without hot water would normally be improved by its supply, here the works were not confined to the demised premises because they involved the affixing of a flue pipe to the underside of the balcony which was not demised to them and remained the property of the landlord." I do not see how that can be an improvement to the demised premises which necessarily extends beyond them and trespasses on the property of the landlords who are not obliged to afford support."[77] Whether the works involve a trespass can be a matter of some difficulty. In *Davies* v. *Yadegar*[78] a house previously in single occupation was divided into two flats and the demise of the upper flat expressly included the roof and the roof space. The tenant converted the roof space into living accommodation by the insertion of dormer windows which protruded into the airspace above the roof. It was held that there was no trespass, because in a demise of premises of this type it was logical to infer that the airspace above the roof was intended to be included. Different considerations could well apply with regard to a block of flats where there were a number

---

[72] At p. 55.
[73] See *Lambert* v. *F. W. Woolworth (No. 2)* [1938] 1 Ch. 883 *per* Greer L.J. at p. 895 & Slesser L.J. at p. 899.
[74] [1938] 1 Ch. 883.
[75] At p. 90.
[76] [1952] 1 All E.R. 1142.
[77] At p. 1147.
[78] [1990] 09 E.G. 67 and see Tomans, *Commercial Leases: The Implications of Alterations*, 1987 L.S.G. 716.

Non-trespassory extensions

of premises, and no tenant had the roof space included in his demise.[79] It may be that the works, while extending to property not included in the demise, do not constitute any trespass; for example, the tenant, having acquired adjoining premises from the landlord or a third party, may wish to use those premises in conjunction with the demised premises. This will involve "knocking through." There has been some controversy as to whether alterations of this type can amount to an improvement within the subsection: while the relevant point of view is that of the tenant, one must, it is argued, take his point of view as tenant *of the demised premises* and not as owner of adjacent properties. Even on this more stringent test, however, it does seem to be established that works of joinder can qualify as improvements. In *F.W. Woolworth & Co. Ltd.* v. *Lambert*[80] the tenant held business premises on a 42 year lease subject to a covenant not to make any structural alterations without the landlord's consent. He wanted to extend the premises onto adjoining land which he had acquired from a third party. This involved knocking down the back wall of the premises and removing the staircase, lavatories, heating and ventilation and locating them in the new extension. Clauson J. had held that the work was not an improvement and that therefore section 19(2) did not apply, but the majority in the Court of Appeal (Lord Wright M.R. and Romer L.J.)[81] found that he had erred. Lord Wright did not accept that the improvement had to be to the demised premises as a self-contained unit; he considered that the word improvement was

Into other property of the tenant

used in a wider sense so as to enable the tenant, consistently with the other conditions of his lease, to get the most beneficial user of the demised premises for the duration of the lease and this may involve using it in conjunction with other premises.[82] Greene L.J. in his dissenting judgment took a narrower view:

> "The real truth of the matter, in my judgment, is this: that the test of what is beneficial to the tenant's business is not the true test. The true test, I suggest, is this, that the improvement must be an improvement to the premises which are the subject-matter of the covenant, and not merely an improvement which derives its character as such from its effect or result upon some composite building."[83]

He considered that the alterations in this case could only be regarded as desirable by reason of their effect upon the composite premises

> "and once you have to bring that consideration in, ... you are introducing something which the section does not authorise you to introduce because the section is concerned

---

[79] *Per* Woolf L.J.
[80] [1937] Ch. 37 C.A.
[81] *Obiter* see *supra.*
[82] *infra.*
[83] At p. 64.

only with improvements to what is the subject matter of the covenant."[84]

While the logical consequence of this argument may appear to be the exclusion from the definition of improvement of all alterations effected for the purpose of joint user, it is clear that he did not take it so far. He did concede that opening up a communication door could amount to an improvement.[85] In the follow up case, *Lambert* v. *F.W. Woolworth No. 2*[86] a differently constituted Court of Appeal was similarly divided. It concerned a second application for consent to the self-same works and the landlord sought a declaration (*inter alia*) that the alterations were not improvements within the subsection, the opinions expressed in the first case being *obiter*. The majority of the Court of Appeal (Slesser and MacKinnon L.JJ.) held that the alterations were improvements within the Act, Greer L.J. dissented, taking the view of Greene L.J. in the first case to its logical conclusion, and opining that, as the question had to be considered from the point of view of the demised premises, apertures which were intended to *join* the two premises, as oppose to simply providing an additional entrance or exit for the demised premises, could not be regarded as improvements. Their beneficial effect could only be seen in relation to the composite building. It is submitted that this is the sensible view, although one well realises the pressures which may have led to the majority taking the opposite one—the undesirability of allowing landlords absolute control over an important aspect of development. The majority, no doubt, felt that the interests of the landlord were still well protected because the fully qualifying phrase allowed him, reasonably, to withhold his consent.[87] There was another strand running through these cases which perhaps deserves a mention: whether, quite apart from the issues referred to above, the works themselves were too destructive of the property demised to be capable of being

Scale of destruction considered improvements. Greene L.J. had no doubts: "I confess that to find described in an Act of Parliament as improvements to demised premises an alteration which involves removing the whole wall up to, say, three storeys on one side, and part of the wall up to three storeys on another; the removal of the staircase; the removal of the lavatories; to find an Act of Parliament referring to those alterations as improvements of the demised premises is to mind something rather startling."[88] Slesser L.J. seems to take the general point but concludes that the works in this case, were not of a sufficiently destructive nature to put them outside the definition of an improvement, and he makes the further point that one cannot reach the conclusion that there would be a destruction of the subject matter of the demise without close regard to the terms of the

Terms of the lease lease. "Thus, on the one hand where what is demised is described merely as land, though there be buildings on it, it

[84] At p. 64.
[85] *Ibid.*
[86] [1938] 1 Ch. 883.
[87] But compare Green L.J. at p. 64 in the first case.
[88] At p. 62.

may well be that under a licence to alter buildings, a complete reconstruction might be permissible though it would have the result of destroying altogether the original building; where on the other hand the demised premises are described with great particularity, as might be the case for example in a building with a defined number of floors, the removal of one floor altogether might be outside the scope of the power given to alter premises, in that what would be done would not be an alteration but a destruction of the subject matter."[89] From the state of the authorities, it may be proper to conclude as follows:

Conclusions

(i) that the definition of an improvement is to be considered from the point of view of the tenant, as tenant of the demised premises,

(ii) the demised premises may be improved by alterations which enable it to be used in conjunction with other premises,

(iii) this will not be so where the alterations involve trespass,

(iv) nor will it be so where the works are destructive of the subject matter of the lease[90]

(v) whether the works are so destructive is a question both of construction of the lease and of the degree of interference,

(vi) Where the works are an improvement, under section 19(2), the landlord can refuse his consent on reasonable grounds.

Consent not to be unreasonably withheld The date at which reasonableness is to be judged depends upon the circumstances.

Relevant Date In an action by the tenant for a declaration, it is the date of the landlord's refusal (if any) or where there has simply been a withholding, the date of the issue of the writ. Where the tenant has gone ahead with the improvement without getting the landlord's consent and the latter has instituted forfeiture proceedings, the relevant date would appear to be that on which the tenant embarked upon the improvement. These issues have been discussed in Chapter VI in connection with disposition

Burden of proof covenants.[91] The burden of proof is upon the tenant to show unreasonableness[92] unless the landlord gives no reason in which case the burden reverses.[93] The Landlord and Tenant Act 1988 section 1(6) which places the burden upon the landlord, is not applicable to alteration covenants. This has further consequences *viz.* that in relation to alteration covenants, the landlord is still under no duty to give reasons or to communicate his decision within a reasonable time.[94] The difficulties to which this gives rise, are considered in Chapter 5. It will clearly be impossible for the tenant to establish that

[89] In the second case at p. 902.
[90] Compare voluntary waste, *supra.*
[91] *Supra*, p. 70. It is submitted that the principles are the same.
[92] See *F. W. Woolworth Ltd.* v. *Lambert* [1937] 1 Ch. 37, *per* Romer L.J. at p. 55 and Greene L.J. at p. 61.
[93] See *Ibid.* [1938] 1 Ch. 883 *per* Slesser L.J. at p. 906.
[94] Compare s.1(3) of the Landlord & Tenant Act 1988.

Consent to be properly sought

consent has been unreasonably withheld, if he has not even asked for it.[95] He must also supply the landlord with sufficient information and sufficient time to enable a decision to be reached.[96] Where the property is subject to a number of superior leases, this can mean that the tenant in possession has to wait for the application to go through a number of hands before he can proceed.[97] Here again the chain of duties imposed upon landlords by the Landlord and Tenant Act 1988 to order to expedite multiple consents[98] is inapplicable to alteration covenants.

Conditions If the landlord attaches conditions to his consent, whether this amounts to an unreasonable withholding, will, in general, depend upon whether those conditions are reasonable. However the subsection itself specifies that certain types of condition will, in principle, be considered reasonable. They are:

Permitted conditions

(i)   the payment of a reasonable sum in respect of damage to or diminution in the value of the premises or any neighbouring premises,

(ii)   the payment of a reasonable sum in respect of any legal or other expenses properly incurred in connection with the licence,

(iii) Where the improvement does not add to the letting value of the premises and such a requirement would be reasonable, an undertaking to reinstate the premises in the condition in which they were before the improvement was executed.

Reasonable sum

In (i) & (ii), it is for the tenant to establish that the sum demanded is unreasonable: it is not a matter which he can refer to the court. In *F.W. Woolworth & Co. Ltd.* v. *Lambert*[99] the defendants asked for £7000 in respect of diminution in the value of the reversion. At the trial of the action before Clauson J. the tenant failed to produce adequate evidence that this was unreasonable and the action was dismissed. On appeal the tenant sought a declaration that consent had been unreasonably withheld and that they were free to alter without it, "paying such sum (if any) as this honourable court shall deem to be reasonable" in respect of the damage. It was held that the court had no jurisdiction to make such a determination.[1] It was for the tenant to satisfy the court that the particular demand which had been made was unreasonable; if he failed to do that, he could not expect the court to bail him out by referring the matter to the official referee. The subsection does not

> "enable the court to say that a particular set of terms or some particular conditions would be the reasonable thing for the lessor to impose in the circumstances. The practical

---

[95] See, *supra* p. 48.
[96] See, *supra* pp. 49–51.
[97] *e.g. Dowse* v. *Davies* (1961) E.G. Dig. 387.
[98] ss.2 & 3 see Chap. 5.
[99] [1937] Ch. 37 C.A.
[1] Compare s.19(3), *infra*.

question which falls to be decided in matters of dispute under this covenant is simply the question, Aye or No, has the covenant been broken; Aye or No, does the covenant or does it not, apply to the particular circumstances of the case?"[2]

The subsection clearly indicates that damage to or diminution in the value of the premise or neighbouring premises is not in itself sufficient ground for refusing consent. If that is the landlords' only complaint, then, as MacKinnon L.J. states in *Lambert* v. *F.W. Woolworth & Co. Ltd. (No. 2)*,[3] they are "obliged by the section to give their consent subject only to a requirement that the defendant should pay them a reasonable sum. ... ". To the tenant's second application, the landlords gave an unconditional refusal which necessarily therefore amounted to an unreasonable refusal. When giving conditional consent the landlords do not have to quantify their loss; they can specify a reasonable sum and agree that any dispute be decided by a competent tribunal. If they do quantify their loss and the tenant establishes that it is too much, then so long as they have made it clear that they would accept less, they will not be held to have unreasonably withheld their consent.[4]

Damages for failure to reinstate
Where the licence is granted subject to a condition for reinstatement[5] under (iii), the failure of the tenants to fulfil the condition at the end of term may give rise to a remedy in damages. The tenant who accepted the condition would obviously be liable. Assignees may also become directly liable if it was provided that the condition was to become a term of the tenancy, or if upon acquiring the lease they entered into a direct covenant with the landlord. Otherwise assignees may become indirectly liable by virtue of some indemnity covenant with the tenant. The measure of damages is the usual contractual one, namely, the loss actually sustained: the reduction in the value of the reversion occasioned by the tenant's breach. The court will not assume such a reduction and automatically quantify it as the cost of reinstatement. This point arose in *James* v. *Hutton & J. Cook Ltd.*[6] where the landlord was claiming the cost of reinstatement although she had no intention of using the money to reinstate and to do so would, in fact, be "a sheer waste of money." In these circumstances it was held that as she had suffered no loss she was entitled to merely nominal damages of one pound (£1). She had argued that the court should assume loss to the extent of the cost of reinstatement by analogy with the special rule which applies to a failure to deliver up premises in repair. Lord Goddard C.J. found that rule to be inapplicable to reinstatement covenants. In the case of breach of a covenant to deliver up in repair, there would obviously be loss because a

---

[2] *Per* Greene L.J. at p. 61.
[3] [1938] 1 Ch. 883, 912.
[4] *Ibid.*
[5] In the absence of express or implied stipulation, a tenant is under no obligation to reinstate: *Never-Stop Railway (Wembley) Ltd.* v. *British Empire Exhibition (1924) Inc.* [1926] 1 Ch. 877.
[6] [1950] 1 K.B. 9 C.A.

"dilapidated house is worth less than a house in good condition"[7] and for convenience the court assessed the loss, not on the basis of the diminution in the value of the reversion which would require extensive enquiries, but as the amount which was necessary to put the property in repair. Breach of a reinstatement covenant was not *per se* indicative of loss, and the court would not assume it here. Had she shown that she or her superior landlord intended to use the premises at the end of the term for a purpose for which the altered shop front would be inappropriate and the old one suitable, she would have shown a loss for which the cost of reinstatement would have been the correct measure.

Other conditions

While the subsection makes it clear that the imposition of conditions complying with the statutory criteria will not amount to an unreasonable withholding of consent, it does not state that other conditions relating to those matters—conditions which do not comply with the statutory criteria—necessarily *do* amount to an unreasonable withholding of consent. As a matter of construction, the subsection indicates that certain conditions are reasonable, but it does not say that all other types of condition on that subject are necessarily unreasonable. For example what of a condition requiring an undertaking for reinstatement regardless of whether the improvement adds to the letting value, or reinstatement to a state other than that referred to in the subsection? Clearly there is no express sanction of such conditions in the subsection and the tenant can challenge them as unreasonable but surely they would not necessarily be so? The tenant may, for example, have covenanted in the lease to reinstate in the terms demanded by the landlord and in these circumstances the condition sought by the landlord would merely secure to him his covenanted rights under the lease.[8] There is some indication that this may not be the position. In *James* v. *Hutton & Cook Ltd.*[9] Goddard C.J. seems to have assumed that if the improvement added to the letting value of the premises and thus fell outside (iii) "the subsection would prevent the landlord requiring the tenant to reinstate at all.[10] The Law Commission make a similar assumption when canvassing and approving a proposal to dispense with the requirement that the improvement must not add to the letting value.[11] Taking the view that the subsection specified the only circumstances under which a condition for reinstatement can be imposed, they commented that it could be unfair to a landlord "if he intends to resume occupation himself at the end of the term [and] is interested not in increasing the letting value but in preserving the layout and amenities which suit him." It is suggested that if the subsection is construed as merely exemplifying the circumstances when a reinstatement condition would be reasonable rather than exhaustively defining

Reinstatement

---

[7] At p. 16.
[8] Compare *Bromley Park Garden Estates Ltd.* v. *Moss* [1982] 2 All E.R. 890; *supra* Chap. 6.
[9] [1950] 1 K.B. 9.
[10] At p. 18.
[11] See Law Com. No. 141 paras. 8.42 *et seq.*

Money payment

them, such a reform would be unnecessary. The same considerations apply to the circumstances in which the landlord can demand a money payment in connection with the grant of a licence. There is a very strong tendency here to regard the subsection as exhaustive because of the policy of the Act as explained by MacKinnon L.J. in *Lambert* v. *F.W. Woolworth & Co. Ltd (No. 2)*[12]: "The mischief aimed at by this section 19(2) is obviously the power of the landlord to exact arbitrary payment—not to use a harsher word—from a tenant as the price for his consent." Requiring payment in excess of the "reasonable sum" referred to in the subsection is not however inevitably arbitrary: the tenant may have agreed to that level of payment in the lease. Thus, it is submitted that conditions relating to the matters dealt with expressly in the subsection, but out of conformity with it, are not automatically unreasonable; their status will depend on the facts and in particular the terms of the lease.

Miscellaneous

The landlord may seek to impose, on the grant of a licence, conditions completely unrelated to those mentioned in the subsection, and whether these are reasonable will depend upon the circumstances. In so far as they secure to the landlord essential information or safeguards they are likely to be reasonable. Such conditions may, for example, require the tenant to submit plans and specifications, to obtain and comply with planning consents and to conform to building regulations. Other conditions may not fall within this category, but it is submitted that they will still be reasonable if they secure to the landlord a right covenanted to him in the lease—as where, for instance, the tenant has agreed that any improvements will be effected in the manner specified by the landlord.

"Aesthetic historic or sentimental"

Types of objection   The subsection indicates that harm of a purely commercial nature to the premises or neighbouring premises of the landlord does not justify an absolute refusal of consent. It only justifies attaching an appropriate condition to the consent. The subsection deals similarly with improvements which do not add to the letting value. On the other hand, harm of an aesthetic, historic or sentimental nature can justify an absolute refusal. This appears to have been so before the 1927 Act and MacKinnon L.J. in *Lambert* v. *F. W. Woolworth Co. Ltd. (No. 2)*[13] opined that it remained unaffected by the Act. "No court, as I believe, will ever hold that, under section 19(2), a landlord must consent to the hideous degradations of the front of his building by a sheet of plate glass, and be satisfied by a money payment for the loss of graceful eighteenth century windows."[14] Slesser L.J., in the same case, was equally vehement in the matter of shop fronts: having given the tenant the benefit of a very wide definition of "improvement"[15] he was keen to redress the balance by allowing the landlord to successfully object on aesthetic grounds. "The wider the

[12] [1938] 1 Ch. 883, 908.
[13] [1938] 1 Ch. 883 at pp. 911, 912.
[14] *Ibid.*
[15] See *supra.*

connotation given to the idea of improvement, the more necessary it may be that the landlord should have his protection. In the present decline of taste and manners, a shop keeper looking at the matter from a purely commercial point of view, may be right in saying that the removal of some beautiful casement and the substitution of a garish window or facade of false marble may prove to be an attraction to the public and so from his point of view an improvement. It is important that the landlord should be able to say that it may be reasonable that he should refuse his consent to the perpetration of the contemplated atrocities."[16] There were no aesthetic considerations in that case: the proposed extension was to the back of the premises and affected only "a confused area of garages, yards and sheds."[17] Aesthetic merit is of course a matter of opinion and therefore the result of any objection based upon this ground is likely to be very uncertain. Such an objection was considered reasonable in *Mosley* v. *Cooper*[18] where the trustees of a management scheme established under section 19 of the Leasehold Reform Act 1967 refused permission for the creation of a hard standing in the front garden of an enfranchised property, inter alia, because it would diminish the appearance and visual amenity of the road as a whole. Historic significance is perhaps less easy for the tenant to denigrate. Reliance upon "sentimental" grounds, or as Slesser L.J. expressed it, "personal" grounds would probably not stand much chance of success as such grounds would often be condemned as attempts to gain collateral/uncovenanted advantages.

Approval by a superior landlord

It may be that the landlord withholds his consent because he himself needs to seek the approval of a superior landlord. The tenant should allow sufficient time for the various parties to consider the application before challenging the withholding as unreasonable. Once this time has elapsed, can he treat further delay by the immediate landlord, who will not respond without clearance from above, as unreasonable? Buckley J. in *Dowse* v. *Davies*[19] was inclined to think that the landlord was entitled to wait until he was clear of risk of forfeiting his own interest as a result of allowing the alteration to go ahead: "to say that somebody who was himself exposed to risk of forfeiting his interest in the property if he allowed the alterations to be made, was acting unreasonably in withholding his consent until he obtained his superior landlord's consent was prima facie a rather extreme view to take."[20] However it can be very frustrating for the tenant to wait upon a landlord who has, in substance, no objection to the alterations and simply wishes to be safe. These issues are discussed in Chapter five in relation to disposition covenants. The reforms effected by the Landlord and Tenant Act 1988 do not apply to alteration covenants.

---

[16] At p. 908.
[17] *Ibid.*
[18] [1990] 23 E.G. 66.
[19] [1961] E.G.D. 387.
[20] At p. 388; but see also *supra*, p. 120.

Alterations constituting a tort

In *Haines* v. *Florensa*[21] the landlord refused his consent because he believed that the loft conversion proposed by the tenant would constitute a trespass to the airspace above the roof and to his adjoining property (scaffolding, deposit of materials) and the interference which would be caused would be an actionable nuisance. In the event there was no trespass to airspace (it had passed to the tenant by the demise), any other trespass could be avoided and the interference was not extensive enough to constitute a nuisance. Had any of these torts been substantiated, the landlord could reasonably have withheld his consent. As they had not been it was considered that the temporary inconvenience to which the landlord may be subjected was outweighed by the benefit to the tenant of increasing his living space.

Changes in estate policy

It may be that in the past consent has been forthcoming for certain types of alteration which in retrospect the landlord considers detrimental. In *Mosley* v. *Cooper*[22] a number of householders had been granted permission to create hardstandings in their front gardens to provide off street parking. By the time Mr. Cooper came to make his application, the trustees had formed the view (which was held reasonable) that this had spoilt the appearance of the road and had a detrimental effect upon parking arrangements. They therefore formally adopted a change of policy and refused Mr. Cooper's application. Mr. T. R. A. Morison, Q.C. took the view that the trustees could reasonably decide "that enough was enough" and announce a change of policy. Such a policy statement did not prevent subsequent applications and in the event of a refusal, the applicant could test the reasonableness of the decision. It may be that in the circumstances of a particular case the implementation of the new policy could be held unreasonable. Mr. Cooper, however, had no legitimate expectation that consent would be granted to him; he had not been mislead by the trustees, the most that could be said was that he had seen hardstandings formed at other houses and thought it would be alright. The refusal of consent was reasonable.

There is a dearth of cases on other types of objection, but it is to some extent possible to rely upon decisions relating to disposition covenants. In relation to objections based upon breaches of covenant by the tenant, his anticipated user of the premises and objections which challenge the continuance of the term reference should therefore be made to Chapter six. Objections based upon harm to other property of the landlord must necessarily be treated differently because of the express reference to this sort of harm in section 19(2). Unless any aesthetic, historic or sentimental consideration can be invoked, it does not justify an absolute refusal of consent; but the landlord can make his consent conditional upon the payment of a reasonable sum in recompense.[23]

---

[21] [1990] 09 E.G. 70 C.A.
[22] [1990] 23 E.G. 66.
[23] See *supra*.

PART 3

9 RESTRICTIONS ON USER

Tenants' basic freedom

Subject to the general law

Subject to restrictions affecting the reversion

In the absence of provision to the contrary the tenant is free to use the premises for any purpose[1] which does not contravene the general law. In relation to the latter, the tenant is obviously subject to the Town and Country Planning Act 1971, the Control of Pollution Act 1974, The Sexual Offences Act 1956,[2] the Tort of Nuisance, the Law of Waste and the many other restraints to which occupiers of premises are subject. Where there is "provision to the contrary," the restriction may be in the tenant's own lease (see *infra*) or it could affect the freehold or leasehold reversion. Enforcement against a tenant of restrictive covenants affecting the reversionary title *other than those made between landlord and tenant* depends, in the case of unregistered land, upon the old doctrine of notice where the covenant was entered into prior to January 1, 1926[3] and upon registration as a Class D(ii) Land Charge where it was entered into on or after that date.[4] In the case of registered land, enforcement will depend upon whether the restrictive covenant was protected by a notice on the register. Under section 50 of the Land Registration Act 1925, such a notice takes the place of registration as a land charge, and results in the proprietor and those deriving title under him[5] having deemed notice of the covenant.[6] This is so even though the notice did not appear upon the lessee's register of title but only upon the register of title relating to the freehold or leasehold reversion which the lessee had no right to inspect.[7] If it is not so protected on the register, the proprietor on first registration[8] or under a

---

[1] See example *Yelloly* v. *Morley* (1910) 27 T.L.R. 20 where the tenant successfully sued the landlord in trespass for entering the premises and ripping down a poster which the tenant had displayed in connection with the parliamentary elections, such a right of entry being limited to non-payment of rent or breach of covenant.

[2] Note s.35(2) which allows a landlord, whose tenant has been convicted of knowingly permitting the premises to be used as a brothel, to require the tenant to assign to someone approved by the landlord, which approval must not be unreasonably withheld.

[3] As to constructive notice of intending lessees and assignees see s.44 of the Law of Property Act 1925 and Woodfall, *Landlord and Tenant*, Vol. 1, 1.1136 & 1.1216.

[4] Land Charges Act 1972, s.2(5)(ii)(ii); by s.4(6) non-registration makes the covenant void against a purchaser of the legal estate for money or moneys worth.

[5] Except incumbrancers or other persons who at the time the notice was entered, were not bound by the covenant.

[6] See s.50(2).

[7] *White* v. *Bijou Mansions Ltd.* [1937] Ch. 610; Ruoff & West, *Concise Land Registration Practice*, (3rd ed.) p. 138.

[8] s.5 of the Land Registration Act 1925.

registered disposition for valuable consideration[9] takes free[10] even if he had actual notice.[11] Enforcement of restrictive covenants made between lessor and lessee and affecting the leasehold reversion are not registrable under the Land Charges Act 1972 nor, in the case of registered land, may they be protected by notice under section 50(1) of the Land Registration Act 1925. Whether they would bind a subtenant would therefore depend upon the old doctrine of notice.[12]

Restrictions in the lease

Effect on rent

Business premises

In the case of business premises, it is in the interests of the landlord to ensure that the tenant retains as much freedom in the use of the premises as possible; restraints upon use do reduce the rent the property can command: initially, upon a rent review and also upon the grant of a new tenancy under the Landlord and Tenant Act 1954.[13] Ideally therefore the tenant should be subject only to the minimum of restrictions and those restrictions should be embodied in a fully qualified covenant.[14] The potential effect of user restrictions upon rents should be considered not only when the lease is granted, but also where it is proposed to execute a deed of variation. In *Lynnthorpe Enterprises Ltd.* v. *Sidney Smith (Chelsea) Ltd.*[15] the lease contained a fully qualified covenant: to use as a wine and snack bar or, with landlord's consent (which was not to be unreasonably withheld), for any other purpose. On the occasion of a subsequent assignment, a deed of variation was executed containing an absolute covenant: to use only as a restaurant. It was held that the deed of variation had effected a permanent change in the terms on which the property was held and would bind future tenants and therefore rent fell to be assessed solely on the basis of the absolute user clause in the deed of variation. This was a case where the variation was to the landlord's detriment; in other circumstances the landlord may wish, by way of variation, to widen the user clause prior to a rent review in order to increase the rent. He cannot do this unilaterally, for example by issuing the tenant with licences for a change in use for which he has not asked.[16] If the landlord foresees the

---

[9] s.20(1); s.23(1) *ibid.*; no valuable consideration, see ss.20(4) & 23(5) *ibid.*

[10] Preston & Newsom, *Restrictive Covenants Affecting Freehold Land*, (7th Ed.) 13.26.

[11] s.59(6) *ibid.*

[12] And see s.44 of the Law of Property Act 1925.

[13] See *e.g. Plinth Property Investments Ltd.* v. *Anderson* (1978) 38 P. & C.R. 361; *Charles Clements (London) Ltd.* v. *Rank City Wall Ltd.* (1978) 246 E.G. 739.

[14] See *infra.*

[15] [1989] E.G.C.S. 63.

[16] See *C & A Pensions Trustees* v. *British Vita Investments Ltd.* (1984) 272 E.G. 63.

consequences of imposing a narrow user clause at the outset, it seems that he can avoid them by providing in the lease that, for the purposes of the rent review clause, a different user, one which maximises the rent, is to be assumed.[17] Restricting the use of residential property does not usually have any effect

Residential premises

upon the rent, because it would in any event be difficult to obtain planning permission for a change to business use.[18]

The scope of the restraint may be defined by specifying what cannot be done, or, alternatively, what can be done—the latter tending to be more restrictive than the former. Thus some covenants list the prohibited uses ("wide" clauses) while others prohibit all uses except the specified ones ("narrow" clauses). Furthermore the activities referred to by both types of user clause, are described in varying degrees of generality. Thus it is common to find covenants by the tenant not to cause a nuisance or annoyance to the landlord or adjoining occupiers or not to carry on an offensive trade, but it has also been the practice expressly to name some trades. So-called "narrow" clauses are equally various, some limiting use generically, *e.g.* to business purposes, others to particular businesses or even to a particular business carried on by the tenant and his associates. *Granada T.V. Network Ltd.* v. *Great Universal*

User limited to business of lessee

Stores[19] is an example of the latter: "not to use the premises . . . except as offices for the business of" Granada T.V. Network Ltd. This has the effect, potentially, of rendering the property unassignable despite the presence of a fully qualified disposition covenant.[20] However, it should not be thought that such clauses are necessarily disastrous for the landlord in the context of a rent review. Where there is a rent review clause which requires the rent to be determined upon an open market basis having regard to the terms of the lease, this is construed as requiring, not an assumption that the lease is unassignable, but rather an assumption that the hypothetical tenant, like the actual one, will only be able to use the property for his particular business at the time of letting. Thus the user clause should be read as containing a blank to be filled in when the name and business of the hypothetical tenant becomes known.[21] Thus it has been said that "a restriction to use by a particular lessee may have less of a depreciatory effect on review than a restriction to use for a particular trade or profession."[22]

---

[17] See Hudgill, *Leases—The effect of a User Restriction*, 1986 L.S.G. 1122; but see *Encyclopedia of Forms and Precedents*, (5th ed.) Vol. 22, para. 83.1 where the tenant is advised not to accept such a clause upon the basis that if he has accepted the problems of a narrow user clause he should benefit from such advantages as they bring on a rent review.

[18] See Law Com. No. 141, para. 4.49.

[19] (1963) 187 E.G. 391.

[20] See *supra*, Chap. 6 "Objections based on Anticipated User" & *infra*.

[21] *Law Land Co. Ltd.* v. *Consumers' Association* [1980] 255 E.G. 617 C.A. "not to use other than as offices of the Consumers' Association and its associated organisations"; *Sterling Land Offices Developments Ltd.* v. *Lloyds Bank plc* [1984] 271 E.G. 894 not to use other than as a branch of Lloyds Bank plc.

[22] Hudgill *ibid.*

Effect on tenant's powers of disposition

Where a lease contains a fully qualified disposition covenant
and a covenant restricting user, it is settled that the landlord
may be able reasonably to object to the assignment, on grounds
of user, although the user proposed by the disponee is within
the permissible limits.[23] However the likelihood of his
objection being found reasonable diminishes the stricter the
user covenant becomes. In *International Drilling Fluids Ltd.* v.
Louisville Investments (Uxbridge) Ltd.[24] there was a narrow user
clause, the tenant covenanting not to use the premises "for any
purpose other than as offices within the meaning of Class II of
the Town and Country Planning (Use Classes) Order 1963 with
ancillary showrooms." The intended user of the proposed
assignee was within this clause and the landlord was held to
have unreasonably withheld his consent. Balcombe L.J.
considered that there "is all the difference in the world between
a case where the user clause prohibits only certain types of use,
so that the tenant is free to use the property in any other way,
and the case where (as here) only one specific type of use is
permitted. In my judgment in that sort of case it is not
reasonable for the landlord to refuse consent to an assignment
on the grounds of user (being within the only specific type of
use), where the result will be that the property is left vacant
and where (as here) the landlord is fully secured for the
payment of rent."[25]

Types of user commonly restricted[26]

**Construction of
restrictions**   On general principles, provisions which restrict the tenant's
rights will be construed against the landlord.[27] It is also clear
that the words used will be interpreted as at the date when the
covenant was made[28]; if at that time, it can fairly be said to
have restricted the relevant use, that use will be a breach of
covenant. It makes no difference that the main thrust of the
covenant was towards other uses which were more prevalent at
the time it was entered into. In *Texaco Antilles* v. *Kernochan*[29]
the covenant, made in 1925, prohibited use as a "public
garage" a term which at that time involved mainly the repair
and storage of vehicles. Petrol *was* sold, but the bulk of the
profit would be derived from the other activities. The question
was whether the covenant prohibited use as a filling station.
The Privy Council refused to interfere with the view of the
lower court that it did.[30] It may of course be a matter of degree
whether the proposed business is to be regarded as an evolved

---

[23] See *supra*, p. 79.
[24] [1986] 1 All E.R. 321.
[25] At p. 327.
[26] See Hill & Redman's *Law of Landlord and Tenant*, (18th Ed.), Vol. 1, paras.
1295–1326.
[27] Compare disposition covenants; see Chap. 2, *supra*.
[28] *Rother* v. *Colchester Corporation* [1969] 1 W.L.R. 720, 729.
[29] [1973] A.C. 609.
[30] At p. 622.

aspect of the prohibited business or whether it should be regarded as an entirely different business outside the scope of the restriction.

"Nuisance" In *Harrison* v. *Good*[31] a covenant not to do or suffer to be done anything which shall be a nuisance to the owners of adjoining property, was held to refer to a nuisance in the legal sense and therefore gave those enjoying the benefit of the covenant no control over uses which fell short of a nuisance at law but which they found to be distasteful, namely the building of a boys' school. Bacon V.-C. refused to construe the word in its wider popular sense because "if I enlarge it in some degree, I must enlarge it perhaps in a greater degree ... and I do not know how I could stop .... That which would be so odious and almost intolerable to one man, others might not care a straw about."[32] This view was doubted by the Court of Appeal in *Tod-Heatley* v. *Benham*[33] but the doubts must be regarded as *obiter* because the covenant in that case additionally restricted users which caused annoyance.[34] Be this as it may, in relation to the construction of the word "nuisance," Cotton L.J. expressly refused to approve *Harrison* v. *Good* and Lindley L.J. doubted whether Bacon V.-C. "gave sufficient weight to the consideration that the whole object of having a covenant against nuisance is to give the covenantee some protection in addition to what he would have had without the covenant, but, for a nuisance in the strict sense, there would be an action, covenant or no covenant." Bowen L.J. doubted whether, in the context of the clause he was considering, which referred to "annoyance, nuisance, grievance or damage" nuisance should be given its strict legal sense.

"Annoyance" It is clear that this term is wider than a legal nuisance.[35] In the *Tod-Heatley* Case Bowen L.J. defined legal nuisance by quoting the definition given in *Walter* v. *Selfe*[36] by Knight-Bruce V.-C. which refers to interference "with the ordinary comfort physically of human existence not merely according to elegant or dainty modes and habits of living but according to plain and sober and simple notions among English people." On the authority of *Aldred's* Case[37] nuisance was concerned to safeguard the necessities of life and provided no remedy for "matters of delight." A covenant which restricts annoyance, however, does go some way towards preserving the delights of life; it does not preserve all of them because what amounts to an annoyance is to be judged not by the subjective view of the landlord but according to the standards of ordinary people and "if you find anything which reasonably troubles the

---

[31] (1871) L.R. 11 Eq. 338.
[32] At p. 350.
[33] (1889) 40 Ch.D. 80.
[34] Which has a wider meaning: see *infra*.
[35] See, *e.g. Errington* v. *Birt* (1911) 105 L.T. 373—a fish shop was not a nuisance but it was an annoyance.
[36] 4 De G. & Sm. 322.
[37] (1610) 9 Co. Rep. 57b at 58b *per* Wray J.

mind or pleasure, not of a fanciful person or of a skilled person who knows the truth, but of the ordinary sensible English inhabitants of a house—if you find anything which reasonably disturbs his peace of mind, that seems to me to be an annoyance, although it may not appear to amount to physical detriment to comfort."[38] It was held ordinary people *would* apprehend risk by way of infectious disease from the opening of a hospital for poor outpatients and would fear that this may lead to a reduction in letting value of properties in the neighbourhood. Such apprehension was not unreasonable and therefore the hospital was an annoyance within the covenant. This test has been applied in subsequent cases like *Benton* v. *Chapman*[39] where it was held that a widow who allowed a man to visit her several times a week and stay the night, was in breach of a covenant not to cause annoyance. The case was also relied on in *Hampstead & Suburban Properties* v. *Diomedous*[40] where the landlord sought an injunction against a noise annoyance. The tenant argued, first, that damages would suffice by way of remedy because the landlord did not live upon the premises, and it was of no consequence to him that his other tenants could not sleep and, second, that the phrase nuisance and annoyance was too uncertain to permit the remedy of injunction to be used, because the number of decibels which would annoy one person would not be noticed by another. Both of these arguments failed: the landlord needs an injunction even if *his* sleep is not disturbed, because the existence of noisy neighbours may make it difficult for him to relet neighbouring properties and the *Tod-Heatley* test provided a means of determining the level of noise which would constitute an annoyance.

"Immoral purposes"   It is clear that using the demised premises as a brothel would contravene a covenant not to use for an immoral purpose.[41] In *Upfill* v. *Wright*[42] it was held that use by a woman for receiving constant visits by her lover (who paid the rent) was an immoral purpose.[42a] However in *Heglibiston Establishment* v. *Heyman*[43] *Upfill* was distinguished as a case which concerned a "kept woman" and it was held that user by a couple living together as man and wife did not involve an immoral purpose. It was also doubted whether *Upfill* would be decided in the same way today.[44] The meaning of immorality is determined as at the date when the covenant was entered into and therefore modern leases may be construed in accordance with the more broad minded outlook of today.

---

[38] *Per* Bowen L.J. at p. 98.
[39] [1953] C.L.Y. 3099.
[40] [1968] 3 All E.R. 545.
[41] Compare *Smith* v. *White* (1866) L.R. 1 Eq. 626; it may also constitute an illegal purpose: see Sexual Offences Act 1956.
[42] [1911] 1 K.B. 506.
[42a] Knowledge of the intended purpose on the part of the landlord's agent precluded the landlord from recovering on the covenant to pay rent.
[43] [1978] 36 P. & C.R. 351 C.A.
[44] *Per* Browne L.J. at pp. 360–1 and Megaw L.J. at p. 362.

Absolute, qualified and fully qualified covenants

Of the three types of covenant with which this book is concerned, it is only user covenants which can still exist in absolute, qualified or fully qualified form.[45] This is because any qualified covenants restricting *dispositions or alterations* automatically become fully qualified under subsections (1) and (2) of section 19 of the Landlord and Tenant Act 1927. Section 19(3) which relates to *user* covenants[46] does not have this effect and thus they can still exist in qualified form.

Absolute and qualified restrictions
Absolute and qualified user covenants are of similar effect: both involve an express prohibition, in both cases that prohibition can be lifted at the landlord's uncontrolled discretion. They differ in form only—an absolute covenant makes no express mention of the possibility of a waiver while a qualified covenant does invite an application for consent. It has been pointed out that qualified user covenants are misleading in two ways: first, they amount to a representation by the landlord that he is willing in principle to consent to a reasonable application for change of use, but under the existing law, he is not bound to do so and second, because the full qualification of disposition and alteration covenants is well known, it is often wrongly assumed that user covenants too are subject to full qualification.[47] The Law Commission have therefore justifiably recommended that in future they be subject to full qualification.[47a] A very keen draftsman may perhaps mourn the passing of the qualified form of covenant—it has been pointed out that "what the words 'without consent' contemplate is that consent may be given under the lease and without a variation of the terms of the lease"[48] and also that, in some circumstances, a qualified covenant makes more sense than an absolute one— for example it would be unfortunate to have an absolute covenant not to use for business purposes followed by a provision which presupposes just such a change. A qualified covenant would make perfect sense in these circumstances whilst maintaining the landlord's absolute discretion. The case of *Pearce* v. *Maryon-Wilson*[49] illustrates other circumstances where the effect of an absolute covenant would not be the same as the effect of a qualified one. It concerned a leasehold building scheme where all the lessees had entered into covenants not to use their properties for certain purposes without the consent in writing of the landlord. The plaintiff argued that the landlord was under an implied duty to withhold his consent to changes of use which would involve a radical departure from the scheme, and sought an injunction to prevent the landlord giving his consent. Luxmore J. held that the landlord was under no such duty: the qualifying words gave him complete freedom to give his consent—even if it harmed

---

[45] For an explanation of these terms see Chap. 1.
[46] Discussed *infra*.
[47] See Law Com. No. 141 paras. 4.69 & 6.14.
[47a] *Ibid.*
[48] *Pearl Assurance plc* v. *Shaw* [1985] 1 E.G.L.R. 92 *per* Vinelott J. at p. 94.
[49] [1935] Ch. 188.

the interests of the other tenants. He opined, however, that had the covenants been in absolute form the landlord would have had no power to vary them at all.

A qualified user covenant will be fully qualified *if the lease so provides*. As has been pointed out, there is no statutory implication. Over the years attempts have been made to argue

Full qualification implied under the general law?

that full qualification can be implied under the general law. In *Viscount Tredegar* v. *Harwood*[50] it was unsuccessfully argued that a covenant to insure in an office approved by the lessor should import a qualification that approval was not to be unreasonably withheld. Lord Blanesburgh dissented, pointing out that the form of covenant chosen gave the tenant an option in the matter of the insurance office, and unless there was imported into it the qualification that consent was not to be unreasonably withheld the landlord could insist, as he was doing in that case, that the tenant uses an insurance company nominated by him. In *Bocardo* v. *S. & M. Hotels*[51] similar sentiments were expressed by Megaw L.J. in discussing the effect of section 19(1): it merely made statutory "an implied term which must already have been implied if the express words were to have any sensible meaning." A qualified provision

> "would, in strict law, be meaningless or ineffective, unless it were to have implied in it some such term as 'such consent not to be unreasonably withheld,' for if the landlord was entitled to refuse consent at his own entirely unrestricted discretion, the provision for assignment with consent would add nothing to, and subtract nothing from, the effect of the law of contract as it would be without those words included."[52]

In short, unless full qualification is implied, it is impossible to distinguish a qualified covenant from an absolute one. This view was relied on by the tenant in *Guardian Assurance Co. Ltd.* v. *Gants Hill Holdings Ltd.*[53] He sought a declaration that a qualified restrictive user covenant was subject to the implication, under the general law, that consent was not to be unreasonably withheld. Mervyn Davies L.J. noted that the statement relied upon from *Bocardo* was *obiter* and he refused to follow it taking the view that (in the absence of special circumstances) he could not imply under the general law something which the statute, by omission, makes plain is not to be implied into covenants restricting user.[54] In *Pearl Assurance plc* v. *Shaw*[55] Vinelott J. followed Mervyn Davies J. in *Guardian* rather than *Bocardo*.[56]

It would however be wrong to assume that the court would never imply the fully qualifying words. In relation to

---

[50] [1929] A.C. 72.
[51] [1979] 3 All E.R. 737, 741.
[52] At p. 741.
[53] [1983] 267 E.G. 678.
[54] At p. 679.
[55] [1985] 1 E.G.L.R. 92.
[56] At p. 94.

**Restrictions of a
regulatory nature**

some types of covenants, of a regulatory nature, such an implication may be inescapable. *Dallman* v. *King*[57] is an early example. Here there was a covenant on the part of the tenant, the effect of which was that the tenant agreed to expend £200 in specified improvements "to be inspected and approved" by the landlord and the latter agreed that the tenant should be entitled to recover the amount by retaining it out of the first year's rent. The tenant completed the work, but the landlord did not approve all parts of it and would not allow the tenant the whole of the agreed retention. Tindal C.J. held that the agreement to do the work subject to the landlord's approval was not a condition precedent of the tenant's right of retention but, even if it had been, the condition had been substantially performed: the work had been completed. All that remained was for the landlord to give his approval and

> "[i]t could never have been intended that he should be allowed capriciously to withhold his approval. That would have been a condition which would go to the destruction of the thing granted, and, if so, according to the well-known rule, the thing granted would pass discharged of the condition."[58]

Thus a covenant which prohibits the tenant from engaging in a particular activity at all unless the landlord consents, must be distinguished from a covenant which either requires or allows the tenant to engage in the activity subject to the landlord's consent in relation to a specified matter. In the latter case the court will be ready to imply that consent is not to be unreasonably withheld. A more recent case in point is *Cryer* v. *Scott Bros. (Sunbury) Ltd.*[59] The covenant, which related to freehold land, was to the effect that all building or other plans were to be submitted for the defendant's approval before building work was commenced. The plaintiff wanted to build a bedroom over his garage and the defendant refused permission. The plaintiff sought a declaration that (*inter alia*) consent could not be unreasonably withheld. The Court of Appeal granted the declaration. Slade L.J. accepted that there was no general principle of law "that whenever a contract requires the consent of one party to be obtained by the other, there is an implied term that such consent is not to be unreasonably withheld"[60] and that therefore such an implication could not *automatically* be made. However, if it was necessary to give business efficacy, there was no reason why it should not be implied. He relied upon an unreported decision of Sir Robert Megarry V.-C., *Clerical, Medical and General Life Assurance Society* v. *Fanfare Properties Ltd.*,[61] where the latter drew a distinction between qualified covenants requiring "general and unrestricted" consent, like a covenant not to carry on any trade upon the premises without the landlord's consent, and covenants which

---

[57] (1837) 4 Bing (N.C.) 105.
[58] At p. 109.
[59] [1988] 55 P. & C.R. 183; and see Adams, 1988 Conveyancer 172.
[60] *Per* Millet J. in *Price* v. *Bouch* (1986) 53 P. & C.R. 257, 260.
[61] June 2, 1981.

require the approval of a specific matter, as when building plans have to be approved in which case "the courts will not permit the party whose consent is required to misuse the requirement to approve the plans which are free from any tenable objection."[62] The covenant, here, as well as covering extensions also covered the initial development of the estate and the "contemplation of both sides was clearly that the land to be transferred would be developed by the transferees. The reservation of a right arbitrarily to withhold approval of the plans would have been liable to defeat the purpose of the grant."[63] Waite J. opined that the question to ask is "whether a capricious or unreasonable withholding of consent would amount to a destruction of the thing granted?"[64] None of these cases concerned user covenants and the extent to which the principle to which they give rise can be applied to user covenants is somewhat limited: however, it is submitted that a covenant to use only for a purpose approved by the landlord may well call for the implication that such approval is not to be unreasonably withheld.

Full qualification and reasonableness

In relation to disposition and alteration covenants[65] section 19 of the Landlord and Tenant Act 1927[66] has a twofold effect: it implies the fully qualifying phrase into qualified covenants from which it is absent, and it neutralises any glosses upon the meaning of reasonableness, which may have been incorporated, by the parties, into covenants which were already in fully qualified form. User covenants experience neither of these effects. There is no statutory implication of full qualification and, if the covenant *is* fully qualified, there is nothing to stop

Covenants which define reasonableness

the parties specifying what will be deemed reasonable. This is what they did in *Berenyi* v. *Watford Borough Council*[67] where the tenants had taken a 97 year building lease from the council and had erected a factory thereon for the business of precision engineering. There was a fully qualified disposition covenant followed by a user covenant (referred to as clause (11)) in these terms:

> "To use the demised premises for the purpose of precision engineering with ancillary office and warehouse accommodation and not to use the demised premises or suffer or permit the same to be used for any purpose whatsoever except with the previous consent of the Corporation which consent shall not be unreasonably withheld howsoever (without prejudice to[68] the generality

---

[62] At p. 194.
[63] At p. 195.
[64] At p. 202.
[65] See Chaps. 4 & 8.
[66] In subsections (1) & (2).
[67] 1980 256 E.G. 271, at p. 273.
[68] It would appear that the draftsman must have meant "notwithstanding."— see Megaw L.J. at p. 278.

of the foregoing) that (*sic*) the Corporation's consent shall
not be treated or construed as being unreasonably withheld
on the grounds or any of the grounds following that is to
say. . . . . (ii) that the trade or business proposed to be
carried on is considered by the Corporation to be one
which would be in conflict with the Corporation's
interpretation of good estate management."

The business prospered and the tenants applied for
planning permission for an extension large enough to
accommodate the current expansion and a further expansion
planned a few years hence. The unwanted space could in the
meantime be sublet. The Council granted planning permission
subject to the condition that no part of the property should be
separately let without the permission of the planning authority.
The reason for the condition was stated to be that the premises
were "unsuitable for dual use having regard to the restricted
access to and from the rear of the site." After a public enquiry
the condition was discharged, the inspector being of the
opinion that "whatever the industrial occupation of the
completed building, it would [not] significantly affect . . . traffic
generation." Then, as Sir Patrick Browne put it,[69] "the council
having missed with the first barrel, then discharged the second
barrel." The tenant applied for their consent to a sublease to a
print finishing and packing firm and to an appropriate change
of use and consent was refused. The minutes of the various
council organs responsible for this decision were in some
considerable disarray but two reasons for the refusal emerged.
First, that the council considered that the trade or business
carried on would be in conflict with councils' interpretation of
good estate management, in that it would lead to an over-
intensification of the use of the site causing traffic congestion.
Second, that the proposal was contrary to the express wishes of
the inspector on the appeal. The second reason was clearly bad.
The trial judge however refused to grant the tenant declarations
that consent to sublet and change the use had been
unreasonably withheld because though, like the inspector, he
thought the anxieties relating to traffic congestion were ill-
conceived, he accepted that the council had *bona fide* reached
the opposite conclusion and, in view of the subjective terms of
the clause, he did not think that he could substitute his own
view of the matter for theirs. The tenant successfully appealed,
the Court of Appeal responding robustly to what Templeman
L.J. described as an "horrendous" lease which the Watford
Borough Council was using to bully the tenants at the expense
of the ratepayers. He pointed out that the user clause was in
two parts: "the first requires the council to be reasonable in
withholding consent for change of use; the second authorises
the council to be unreasonable in certain circumstances." As,
objectively, the refusal was unreasonable, the only way that the
council could maintain their objection was to bring it within
the second part—and that was construed narrowly. For the
purposes of clause (11)(ii) the council had to show that they

[69] At p. 272.

had considered *"the trade or business"* proposed to be carried on and found it to be in conflict with their own interpretation of good estate management. The ground applied where there was some objection to the *nature* of the business proposed and no objection had been raised to the nature of the proposed subtenant's business. The traffic intensification was never linked to the nature of the subtenant's business for the simple reason that it was not the nature of the business to which the council objected, it was the fact of subletting at all—to anyone.[70] The council could not therefore rely upon the second part of the user clause which allowed them to be unreasonable, they had to rely upon the first part which required them to be *reasonable* and in view of the inspectors' findings they certainly had not been. Templeman L.J. and Megaw L.J. gave an additional ground for their decision—the proffering of a reason that was manifestly bad. That bad reason—that the inspector was against the proposal—affected the mind of the council in arriving at its decision to refuse consent and that "being shown, the purported refusal of consent must be a bad refusal of consent."[71] It is clear from this case that the lease can specify that certain grounds are to be deemed reasonable and also that the landlord's discretion can be increased still further by drafting these grounds in subjective terms. Should the landlord seek to rely upon such a ground he must link the reason for his refusal very closely to it and if it requires him to form a subjective view, that view must be shown to have been reached *bona fide* and independently of erroneous impressions. While the landlord is under no duty to give his reasons[72] failure to do so may reverse the burden of proof[73] or make the court more ready to infer that the withholding had been unreasonable.[74]

Other fully qualified covenants   In the absence of sub-clauses defining the meaning of reasonableness, it is determined upon principles similar to those applicable to disposition and alteration covenants.[75] Thus consent cannot be refused in order to gain an uncovenanted advantage.[76] In *Anglia Building Society* v. *Sheffield City Council*[77] the council had granted a 20 year lease of business premises subject to fully qualified disposition and change of user covenants. The council had refused their consent to an assignment and change of use in favour of the Anglia Building Society. The refusal relating to the assignment had already been held unreasonable but the question of the reasonableness of the refusal of a change of user was left over to be decided in other proceedings. The relevant covenant provides as follows:

---

[70] See Sir Patrick Browne at p. 277, Templeman L.J. at p. 277, Megaw L.J. at p. 278; two previous applications for consent to sublet by the tenant had also been refused.
[71] Megaw L.J. at p. 278; see also Templeman L.J. at p. 277.
[72] Compare s.1(3)(*b*)(ii) Landlord and Tenant Act 1988.
[73] See *supra*, Chap. 4.
[74] See *Tollbench Ltd.* v. *Plymouth City Council* (1988) 56 P. & C.R. 194.
[75] See Chaps. 6 & 8.
[76] *Bromley Park Garden Estates Ltd.* v. *Moss* [1982] 1 W.L.R. 1019.
[77] (1983) 266 E.G. 311.

"Not at any time during the said term without the consent in writing of the Corporation to carry on . . . any trade or business . . . other than as a travel and employment bureau and theatre ticket agency . . . except that the use may be changed with the consent of the Corporation . . . such consent not to be unreasonably withheld."

The Corporation refused consent because, in the interests of good estate management, they wanted any assignment to be for the purposes of a retail shop. There was evidence that the presence of a retail shop would increase the rent which they could charge for other premises in the area and they argued that they had a duty to the ratepayers of Sheffield to maximise rents. The trial judge held that they had acted reasonably but, on appeal, the Court of Appeal found otherwise. Slade L.J. considered that two questions had to be addressed: what were the reasons which had in fact prompted the council to refuse their consent and did those reasons constitute reasonable grounds for refusing consent? Though others were urged at the trial, the true reason was found to be that the council wished to restrict the use of the premises to that of a retail shop. That however was not in the contemplation of the parties when the lease was made: the user restriction in the lease indicated that service use was what was then contemplated. The proposed use was a service use and there was no evidence to show that use as a building society would be any more detrimental to the council's interests than the use for which they had expressly let property. The fact that the council now realised that they may have made a mistake in letting the property for a service use in the first place did not now enable them to avail themselves of an application for a change of use in order to force a change to retail trade: that would be an attempt to secure "a collateral advantage for themselves, quite dissociated from the bargain made between the original parties."[78]

Payments to the landlord

Where the landlord asks for a fine, *i.e.* a sum demanded other than as compensation for the matters expressly referred to in section 19(3) of the Landlord and Tenant Act 1927, as a condition of granting his consent, it is thought that this amounts to an unreasonable refusal of consent. Thus the tenant would be entitled to change the use without consent and without payment of the sum demanded. The position where the landlord demands a sum in respect of the matters referred to in section 19(3), but the tenant considers that he is asking too much, is not clear. Here too it could be argued that asking for an excessive amount by way of compensation amounts to an unreasonable refusal of consent and therefore the tenant could change the use without consent and without paying *any* of the amount sought. Section 19(3) seems however to envisage a rather different outcome, namely, that the tenant should apply to the court to have a reasonable sum by way of compensation determined and that he should then pay that sum whereupon the landlord becomes bound to grant the consent.[79]

---

[78] *Per* Slade L.J. at p. 315.
[79] See Woodfall, *Landlord and Tenant*, Vol. 1, para. 1–1221; s.19(3) *infra*.

Statutory regulation of terms

Section 19(3) of the Landlord and Tenant Act 1927, which will be discussed here, implies into restrictions on user, in certain circumstances, a proviso against the payment of a fine. Section 610 of the Housing Act 1985 and section 84 of the Law of Property Act 1925 make provision for the discharge or modification of such restrictions and their substance has already been discussed in Chapter 8.

Section 19(3) Landlord and Tenant Act 1927

In all leases[80] whether made before or after the commencement of this Act containing a covenant condition or agreement[81] against alteration of the user of the demised premises, without licence or consent, such covenant conditions or agreement shall, if the alteration does not involve any structural alteration of the premises, be deemed, notwithstanding any express provision to the contrary, to be subject to a proviso that no fine or sum of money in the nature of a fine, whether by way of increase of rent or otherwise, shall be payable for or in respect of such licence or consent; but this proviso does not preclude the right of the landlord to require payment of a reasonable sum in respect of any damage to or diminution in the value of the premises or any neighbouring premises belonging to him and of any legal or other expenses incurred in connection with such licence or consent.

Where a dispute as to the reasonableness of any such sum has been determined by a court of competent jurisdiction, the landlord shall be bound to grant the licence or consent on payment of the sum so determined to be reasonable.

Application

This sub-section applies to restrictions on alteration of user "without licence or consent" and its effect is limited therefore to qualified and fully qualified covenants. In the case of an absolute covenant, the landlord can name his price for a licence to change user. Qualified and fully qualified covenants, on the other hand, are subject to the proviso that no fine etc. shall be payable. An increase in rent is expressed to be within the

"Fine"

definition of a fine and other types of demand have also been held to amount to a fine.[82] It is submitted that the tenant is entitled to treat as a fine any sum demanded by the landlord unless the demand is clearly linked to the compensatory payments referred to in the latter part of the subsection. On general principles of construction, the addition of the proviso

---

[80] See s.25 & Chap. 4 *supra*.
[81] See Chap. 1.
[82] *e.g.* a "tie" to a brewer, see *Gardner & Co. Ltd.* v. *Cone* [1928] Ch. 955; assignment by tenant of local authority compensation rights, *Comber* v. *Fleet Electronics* [1955] 1 W.L.R. 566.

Effect of landlord demanding a fine

Irrecoverable

Promise unenforceable

limits the generality of the covenant[83]: the tenant does not covenant that he will never alter the use without consent, but that he will not alter the use without consent where the landlord refrains from demanding a fine. If the landlord does demand[84] a fine, then the tenant, without breach of covenant, can change the use without paying and without consent.[85] Where a fine is demanded and paid, it cannot be recovered by the tenant subsequently[86]; however where a fine is merely agreed to be paid and the landlord grants his licence on that basis, the promise of the fine is unenforceable. In *Comber* v. *Fleet Electronics*[87] the tenant needed three licences: to assign to **X** who would sublet to **Y** who would change the user. At that time the local authority was, by way of compulsory purchase, desirous of slicing several feet off the front of the demised premises and the tenant agreed with the landlord that, as the price of the licences, he would assign his share of the compensation to the landlord. The landlord then granted the licences but when the compensation became payable the tenant refused to assign his rights. Vaisey J. held that though the landlord could have kept the amount had it been paid, he could not enforce the undertaking though the merits of the case were all on his side.

Evasion

The basic principle underlying section 19(3) is that licences for change of use should, if granted, be gratuitous and that this should be so whatever attempts the parties may have made to provide otherwise.[88] It has been strongly criticised as a provision "which interferes fundamentally with the ordinary rights of the subjects of Her Majesty to make contracts in this respect according to their wishes and inclinations."[89] Where the covenant is merely qualified however it may be possible for the landlord to obtain a financial benefit indirectly: he can exercise his right to refuse consent out of hand and thereafter make it clear to the tenant that he is prepared to grant a new lease allowing the change of user but only upon the payment of a premium or at a higher rent or on more onerous terms.[90] The same device could in theory apply in the case of a fully qualified covenant, but the landlord would first have to find a reasonable ground for refusing his consent and he would also have to convince the court that the ground relied on was the true ground rather than a determination to exact a fine.

---

[83] See *Treloar* v. *Bigge* (1874) L.R. 9 Ex 151, 156 *per* Amphlett B.
[84] The fact that the payment of a fine was canvassed in negotiations will not amount to such a demand where consent was ultimately refused outright: see *Gardner & Co. Ltd.* v. *Cone* [1928] Ch. 955.
[85] Compare *West* v. *Gwynne* [1911] 2 Ch. 1 which relates to the similarly worded s.144 of the Law of Property Act 1925.
[86] *Comber* v. *Fleet Electronics ibid.*; *Memvale Securities Ltd.'s Application* [1975] 233 E.G. 689, 718.
[87] *Ibid.*
[88] In this respect it goes beyond s.144 of the Law of Property Act which implies a proviso against fines into disposition covenants but only if the lease contains no provision to the contrary.
[89] *Comber* v. *Fleet Electronics ibid. per* Vaisey J. at p. 570.
[90] Law Com. No. 141 para. 3.26.

Exclusions

The subsection does not apply to agricultural or mining leases,[91] nor does it apply where the change of use involves structural alterations. The latter limitation has been described as "puzzling."[92] If the change of use involves structural alterations, the proviso against fines is not to be implied. In such circumstances, in the case of a qualified covenant, the landlord is free to demand a fine. In the case of a fully qualified covenant the landlord can demand one where it is reasonable for him to do so. The landlord may also be able to demand a fine in respect of a licence to effect the alterations; this would be so where there was an absolute covenant against making alterations or possibly[93] where there was a fully qualified[94] covenant and the fine could be shown to be reasonable.

Permissible monetary demands

Where the landlord requires payment in respect of diminution in the value of his property or his legal or other expenses, this does not offend the proviso and, it is submitted, the tenant is not entitled, even if he regards the sum demanded as exorbitant, to change the use without consent. His rights in this situation are set out in the last paragraph of the subsection: he must apply to the court to have a reasonable sum determined and on payment of that sum the landlord is bound to grant the licence. It would appear that only the High Court has jurisdiction to make a declaration, unaccompanied by other relief, as to the reasonableness of the sum claimed.[95] Section 53 of the Landlord and Tenant Act 1954 which gives the county court concurrent jurisdiction to make declarations relating to the reasonableness of a *withholding of consent*, unaccompanied by other relief, does not make any reference to declarations under section 19(3) as to the reasonableness of *a sum claimed by way of compensation*. It has been suggested[96] that this deficiency in the jurisdiction of the county court has been cured by section 14 of the Administration of Justice Act 1977 but acceptance of this view depends upon whether one can construe a declaration as to the reasonableness of the sum required as being a declaration "in respect of, or relating to, any land, or the possession, occupation, use or enjoyment of any land."[97] Such a construction seems very strained.[98]

Other regulation

Restraint of trade

In *Esso Petroleum Ltd.* v. *Harpers Garage (Stourport) Ltd.*[99] it was held that the doctrine of restraint of trade, which requires

---

[91] s.19(4).
[92] Law Com. No. 141 para. 6.16.
[93] See *supra*, Chap. 8, pp. 169–172.
[94] Note the effect of s.19(2) is to make qualified covenants fully qualified.
[95] See Hill and Redman's *Law of Landlord and Tenant*, (18th Ed.), Vol. 1, para. 1284 n. 13.
[96] See Woodfall, *Landlord and Tenant*, Vol. 1, para. 1–1221 n. 86a.
[97] See s.51A(1) of the County Courts Act 1959 as amended by s.14 of the Administration of Justice Act 1977.
[98] In Law Com. 141, para. 8.32, the limited terms of s.53 were noted and it was recommended that the county court be given jurisdiction in relation to declarations as to the reasonableness of compensation.
[99] 1968 A.C. 269.

the restraint to be reasonable as between the parties and not injurious to the public interest, *can* apply to a covenant in a lease which restricts the trading use of the demised premises. It will only do so, however, where the tenant gives up some freedom which he previously enjoyed, as in the case of a sale and lease-back or lease and lease-back arrangement where "you are subjecting yourself to restrictions as to the use to be made of your own land so that you can no longer do what you were doing before."[1] Where this is so, the doctrine cannot be evaded by ensuring that the lease-back is not to the original corporate owner but to its shareholders.[2] Normally though, the doctrine does not apply because the tenant had no previous right to trade on the land at all. In the words of Lord Morris of Borth-Y-Gest

> "If one who seeks to take a lease of land knows that the only lease which is available to him is a lease with a restriction, then he must either take what is offered ... or he must seek a lease elsewhere. No feature of public policy requires that if he freely contracted he should be excused from honouring his contract. In no rational sense could it be said that if he took a lease with a restriction as to trading he was entering into a contract that interfered with the free exercise of his trade or business or with his 'individual liberty of action in trading.' His freedom to pursue his trade or earn his living is not impaired merely because there is some land belonging to someone else upon which he cannot enter for the purposes of his trade or business. In such a situation (that is of voluntarily taking a lease of land with a restrictive covenant) it would not seem sensible to regard the doctrine of restraint of trade as having application."[3]

Further, for similar reasons, most leases will not be regarded as restrictive agreements requiring registration under the Restrictive Trade Practices Act 1976.[4]

---

[1] *Per* Lord Hodson at p. 317.
[2] See *Alec Lobb Garages Ltd.* v. *Total Oil (Great Britain) Ltd.* [1985] 1 W.L.R. 173 where the court lifted the corporate veil.
[3] At p. 309.
[4] See *Ravenseft Properties Ltd.* v. *Director General of Fair Trading* [1977] 1 All E.R. 47.

PART 4

10 CONTRACTS AND CONSENTS

Usual covenants

The question of whether a particular covenant is usual may arise where there is an open contract to grant a lease[1] and there is a dispute as to its contents or where there is a contract to assign an existing lease and the assignee alleges that an unusual covenant has not been disclosed. Usual covenants are incorporated into an open contract for the grant of a lease (subject to express provision to the contrary) and they do not have to be disclosed by a vendor prior to a contract to assign a lease. The test of what is usual is the same in whichever manner the question arises.[2]

Characteristics of usual covenants

Certain covenants are always treated as usual by the court: covenants by the lessee to pay the rent, to pay taxes except where expressly made payable by the lessor, to keep and deliver up the premises in repair and to allow the landlord to enter and view the state of repair and a covenant by the lessor for quiet enjoyment.[3] A proviso for re-entry on non-payment of rent has also been deemed usual.[4] It is submitted that the characterisation of these covenants as usual depends both on the frequency with which they are encountered and the fact that they are "essential to perfect the contract between the parties," in the sense that the grant of the property would not be effectual without them.[5] Covenants other than those mentioned above may, in particular categories of lease, be properly characterised as "usual." Thus in *Hodgkinson* v. *Crowe*.[6] Sir James Bacon V.C. considered that in mining leases the court will imply customary covenants and provisions *applicable to mining operations*, for example as to the manner and time of working and protection against influx of water. Such covenants, "mining clauses," as he calls them, are necessary to give business efficacy to that particular type of agreement; but, he opined, a covenant restricting assignment is not a mining clause and is no more necessary to a mining lease than it is to any other sort of lease. It could not therefore be regarded as usual however often, in fact, parties to mining leases agreed to insert it.[7] Another similar situation arises in

[1] Or a contract which provides that the lease is to contain "usual and proper" covenants: *Blakesley* v. *Whieldon* (1841) Hare 176; *Church* v. *Browne* (1808) 15 Ves. 258, 272.
[2] *Chester* v. *Buckingham Travel Ltd.* [1981] 1 ALL E.R. 386, 390.
[3] *Hampshire* v. *Wickens* (1978) 7 Ch.D. 258, 264.
[4] See *Hodgkinson* v. *Crowe* (1875) 10 Ch.App. 622, 626; *per* Sir W. M. James, L.J.
[5] See Sir James Wigram in *Blakesley* v. *Whieldon* (1841) 1 Hare 176, 180.
[6] (1875) L.R. 19 Eq. 591.
[7] *Ibid.*

relation to covenants not to cause a nuisance or annoyance to
adjoining property owners. Where the property is comprised in
a building estate or in a building in multiple occupation over
which the landlord is seeking to maintain overall control in the
interests of all, such a covenant is a necessary; in other
circumstances where the landlord seeks to impose it it will not
be usual.[8] A number of the early cases take a rather different,
but nonetheless strict, view as to the recognition of covenants
as "usual." Thus in *Henderson* v. *Hay*[9] Lord Thurlow
considered that the fact that a covenant was usual in the
colloquial sense did not suffice to justify its implication into the
lease: the covenant had also to be "incidental to the lease."
This seems to mean, relying upon Lord Eldon's interpretation
in *Church* v. *Browne*[10] that the covenant must be seen to flow
out of the incidents of the estate granted, rather than to
contradict them. As alienability is an incident of a lease[11] a
provision curtailing alienation could not qualify as a usual
covenant.[12] Lord Eldon was insistent that "nothing which flows
out of [the lease], as an incident, is to be done away with by
loose expressions to be construed by facts more loose."[13] It was
safer to have a rule that incidents can only be restricted by
express provision

> "than for Courts of Equity to hold, that contracting parties
> shall insert, not restraints expressed by the contract, or
> implied by Law, but such, more or less in number, as
> individual conveyancers shall from day to day prescribe, as
> proper to be imposed upon the lessee and that all those
> restraints so imposed from time to time are to be
> introduced as the aggregate of the agreement."[14]

It is apparent from the foregoing cases that there has, in
the past, been a desire to put some brake upon the
development of usual covenants by not characterising them
exclusively by reference to the frequency with which they are
A Change of used. That new usual covenants can arise has long been
Approach admitted. Jessel M.R. in *Hampshire* v. *Wickens*[15] took the view
that

> "usual covenants may vary in different generations. The
> law declares what are usual covenants according to the
> then knowledge of mankind ... Now, what is well-known
> at one time may not be well-known at another, so you
> cannot say usual covenants never change."[16]

However such new usual covenants should, it is submitted
and indeed as some of the cases referred to above show, be
capable of justification by evidence additional to that relating to

---

[8] See *Flexman* v. *Corbett* [1930] 1 Ch. 672, 680.
[9] (1792) 3 Bro. C.C. 632.
[10] (1808) 15 Ves. 258, 264.
[11] See Chap. 1.
[12] At p. 270.
[13] At p. 269.
[14] *Ibid.*
[15] (1878) 7 Ch.D. 555.
[16] p. 561.

the frequency of their imposition. What parties commonly agree to, is not the same as what should be foisted on them in the absence of evidence that they have agreed[17]: the latter situation merits a more cautious approach. It should also be remembered that evidence of frequency is gleaned from taking the opinion of the conveyancers called by either side and by a perusal of the precedent books. Thus, as is pertinently pointed out in Woodfall on *Landlord and Tenant*[18] different evidence may be given in different cases giving rise to the risk of inconsistent decisions. It may also be remarked that precedent books often present a basic clause with a number of possible variations in square brackets: is the clause to be considered usual in all its possible variations? Furthermore, in relation to types of lease where there is inequality of bargaining power, adopting as usual covenants those which are imposed in the majority of cases,[19] becomes progressively more unfair. It is with such considerations in mind, that one may approach the cases of *Flexman* v. *Corbett* and *Chester* v. *Buckingham Travel Ltd.*[20]

In the former case, Maugham J. indicated that he thought it "proper to take the evidence of conveyancers and others familiar with the practice in reference to leases and also ... to examine books of precedent."[21] He went on to say, in effect, that such evidence should be made "case specific" by relating it "to the nature of the property and to the place where it is situated and to the purposes for which the premises are to be used.[22] If "it is established that (to put a strong case) in nine cases out of ten the covenant would be found in a lease of premises of that nature, for that purpose and in that district, I think the court is bound to hold the covenant usual." This is the flexible *Flexman* approach: an approach free from the restraints imported by notions of business efficacy and the "incidents inherent" in leasehold property. It was in this case that Maugham J. considered the status of a proviso for re-entry for breach of *any* covenant in the lease.[23] He in fact followed authority, and held that it was not, but he did comment that the question may need to be reconsidered in the future.[24] His general approach, and that opinion, form the basis for the decision of Foster J., in *Chester* v. *Buckingham*,[25] that what constitutes a usual covenant is a question of present fact: does the covenant occur in ordinary use? Business efficacy and related notions were irrelevant.[26] Thus, as it was rare, in 1971

---

[17] It always remains open to the court, on the basis of substantial evidence of intention, to find that particular covenants, though not expressed, were intended to be implied into the agreement.

[18] Para. 1.0422.

[19] *Flexman* v. *Corbett ibid.* at p. 679.

[20] [1981] 1 All E.R. 386; (1981) 97 L.Q.R. 385 (Woodman); (1981) 131 N.L.J. 545 (Wilkinson).

[21] At p. 678.

[22] *Ibid.*

[23] As opposed to simply non-payment of rent which had long been held usual. See *supra.*

[24] At p. 680.

[25] *Ibid.*

[26] At p. 390.

when the agreement was made, to find a right of re-entry which was limited to non-payment of rent and every precedent consulted extended the right to breaches of covenant generally, the wider form of right was now considered to be usual.[27] He also considered the status of covenants restricting alienation, user and alterations. These will be considered more specifically below. It is submitted that the *Flexman* approach is ill-considered and should not be followed, though it seems to have been widely accepted by text book writers. However, Woodfall,[28] does warn the reader that in view of the danger of inconsistent decisions the court will be slow to extend the category of usual covenants much further than Foster J. was prepared to go. Should he have gone so far?

Covenants against assignment

Early cases indicate that a covenant against assignment is not usual[29] notwithstanding the frequency of its imposition.[30] The right of assignment is an incident of the estate granted to the tenant and it cannot be "shut out" unless there is an express contract.[31] Were a covenant against assignment to be held usual, other restraints, on underletting and parting with possession may be similarly classified and there is no justification for confering such a benefit upon a party who has foreborne expressly to insert such restrictions.[32] It has been held that it makes no difference whether or not the agreement contained a reference to the tenant's "assigns": the absence of such reference did not warrant the introduction of a covenant against alienation.[33]

In *Hampshire* v. *Wickens*[34] a more open view was taken as to status of a covenant against assignment. Jessel M.R. was prepared to entertain the suggestion that what constitutes a usual covenant may change with the times. He did not appear to rule out the possibility that a covenant against assignment could be usual, but found after consulting text books and books of precedent that it had not in fact become so. This more open attitude influenced Foster J. in *Chester* v. *Buckingham Travel*. He paid regard to the fact that the lease was of business premises for approximately 14 years extendable by statute. He found that covenants regulating alienation, appearing in the precedent books, differed considerably and that the covenant in this particular case could not be said to be usual.[35] It restricted assignment, underletting and parting with possession or occupation without the consent of both the landlord and the superior landlord, in the case of the landlord,

---

[27] At p. 394.
[28] *Landlord and Tenant*, Vol. 1, para. 1.0422.
[29] *De Soysa* v. *De Pless Pol* [1912] A.C. 194 P.C.; no more is a covenant to register assignments with the lessor: *Brookes* v. *Drysdale* (1877) 3 C.P.D. 52.
[30] *Henderson* v. *Hay supra*.
[31] *Church* v. *Brown supra* at pp. 264, 270; *Hodgkinson* v. *Crowe supra*.
[32] *Church* v. *Brown ibid*.
[33] *Buckland* v. *Papillon* (1866) L.R. 1 Eq. 477.
[34] [1878] 7 Ch.D. 555.
[35] At p. 393.

such consent not to be unreasonably withheld. Foster J. did not appear to recognise any difficulty of principle in admitting alienation covenants as usual: it simply had to be established that such a covenant as the one sought to be included was in common use in the circumstances in question. It is submitted that this is a regrettable trend and ought to be reversed.

While a covenant against alienation may not qualify as a usual covenant, it is always possible to imply it if there is evidence that the parties intended it. Thus in *Bill* v. *Barchard*[36] a landlord cancelled a farming lease in order to grant another one, more beneficial to the tenant: he was a very good tenant and the landlord wished to encourage "his general industry." The first lease contained a covenant against assignment, etc. The landlord died before the new lease was granted and a dispute arose between the tenant and his personal representatives as to its terms, the tenant arguing that not only was he to have the benefit of a lower rent but also he was to be free to underlet. Sir John Romilly opined that where there had been previous relations between the parties, the agreement must be construed in the light of those relations though "such construction may differ from what it would have been, if the parties had had no dealing previous."[37] He held that as the new lease was to reward and encourage the tenant personally it would wrong to construe the contract as conferring upon him a power of underletting.[38]

Covenants restricting alterations

In *Chester* v. *Buckingham Travel Ltd.*[39] it was sought to include a qualified covenant against alterations. There was no fully qualifying phrase that consent was not to be unreasonably withheld but this could be implied in any event under section 19(2) of the Landlord and Tenant Act 1927.[40] Foster J. was referred to a precedent of a lease of a garage,[41] the type of premises involved in this particular case, which contained a similar clause, and also an affidavit, filed on behalf of the landlord, sworn by a solicitor specialising in commercial leases to the effect that it was reasonable and usual for a landlord, in the case of a commercial lease where there were to be full repairing covenants by the tenants and the building was used by persons other than the tenants, for the landlord to retain some control by way of a prohibition, absolute or qualified, on alterations. On this basis, and also taking into account that the lease was to be a short one, he found that the covenant was usual as long as the fully qualifying phrase was expressly included. Had the covenant not been found usual the tenant would have been free to alter the premises, subject to the law of waste.[42] For the

---

[36] (1852) 16 Beav. 8.
[37] At p. 10.
[38] At p. 11.
[39] *Ibid.*
[40] So long as the alteration was an "improvement": see Chap. 8.
[41] *Encyclopedia of Forms and Precedents* (4th Ed.), vol 12, form 10:2, cl. 2(7) p. 1006.
[42] See *supra* Chap. 8.

reasons given earlier, it is submitted that the courts should not be facilitating the expansion of the category of usual covenants in this way.

Covenants restricting user

Covenants restricting trade, in absolute form, have been held not to be usual in a number of circumstances. In *Van* v. *Corpe*[43] a covenant restricting all trade was held not to be usual in an agreement for the lease of a house. In *Wilbraham* v. *Livesey*[44] it was held that a covenant against carrying on obnoxious trades was not usual in an agreement for a business lease in a trading locality. In *Chester* v. *Buckingham Travel Ltd.*[45] the landlord sought to include a covenant, in absolute form, limiting use to a garage or workshops in connection with the tenant's business. After listening to expert evidence on behalf of the landlord[46] and noting that the clause could be found, in qualified form, in the precedent books,[47] Foster J. held that a qualified covenant would be usual here, so long as the further words "such consent not to be unreasonably withheld" were added. In the case of user covenants this is an addition of substance. The fully qualifying phrase would not have been implied under the Landlord and Tenant Act 1927. He appears to have added it solely on his own initiative.

   Covenants not to cause a nuisance or annoyance have in the past been held to be usual only in limited circumstances.[48] The circumstances in *Chester* v. *Buckingham Travel Ltd.* may conceivably fall within that limited range as the premises were apparently enjoyed by other users but the reasons Foster J. gave were not connected with this—rather they were based again on the expert evidence submitted by the landlord. He did baulk at the addition of the word "discomfort" though having allowed in a word as vague as "annoyance" this may have been rather pointless.

Lack of consent

Contract not Conditional

Under the general law, the fact that a contract to assign a lease is subject to the landlord's consent being obtained, will not generally[49] be construed as making the contract conditional on consent; obtaining consent is not a condition precedent to the formation of a contract, and so failure to obtain consent does not discharge the vendor from contractual liability. The necessity for consent does not affect the *existence* of the contract

---

[43] (1834) 3 My. & K. 269.
[44] (1854) 18 Beav. 206, 210.
[45] *Supra.*
[46] See *supra* Covenants against Alterations.
[47] *Encyclopedia of Forms and Precedents* (4th Ed.) vol. 12, form 10:2, cl. 2(15), p. 1007 & form 9:1 cl. 3(7) p. 883.
[48] See *supra* "Characteristics of Usual Covenants."
[49] The contract could expressly provide that it is to be conditional: in which case the vendor would be discharged by a failure to obtain consent assuming that he has used his best endeavours.

but "merely the machinery for carrying out the contract."[50] Thus, the contract subsists and the vendor's failure to get consent may put him in breach.

Vendor's liability for breach of contract

Whether the Vendor is, in fact, liable in breach of contract depends upon whether the purchaser has given all due co-operation and whether or not the consent was, in law, required.

Duty of Purchaser   In relation to the former, the purchaser is under implied obligation to supply the landlord with references etc. to enable the landlord to discharge his obligations and a failure to do this may shift the breach onto the purchaser. The purchaser's obligation is, however, a limited one. In *Butler* v. *Croft*[51] it was argued that the purchaser was in breach of duty in failing to provide a guarantor but Templeman J. dismissed this suggestion saying "[o]f course he must do his best not to frustrate the contract, or go around and find people who will say bad things about him; he must do his best to obtain the best references he can obtain, and he must send them in, but further than that, that there is an obligation upon anyone to get a guarantee, that seems to me to be going far beyond the duty of any purchaser of leasehold property."[52]

Consent was   In relation to the latter, if the requirement for consent
Required   originated in an absolute covenant, a consent will be required in all circumstances to discharge the vendor's obligation to convey "good title"; on the other hand, where it originated in a fully qualified covenant, consent will only be required to discharge the vendor's obligation as to title where the landlord could reasonably have withheld it.[53]

Consent required   Where consent is required, it is regarded, somewhat anomalously, as simply a defect of conveyance and consequently the purchaser cannot repudiate the contract on account of its absence until the time for completion has arrived.
Time allowed   In *Ellis* v. *Rogers*[54] the purchaser claimed the right to repudiate the contract earlier but both Cotton L.J.[55] and Fry L.J.[56] expressed the view that there was no such right.[57] In this case

> "the vendor up to the time when the purchaser refused to go on, had been ready and willing to do all that was required to be done by him . . . and the proceedings had

---

[50] *Per* Sachs L.J. in *Property and Bloodstock Ltd.* v. *Emerton* [1967] 3 All E.R. 321, 330.

[51] [1974] 27 P. & C.R. 1.

[52] At p. 9; compare *Sheggia* v. *Gradwell* [1963] 3 All E.R. 114, 121; and see *infra* where the purchaser's duty is discussed further in relation to the Conditions of Sale.

[53] For the position where the landlord could not reasonably withhold it, see *infra*; for the effect of a fully qualified covenant see *supra* Chap. 4.

[54] (1885) 29 Ch.D. 661.

[55] At p. 671.

[56] At p. 672.

[57] This was unnecessary for the decision because the purchaser was allowed to repudiate immediately due to the existence of unextinguished restrictive covenants.

not reached the stage when it was necessary for [the purchaser] to be furnished with a licence to assign."[58] "Without giving a concluded opinion on the point, I may state my present view to be that this defence would not avail [the purchaser] the time not having arrived when a licence was wanted, as the title had not been accepted nor a conveyance tendered."[59]

The well accepted view is therefore that the vendor has until completion to get the licence and that he only goes into breach of contract if upon completion he has not obtained it. Two comments can perhaps be made. First, in some circumstances, it would seem quite wrong to make the purchaser wait, as, indeed, was recognised in *Smith* v. *Butler*[60] where the consent of a mortgagee was required to the assignment of a lease of a public house. The mortgagee, at a meeting with the assignor and the assignee, sought to impose a condition upon his consent which the assignee found unacceptable. The assignee treated this as a final refusal of consent and repudiated the contract—in advance of completion. It was held, here, that he could not recover his deposit, Romer L.J. referring to the general rule that the vendor "has until the time fixed for completion, or if no time is fixed for completion, then a reasonable time, in which to procure the assent."[61] However he went on to concede that the purchaser was not always bound to wait and gave a list, not intended to be exhaustive, of circumstances in which the purchaser could repudiate in advance of completion, namely, if he could show:

(1)   that the condition could not practically be fulfilled by the date fixed, or,
(2)   that the vendor had admitted that the condition was incapable of fulfilment, or,
(3)   that there was an express or implied agreement between the vendor and the purchaser that a particular refusal be treated as final, or,
(4)   that a refusal had been so treated by the vendor as to justify the purchaser in regarding the matter as at an end.[62]

Second, it is a pity that it ever came to be accepted that the lack of consent was a mere defect of conveyance—a defect which, by definition, the vendor can *as of right* correct. It is clearly no such thing. He is completely at the mercy of the landlord where the covenant is absolute; if it is fully qualified, he is at the mercy of the landlord where the latter could reasonably refuse his consent, or of the court where consent could not reasonably be withheld because he will need a declaration (See *infra*). It really would be preferable if the need for a licence were reclassified as a defect of title. This would

[58] Cotton L.J. *ibid.*
[59] Fry L.J. *ibid.*
[60] [1900] 1 Q.B. 694.
[61] At p. 699.
[62] *Ibid.*

have the consequence of bringing it within the vendor's pre-contractual duty of disclosure and in the event of non-disclosure the purchaser would have, if he so wished, the right of immediate repudiation once the requirement came to light.

Specific performance

If once the time for completion arrives, no consent is forthcoming, there is no question of either party obtaining an order for specific performance. The vendor clearly cannot force the purchaser to complete in circumstances where the assignment would constitute a breach of the disposition covenant in the lease, leading potentially to forfeiture. Nor may the purchaser waive the defect and force the vendor to complete because, Equity will not order specific performance of a contract if it would result in a breach of a pre-existing contract. In *Warmington* v. *Miller*[63] a tenant contracted to grant an underlease in the face of an absolute covenant against underletting. The underlessee unsuccessfully sought specific performance of the agreement. Stamp J. indicated that to make such an order would necessitate a breach by the tenant of his contract with a third party[64] which "would quite pass by the object of the court in exercising the jurisdiction which is to do more complete justice".[65] If despite the lack of a required licence, both parties are willing to complete they may of course do so and there is no doubt the assignment will be effective to vest the lease in the assignee but subject to possible forfeiture.[66] Where both parties agree to proceed, it may even be possible to re-cast the transaction in a form which would involve no breach of the disposition covenant and so no risk of forfeiture. This will depend upon the scope of the disposition covenant.[67] Thus a prohibition on assignment is construed as referring to a legal assignment, and would not therefore encompass a declaration of trust by the vendor in favour of the purchaser.[68]

Damages

Where, as is frequently the case, the purchaser cannot be persuaded to proceed, then he would be entitled to damages for breach of contract. In the past, unless the case was exceptional[69] he would only be able to recover for his wasted expenditure because of the Rule in *Bain* v. *Fothergill*.[70] After much criticism,[71] the Rule has now been abolished by the Law of Property (Miscellaneous Provisions) Act 1989 section 3,[72]

---

[63] [1973] 2 All E.R. 372 C.A.

[64] At p. 377.

[65] At p. 377, quoting Fry on Specific Performance 6th Ed. 1921, p. 194.

[66] *Old Grovebury Farm Ltd.* v. *W. Seymour Plant Sales & Hire Ltd.* (*No. 2*) [1979] 1 W.L.R. 1397 *per* Lord Russell at pp. 1399, 1400 and see *supra* Chap. 1.

[67] See *supra* Chap. 2.

[68] See *Gentle* v. *Faulkner* [1900] 2 Q.B. 267; *Pincott* v. *Moorstons Ltd.* [1937] All E.R. 513 C.A.

[69] See for example: *Lock* v. *Furze* [1866] L.R. 1 C.P. 441; *Wroth* v. *Tyler* [1973] 1 All E.R. 891; *Day* v. *Singleton* (1899) 2 Ch. 320; *Sharneyford Supplies Ltd.* v. *Edge* [1987] 1 All E.R. 588; *Goffin* v. *Houlder* (1920) 90 L.J. Ch. 488.

[70] (1874) L.R. 7 H.L. 158; for the purposes of the Rule lack of the landlord's consent was regarded as a defect of title.

[71] See for example Law. Com. No. 166 (1978).

[72] Which applies in relation to contracts made after September 27, 1989.

which has the effect of restoring to the purchaser the right to elect between, on the one hand, damages for wasted expenditure[73] and, on the other hand, damages for loss of bargain and/or, loss of profit. Loss of profit will only be recoverable if it was within the contemplation of the parties, as a serious possibility, that the purchaser would carry on business there.[74] As a result of this change the vendor is at risk of paying heavier damages than previously. It is of course possible for the contract to incorporate an express term limiting the vendors liability in respect of defects of title[75] and duplicating the situation under the previous law. It is also possible that a failure to do this will render the purchaser's solicitor liable to his client in Negligence. The need for a licence will be apparent pre-contract and thus

> "[S]hould the legal adviser have failed to exercise proper care in drafting the contract, by not discovering and dealing with discoverable defects of title, it seems he would be liable to his client for the loss the latter has suffered in having to pay damages to the purchaser."[76]

Waiver by purchaser Where the vendor is in breach of contract in failing to secure a required consent, the purchaser's consequent right to repudiate the contract may, on general principles, be lost by waiver. It was held in *Butler* v. *Croft*[77] that the fact of the purchaser going into possession, prior to completion, having paid the whole purchase price did not, in the circumstances of that case, constitute a waiver because.

> "both parties proceeded upon the footing that the landlord's consent could, and would, be obtained and the mere act of going in and paying money, if that was all that had happened, would not be sufficient . . . to get rid of the requirement for the landlord's consent or the rights of the plaintiff if it were not obtained."[78]

Consent not required It may be that in strict law, a consent is not required in the particular circumstances. This would be so in the case of a fully qualified covenant where the landlord has unreasonably withheld his consent.[79] In such a case,

---

[73] Under the following heads: (1) Legal costs of approving and executing the contract; (2) Cost of performing acts required to be done by the contract notwithstanding that they are done in anticipation of the contract; (3) any other loss which ought to be regarded as having been in the contemplation of the parties, see *Lloyd* v. *Stanbury* [1971] 1 W.L.R. 535.

[74] Compare *Diamond* v. *Campbell-Jones* [1961] Ch. 22 and *Cottrill* v. *Steyning & Littlehampton Building Society* [1966] 1 W.L.R. 753.

[75] See Law Com. No. 166, 3, 25 where it is pointed out that the Unfair Contract Terms Act 1977 does not apply to contracts for the sale of land: see para. 1(b) of Schedule 1.

[76] *Ibid.* para. 3.17.

[77] (1974) 27 P. & C.R. 1.

[78] At p. 8.

[79] See *supra* Chap. 6.

Specific
Performance

technically the vendor will have complied with his duty in
relation to title and superficially therefore completion should
take place. However because of the uncertainty which
enshrouds the issue of reasonableness, Equity will not in fact
grant specific performance *against the purchaser* "if there is a
reasonably decent probability of litigation"[80] which there easily
could be, because even if the lessor's objection was
unreasonable, he may have others which he is not estopped
from raising and the court should only force the title upon the
purchaser if satisfied that any action by the landlord after
completion would certainly be unsuccessful.[81] The best way of
satisfying the court as to this is for the vendor to seek and
obtain a declaration that consent has been unreasonably
withheld[82] whereupon specific performance can be granted. It
is also clear that Equity will not grant specific performance
against the vendor unless, that is, the purchaser can show that
the grounds for refusal offered by the landlord were "so
unreasonable that the [vendor] might clearly assign . . . without
consent."[83] A declaration of unreasonableness would obviously
be helpful in these circumstances, but it is not clear that a
purchaser can bring an action for such a declaration as he does
not yet enjoy the status of a tenant.[84] Where both parties are
content to complete, any assignment will be effective to vest
the lease in the purchaser subject of course to the risk of
forfeiture, which in these circumstances should be slight. If the
purchaser is subsequently menaced by the landlord, he is then
entitled to bring an action for a declaration and there appears
to be no necessity to join the assignor. In *Theodorou* v. *Bloom*[85]
Ungoed Thomas J. held that the lease was properly vested in
the purchaser and that he was entitled to have a dispute
between himself and the landlord resolved. The dispute was
resolved in the purchaser's favour[86] and a declaration was
granted that the assignment to the assignee was "not
invalidated by reason of it having been made without the
consent of the landlord." This form of declaration is obviously
unsatisfactory in view of the fact that, whether or not there was
consent, the assignment would have been *valid*[87]; more
appropriate would have been something which made it clear
that the assignment gave rise to no grounds for forfeiture.
Where the assignor is not a party to the proceedings, the
declaration is not conclusive between him and the landlord and
should not refer to him.[88] Thus, theoretically, there is a
possibility of proceedings against the assignor by the landlord

---

[80] *Per* Alderson B. in *Cattell* v. *Corral* (1840) 4 Y. & C. 228, 237.

[81] Byrne J. in *Re Marshall & Salt's Contract* [1900] 2 Ch. 202, 205.

[82] See *infra* Chap. 11.

[83] *Per* Maugham J. in *Curtis Moffat Ltd.* v. *Wheeler* [1929] 2 Ch. 224, 236.
This was a case where burden upon the landlord to consent was greater than
is usual, the covenant being in *Moat* v. *Martin* form: see Chap. 4.

[84] See s.53 of the Landlord and Tenant Act 1953 as amended by County
Courts Act 1984, Sched. 2 Pt. V.

[85] [1964] 3 All E.R. 399.

[86] The covenant in this case was in *Moat* v. *Martin* form; see *supra* Chap. 4.

[87] See *supra Old Grovebury Farm Ltd.* v. *Seymour Plant Sales & Hire Ltd. (No.
2)* and Chap. 2.

[88] *Supra Theodorou* at p. 400.

for damages for breach of covenant, but as such an action could not affect the title of the assignee, it was considered an insufficient reason for requiring the assignor to be made a party to the proceedings.[89]

As, in the circumstances under discussion, the vendor is not in breach of any obligation under the contract, it is hard to see how he could be liable in damages.

Damages

Conditions of Sale

Shortcomings of the general law

The position under the general law as outlined above is tolerably clear; it is, however, in a number of respects, unsatisfactory. Where consent is lacking the position of the parties depends upon whether the consent was, as a matter of law, required, which in turn, in the case of the ubiquitous fully qualified covenant, depends upon whether the landlord has unreasonably withheld his consent—a matter which even after Balcombe J.'s helpful summary in *International Drilling Fluids Ltd.* v. *Louisville Investments*[90] often cannot be resolved without litigation. Thus there is often no ready answer to the question of whether the purchaser is entitled to damages for breach of contract or not, or whether the vendor is in a position to insist upon performance. There may also be considerable difficulty in determining the point in time when the vendor is entitled or permitted to abandon his endeavours to obtain the consent. As time is not usually of the essence,[91] the completion date, is not a very reliable guide, indicating merely that completion should take place within a reasonable time of the specified date.[92] Where no completion date is specified the purchaser can rescind if there has been unreasonable delay.[93] Bearing in mind these difficulties, it is clear that any attempt to regulate the open contract position must ensure a crisp deadline by which consent has to be obtained and render it unnecessary to decide, in order to determine the parties rights, whether consent has been unreasonably withheld. Both the *National Conditions of Sale*, 20th Edition, (1981), Condition 11(5), and the Law Society's *Conditions of Sale* (1984 Revision) Condition 8(4) attempt to improve upon the open contract situation.[94] It is generally accepted that the Law Society condition has been the more successful.

---

[89] *Ibid.*
[90] [1986] 1 All E.R. 321, 325; see Chap. 6 and Appendix 3.
[91] *Stickney* v. *Keeble* [1915] A.C. 386; s.41 of the Law of Property Act 1925; Equity infers an intention that time is to be of the essence in certain circumstances including the sale of wasting assets; a lease close to its term date would come within this category (*Hudson* v. *Temple* (1860) 30 L.J. Ch. 251) but it is not clear how close the term date must be before the equitable inference will arise; probably close enough for delay to affect the value of the term.
[92] *Stickney* v. *Keeble ibid.*; Completion Notices are discussed *infra.*
[93] *Inns* v. *D. Miles Griffiths, Piercy & Co.* (1980) 255 E.G. 625.
[94] Both apply only to licences to assign, not licences to sublet etc.; compare the *Standard Conditions of Sale*, (1st Ed) 1990 (see *infra*) which are destined to replace them.

**National
Conditions of Sale
11(5)**

National Condition 11(5) provides that:

"The sale is subject to the reversioner's licence being obtained, where necessary. The purchaser supplying such information and references, if any, as may reasonably be required of him, the vendor will use his best endeavours to obtain such licence and will pay the fee for the same. But if the licence cannot be obtained, the vendor may rescind the contract on the same terms as if the purchaser had persisted in an objection to the title which the vendor was unable to remove."

At the outset it may observed that this condition, allowing the vendor (only) to rescind, applies where a licence is

**"Where
necessary"**

"necessary." If this were to be interpreted as *legally* necessary, it would be impossible to use the condition, in the case of a fully qualified covenant, until it had been established that the landlord had reasonably withheld his consent. If he had unreasonably withheld it, the consent is not legally necessary and therefore the condition would be innapplicable. The preliminary investigation that this implies would introduce all the uncertainties which infect the open contract field. It is with some relief therefore that it can be noted that a wider meaning has been attributed to the word "necessary." In *Bickel* v. *Courtenay Investments (Nominees) Ltd.*[95] the vendor of a lease, having failed to secure the landlord's licence, sought to rely upon condition 11(5) to rescind the contract. The purchasers argued that it could only be relied on where the landlord's licence was "necessary" and here it was not, because, they claimed, the landlord had unreasonably withheld it. Warner J. opined that although there was a bona fide issue between the parties whether the landlord's consent had been unreasonably withheld, it was irrelevant for the purposes of applying 11(5). This was because the condition applied wherever, under the lease, the consent of the landlord had to be sought. It therefore applied where there was a fully qualified covenant without the need to investigate the grounds of any refusal: the words "where necessary" did not mean:

"where necessary as between the landlord and the tenant from time to time during the subsistence of the contract so that, if the landlord's consent ceases to be necessary, because the landlord unreasonably withholds it, the contract ceases to be subject to that consent being obtained." Rather "the question whether the landlord's consent is necessary is to answered only by looking at the lease; necessary ... means necessary under the lease and does not invite an inquiry whether at some stage between contract and completion, the landlord has by his conduct, rendered his consent unnecessary."[96]

He accordingly agreed with counsel for the vendor that a vendor, to use the condition, merely had to show that *under the lease* the landlord's consent was necessary, that he had used his best endeavours to obtain it and that it could not be obtained.

[95] [1984] 1 All E.R. 657.
[96] At p. 660.

Any other view would seriously limit the operation of the
condition and could not accord with the intention of the
authors of the National Conditions or those who use them,[97]
namely, to afford security to the vendor and a quick remedy.

**Vendor to use
"best endeavours"**

The vendor's right to rescind under 11(5) is conditional
upon him having used his best endeavours to obtain the
consent and that duty, in its turn, is conditional upon the
purchaser supplying such information and references as may
reasonably be required of him. These requirements will be
considered in turn. A vendor may be held to have used his best
endeavours even though fairly obvious avenues remain
unexplored. In *Lipmans Wallpaper Ltd.* v. *Mason & Hodghton
Ltd.*[98] the vendor rescinded under 11(5) because the immediate
landlord had refused his consent upon the ground that the
proposed user would be a breach of a user clause in the head
lease. The purchaser argued that the vendor was then under a
duty to apply to the head-landlord for a licence for a change of
use (or give the purchaser the opportunity to do so) or, at the
very least, to ask the immediate landlord whether the obtaining
of such a licence would cause him to change his mind. Despite
the fact that in the past the head-landlord had been known to
grant licences for a change of use in relation to the property,
Goff J. refused to burden the vendor with the obligation
himself to take the suggested steps, and saw no good reason
why the vendor should allow the purchaser the time to take
them.

> "As it seems to me, [the vendors] were not under any duty
> themselves to approach [the head-landlord]. Their duty to
> try and obtain the licence of [the immediate landlord] to
> assign could not, I think, involve obtaining a licence or
> consent to a change of use from someone else. If that be
> right, it is difficult to see how [the vendors] could be
> obliged to allow [the purchasers] an opportunity for so
> doing. If they were, then the question must arise at once,
> how long must they wait?"[99]

Thus while the vendor must diligently pursue the primary
licence, this does not involve him in embarking upon a quest
for some secondary licence or allowing the purchaser the time
to do so. This is not only a rational line to draw, but it also
ensures that the purchaser cannot introduce delay into the
operation of the condition by insisting that every lead be
followed up. Furthermore, in *Bickel* v. *Courtenay Investments
(Nominees) Ltd.*[1] Warner J. made it clear that the vendor's
conduct would be viewed in the round, and the mere fact that
at some point he had failed to take a desirable step would not
prevent him using the condition if he could show, as in that
case, that throughout the relevant period he had made
"repeated and strenuous efforts."[2] The vendor is under no

---

[97] *Ibid.*
[98] [1968] 1 All E.R. 1123.
[99] At p. 1129.
[1] *Supra* n. 95.
[2] At p. 660.

duty to institute proceedings against the landlord in relation to
the failure to consent.[3]

The supply of information and references by the purchaser
is, under the terms of 11(5), a condition which qualifies the

**Supply of
"information and
references" by
purchaser**

vendor's duty to use his best endeavours; it does not amount
to a covenant by the tenant.[4] What information, etc., may
"reasonably be required of him" refers not only to what the
reversioner might reasonably seek but also to what it is
reasonable to ask of the particular purchaser in the particular
circumstances of the case.[5] It has been held reasonable to
require him to supply financial as well as personal references[6]
but not to require him to obtain a guarantor.[7] Nor need the
purchaser submit to an interview with the landlord's agents. In
Elfer v. *Beynon-Lewis*[8] the purchaser, having refused to submit
to such an interview, brought an action for return of his
deposit when the landlord's consent could not be obtained. It
was held by Plowman J. that the purchaser was entitled to
recover the deposit because under the condition[9] the extent of
the assistance to be provided by the purchaser, was expressly
limited to the supply of information and references and this
excluded any further implications. In *Shires* v. *Brock*[10] it was
argued that while under the general law the purchaser had a
duty merely to do his best to enable the vendor to obtain the
landlord's consent, under the condition he had a more
extensive duty, namely, to supply information and references
which will satisfy the landlord that he is a satisfactory tenant.
The result of this would have been that if the purchaser,
having supplied the best information he could, turned out to be
financially unacceptable to the landlord, the vendor could
forfeit his deposit. This argument was rejected, Scarman L.J.
opining that the purchaser has "no greater, and indeed no less,
responsibility than that of providing full, honest and truthful
information and proper and credible references about the true
state of his financial position. If, unfortunately, that
information, having been reasonably required by the vendor,
and then submitted by the vendor to the landlord, does not
succeed in persuading the landlord to grant his licence, that is
too bad. The purchaser has done all that he has undertaken to
do. . . . "[11]

**"Cannot be
obtained"**

If despite the vendor's best endeavours the licence "cannot
be obtained," he can rescind. The condition sets no time limit
and therefore the vendor has to make a nice judgment as to the
point at which he may exercise his right. The fact that a
contractual completion date (not of the essence) has passed will
not entitle the vendor to rescind: at whatever date he purports

---

[3] *Lehmann* v. *McArthur* (1868) L.R. 3 Ch. 496.
[4] *Shires* v. *Brock* (1978) 24 E.G. 127 C.A. *per* Goff L.J. at p. 131 & Buckley
L.J. at p. 133; compare Scarman L.J. at p. 133.
[5] *Ibid. per* Goff L.J. at p. 131 *obiter.*
[6] *Sheggia* v. *Gradwell* [1963] 3 All E.R. 114, 121 & 123.
[7] *Butler* v. *Croft* [1974] 27 P. & C.R. 1—discussed *supra* p. 203.
[8] [1972] E.G. Dig. 516.
[9] Then 10(5).
[10] [1978] 24 E.G. 127 C.A.
[11] At p. 133.

to exercise his right he must show that consent "cannot be
obtained." It is not enough that it *has* not been obtained. In *29
Equities Ltd*. v. *Leumi (UK) Ltd*.[12] the landlord had required
the proposed assignee to supply the names of two guarantors
together with bank references for them. After some delay, and
one day before the contractual completion date, the names were
supplied and it was indicated that bank references would
follow. There was every indication, in this case that the
landlord would grant the licence on having his request met.
Two days after the contractual completion date, no licence
having arrived, the vendor rescinded the contract.
Subsequently the licence arrived. It was held that the vendor
was not entitled to rescind when he did and specific
performance was granted to the purchaser. Dillon L.J.
considered that the natural construction of the condition
"requires one to look at the date when the vendor has
purported to exercise his right to rescind. The court has to
consider whether at that date it can fairly be said that the
licence cannot obtained"[13] and in this case it was impossible to
say that. The notion that mere failure to obtain the licence by
the contractual completion date entitled the vendor to rescind,
was expressly rejected and, as a matter of construction, rightly
so. The decision does however leave parties contracting under
the National Conditions of Sale subject to unwelcome
uncertainty: where there is hope there is no right to rescind,
and the fact that a landlord is dilatory keeps hope alive. At this
point it becomes relevant to consider whether the vendor could
end his waiting by utilising a Completion Notice under
Condition 22.

**Completion
Notice?**
Such a notice was served in *Shires* v. *Brock*[14] but was
described by Goff L.J. as "a misconceived step" because the
vendor "not having been able to get the reversioners licence,
was not in a position to perform her part of the contract."[15] In
Jneid v. *Mirza*[16] Fox L.J. opined that

> "if the vendors ... were never in a position before, during
> or on the expiration of the notice to complete, to produce
> [the licence] at any time, then the vendors were quite
> plainly never ready at any material time to fulfil their
> obligations under this contract."

In *29 Equities Ltd*. v. *Leumi*[17] no Notice to Complete had
in fact been served and Dillon L.J. and Balcombe L.J., having
taken note of the earlier decisions, expressly reserved their
opinion on whether the vendor should be able to serve one.
The situation they were concerned about was where the vendor
"is locked into the contract, where the landlords are not
refusing to grant their consent but are being dilatory in
granting it."[18] The condition requires the vendor to be "ready

[12] [1987] 1 All E.R. 108 C.A.
[13] At p. 113.
[14] (1978) 247 E.G. 127 C.A.
[15] At p. 129.
[16] 1981 C.A. Unreported.
[17] [1987] 1 All E.R. 108.
[18] *Per* Balcombe L.J. at p. 114.

and willing" to fulfil his obligations—not necessarily *able*.[19]
Should the vendor be able to serve the Notice, which is without
prejudice to the purchaser's right to rescind,[20] and thus force
the purchaser to rescind, to complete without a licence or to
forfeit his deposit? The case is not compelling.

Rescission

Where the vendor can rescind under condition 11(5), the
terms upon which he may do so are the same "as if the
purchaser had persisted in an objection to the title which the
vendor was unable to remove." This is a cross reference to
condition 10—but only to that part of it which relates to the
terms upon which the right of rescission can be exercised,
namely, 10(2), which provides that the vendor shall return the
deposit, but without interest or the costs of investigating title
or other compensation or payment, and the purchaser shall
return the abstract and other papers furnished to him.[21] It was
argued, unsuccessfully, in *Lipman's Wallpaper Ltd.* v. *Mason &
Hodghton Ltd.*[22] that 10(1) was incorporated also, with the
result that the vendor could not rescind immediately it became
apparent that consent could not be obtained but had to wait 10
days to give the purchaser an opportunity to withdraw his
objection to the title. Goff J. pointed out that the purpose of
the reference to condition 10 was purely to define the terms of
rescission and only 10(2) related to this—10(1) dealt with when
the right to rescission arose and in the case of lack of consent
this was already fully defined in condition 11 itself.

**Law Society
Condition 8(4)**

Law Society Condition 8(4) provides:

Where any consent to assign is necessary:

(c) if any such consent is not granted at least five working days
before contractual completion date, or is subject to any
condition to which the purchaser may reasonably object, either
party may rescind the contract by notice to the other.

Due, no doubt, to the efficiency of this condition there
would appear to be no decisions upon its construction. The
word "necessary" should doubtless be construed in the same
manner as in 11(5) of the National Conditions and for the same
reasons.[23] The firm deadline of five working days before
completion and the mutual rights of rescission make it
preferable to 11(5).[24] Although 8(4) does not refer to condition
16(2), the latter does, in fact, govern the terms of rescission
and states that the vendor is to repay any deposit with interest
at the contract rate from four working days after recission until
payment, and the purchaser will return all documents delivered
to him by the vendor and at his own expense procure the
cancellation of any entry relating to the contract in any register.

---

[19] A point put by counsel in *Jneid* v. *Mirza supra.*

[20] Condition 22(2).

[21] Thus the position is as if the contract was discharged upon failure to satisfy
a condition precedent and, if *Shires* v. *Brock* is correct, it seems that this is
indeed what has happened—both Scarman L.J. (p. 133) and Buckley L.J.
(p. 135) state that under 11(5), then 10(5), the contract is conditional upon
consent being obtained. Compare the position under the general law, *supra.*

[22] [1968] 1 All E.R. 1123.

[23] See *supra.*

[24] But see (1981) 45 Conv. 5 where it is noted that should the contract fail to
include a specified completion date, completion will be 25 days after the
contract—leaving rather a short time to get the consent.

The condition embodies a duty on the part of the vendor to use his best endeavours to obtain the consent[25] and upon the purchaser to supply such information and references as may reasonably be required by the reversioner.[26] These mutual duties are in contrast to the National Conditions of Sale, where the supply of information by the purchaser is merely a condition which qualifies the vendors duty to use his best endeavours and therefore does not constitute an independent duty on the purchaser's part.[27] One possible cause of difficulty with this condition could arise where a consent *has* been obtained by the relevant date but is subject to a condition. Only if the purchaser reasonably objects to the condition can he rescind; if the vendor challenges the reasonableness of his objection, litigation would seem to be the only way out.[28]

Standard Condition 8(3)   The Standard Conditions of Sale, to be incorporated into contracts concluded under the Law Society's Transaction Scheme[28a], provide in condition 8.3, as follows:

> 8.3.1. The following provisions apply if a consent to assign or sublet is required.
> 8.3.2. (a) The seller is to apply for the consent at his expense, and to use his best efforts to obtain it.
> (b) The buyer is to provide all information and references reasonably required.
> 8.3.3. Unless he is in breach of his obligation under 8.3.2. either party may rescind the contract by notice to the other party if three working days before completion date:
> (a) the consent has not been given: or
> (b) the consent has been given subject to a condition to which the buyer reasonably objects

Unlike either of the other sets of conditions, it applies to licences to sublet as well as to assign. It follows closely the format of the Law Society condition; but here again one may assume that the pre-requisite for its application, viz. that consent is "required" will be construed in the same manner as in 11(5) of the National Conditions of Sale. As with Law Society condition 8(4), buyer and seller owe mutual duties, thought it may be noted that condition 8(4) refers to the supply of information reasonably required *by the reversioner*. Both the buyer and seller, so long as they have complied with their duty, have a right to rescind exercisable by a specified date (three working days before completion, as opposed to five in Law Society condition 8(4).

Where the vendor loses a sale under any of these conditions, due to the unreasonable withholding of consent by

---

[25] 8(4)(*a*); see *supra*, p. 210, for the scope of this duty.

[26] 8(4)(*b*).

[27] *Shires* v. *Brock* (1978) 247 E.G. 127, 133.

[28] Note also the Conveyancing Lawyers' Conditions of Sale, condition 9 of which allows the purchaser, after completion date has passed, to serve a warning notice on the vendor that he will rescind after 14 days if consent has not been obtained. The purchaser then has a further seven days to exercise the right of rescission, see (1981) 45 Conv. 38, 48.

[28a] And constituting the 21st Edition of the National Conditions of Sale and the 1990 Revision of the Law Society's Conditions of Sale.

the landlord or on account of an unreasonable delay on the
landlord's part, the vendor may be able to sue him for breach
of statutory duty under the Landlord and Tenant Act 1988.[29]

Costs

**Expense of
making title**

The cost of obtaining a licence is an expense of making title
and as such is to be borne by the vendor. This principle is
followed in the Law Society's *Conditions of Sale*, (1984
Revision) 8(4)(*a*), the *National Conditions of Sale* (20th Ed)
1981 11(5) and the *Standard Conditions of Sale*, 8.3.2. It seems
that if the landlord requires the vendor to put the property in
repair before granting the licence, even this would be regarded
as an expense of making title which the vendor has to bear.
Where however the purchaser has bought the property as it
stands, the vendor would be entitled to specific performance on
the basis that the purchaser reimburses him the cost, because
although it is an expense of making title, it is one which the
purchaser has agreed to bear.[30] In *Re Davies' Agreement*[31] the
facts were a little different. When the vendor sought consent,
the landlord did not ask him to do the repairs but to put up a
deposit of £4,910 to cover the cost of the work, the idea being
that this would be recoverable by him when the purchaser
executed the repairs, for which, under the contract, he was
responsible. The vendor sought a declaration that the purchaser
should be the one to put up the deposit. Stamp J. refused to
grant it, because the deposit was not an amount which the
purchaser had agreed to pay: it may turn out to be either more
or less than the amount of the repairs. It could properly be
regarded as an expense of making title, which, under the
ordinary rule, the vendor was bound to bear.

Landlord's Costs

The cost to the vendor of obtaining the licence may, and
usually will, include paying the landlord's costs. Where a
disposition covenant is absolute, the landlord can clearly
require this as a condition of his consent. Where a disposition
covenant is fully qualified the landlord's right to his costs in
connection with granting a licence is preserved: the prohibition
on fines in section 144 of the Law of Property Act 1925 does
not "preclude the right to require payment of a reasonable sum
in respect of any legal or other expenses in relation to such
licence or consent." Subsections 19(1)(*a*) and (2) of the
Landlord and Tenant Act 1927 which provide for full
qualification of disposition and improvement covenants, are
similarly worded and again do not preclude the landlord from
requiring a reasonable sum in respect of legal and other
expenses "in connection with" the licence. Subsection 19(1)(3)
which prohibits fines in relation to licences for an alteration in
user, is equally permissive. What is permitted is a reasonable
sum "in relation to" or "in connection with" such licence or

---

[29] See *supra* and Chap. 5.
[30] *Lockharts* v. *Bernard Rosen & Co.* [1922] 1 Ch. 433; *Re Davies' Agreement*
(1970) 20 P. & C.R. 328.
[31] *Ibid.*

Consent not granted?

consent; but what if the landlord asked for his expenses *whether or not the licence was ever granted?* Would such a demand be a fine or amount to an unreasonable withholding of consent? Or, are such demands contemplated by the relevant statutory provisions? This is not clear though it was inconclusively discussed in *Goldman* v. *Abbott*[32] where Kerr L.J., remarked that, though the first part of section 144 of the Law of Property Act 1925 referred to the situation where the licence was granted, it would be wrong to conclude that the proviso, allowing expenses, was similarly limited because in fact it employs wider words: "whereas the first part refers to a fine payable 'for or in respect of such licence or consent,' the concluding words are 'in respect of any legal or other expenses in relation to such licence or consent.' " He did not therefore think that it could be concluded with confidence that the provision is necessarily confined to cases where a licence was in fact granted.[33] The position under section 19(1)(a) was equally unclear. The issue did not arise in stark form in this case: the tenant's solicitor had given the landlord an undertaking to "pay your reasonable costs in relation to the licence" deliberately reproducing the vague expression in section 144. Having noted that the meaning of section 144 was a vexed matter which had not previously arisen, Kerr L.J. took grateful refuge in the conviction that the undertaking had to be construed against the background of the correspondence as a whole, which in this case indicated that the landlord had always intended to have his costs paid whether the licence was granted or not, and the tenant's solicitor, in drafting his final form of undertaking, had not clearly shown a more limited intention. This being so, in the context of the correspondence as a whole, the words were wide enough to mean "In relation to an application for a licence" or "for the grant of a licence" or "in relation to a contemplated or proposed licence."[34] He considered himself lucky, in this case, to have the "elucidating context."

Registered title and consents

Leases granted for more than 21 years are subject to substantive registration.[35] Where absolute title is sought, the reversionary title must be approved by the Chief Land Registrar to ensure that the lessor had the right to grant the lease. Unless the reversionary title is already registered, this involves the lessee in deducing title under the unregistered system. Where it is clear from the reversionary title, registered or unregistered, that the consent of some person, a mortgagee or a landlord, is required to the grant of the lease, absolute title cannot be granted without production of such consents.[36] If the lease itself contains an absolute or qualified restriction on

---

[32] 1989 N.L.J. 828.
[33] At p. 829.
[34] At p. 830.
[35] Land Registration Act 1925 ss. 19, 20, 22(2).
[36] Ruoff & Roper, Registered Conveyancing, 5th Ed. pp. 90–91.

disposition, this necessitates an entry on the Register.[37] The entry appears on the Proprietorship Register and states:

> There are excepted from the effect of registration all estates, rights, interests, powers and remedies under the lease at any time arising from any alienation prohibitted or restricted by the lease.

The entry is made regardless of the grade of title. Its effect is to absolve the Land Registry from any liability arising as a result of a subsequent disposition in breach of a covenant restricting or prohibitting dispositions. It is the responsibility of successive purchasers to satisfy themselves that necessary licenses have been obtained.[38]

---

[37] Land Registration Act 1925 s. 8(2) as substituted by Land Registration Act 1986 s. 3(1) and r. 45.
[38] Ruoff and Roper, Registered Conveyancing, 15th ed. pp. 92–93, 520–521.

11 REMEDIES

In the case of a fully qualified covenant, should consent be unreasonably withheld, the tenant can, as a matter of construction, proceed with the disposition, alteration or change of user, without it.[1] However to put the matter beyond doubt, the tenant can take the precaution of seeking a declaration from the court that the landlord has unreasonably withheld his consent and that he is free to proceed without it.[2] Under the usual form of fully qualified covenant, the tenant cannot claim damages from a landlord who has unreasonably withheld his consent to the restricted activity[3] and it is only in relation to fully qualified *disposition* covenants that the legislature has provided such a remedy: under section 1(3) of the Landlord and Tenant Act 1988 the landlord, upon whom is served[4] a written application for consent to a proposed transaction,[5] owes a duty to the tenant within a reasonable time, (*inter alia*), "to give consent, except in a case where it is reasonable not to give consent" and, by section 4, a breach of this duty may be made the subject of civil proceedings "in like manner as any other claim in tort for breach of statutory duty."

Declarations

An action for a declaration may be brought in the High Court, by writ or originating summons,[6] the latter being appropriate where the facts "can conveniently be placed before the court by affidavit evidence."[7] The jurisdiction extends to cases where no other relief is, or could be claimed.[8] The County Court, on the other hand, would normally have power to grant a declaration only where it would be ancillary to a claim for money or other relief within its substantive jurisdiction.[9] However, for present purposes it is given wider jurisdiction by section 53 of the Landlord and Tenant Act 1954[10] which provides as follows:

(1) Where a landlord withholds his licence or consent—
    (a) to an assignment of the tenancy or a subletting, charging or parting with the

---

[1] *Treloar* v. *Bigge* (1874) L.R. 9 Ex. 151; *supra* Chap. 4.
[2] The vendor of a lease would not be granted specific performance without such a declaration: see Chap. 10.
[3] See *supra*, p. 33.
[4] In any manner provided by the tenancy or, where the tenancy makes no provision, as provided by s.23 of the Landlord & Tenant Act 1927: s.5(2).
[5] See s.1(1)—assignment, underlease, charge, a parting with possession.
[6] Rules of the Supreme Court, Order 5, The Supreme Court Practice 1988 p. 29.
[7] See Woodfall, *Landlord and Tenant*, Vol. 1, 1–1264.
[8] Order 15, r. 16, *ibid.* p. 224.
[9] See s.38 of the County Courts Act 1985, Pt. 1; County Court Practice 1989 p. 1558.
[10] As amended by the County Court Act 1984, s.148(1) Sched. 2, Part V, para. 23.

possession of the demised property or any part
thereof, or

(b)   to the making of an improvement[11] on the
       demised property or any part thereof, or

(c)   to a change in the use of the demised property
       or any part thereof, or to the making a
       specified use of that property,

and the High Court has jurisdiction to make a
declaration that the licence or consent was
unreasonably withheld then without prejudice to the
jurisdiction of the High Court the County Court shall
have the like jurisdiction whatever the net annual value
for rating of the demised property is taken to be for
the purposes of the County Courts Act 1984, or the
rent payable under the tenancy and notwithstanding
that the tenant does not seek any relief other than the
declaration.

The wider jurisdiction exists regardless both of when the
tenancy was created and when the refusal occurred.[12]
Proceedings are by originating application and the respondent
must file an answer[13] stating whether he intends to resist the
application, and if so upon what grounds, and complying with
the formal requirements of Order 9, rule 18.[14]

Proceedings may be brought by the tenant, or, in the case
of a disposition covenant, by an assignee. In the former case,
the declaration sought is to the effect that the landlord's
withholding of consent is unreasonable and that the tenant is
entitled to proceed with the disposition, improvement, change
of user, without it. Where the consent of a superior landlord
has also been withheld, no declaration can be made against him
unless he has been made party to the action.[15] Where the
action is brought by an assignee, it is not necessary that the
assignor be made a party to the proceedings but the
declaration, in these circumstances, would not be conclusive as
between the assignor and the landlord and it should not
therefore state that the assignor was entitled to assign the lease
to the plaintiff without consent but rather that the assignment
to the plaintiff was not invalidated by reason of it being made
without the consent of the landlord.[16]

Breach of statutory duty

Such an action only exists in relation to disposition covenants[17]
and it arises where the landlord[18] has failed to comply with any

---

[11] See *supra* Chap. 8.
[12] s.53(3).
[13] Ord. 43 r. 2; County Court Practice 1989 p. 1571.
[14] See County Court Practice 1989 p. 254.
[15] *Vienit Ltd.* v. *W. Williams & Sons (Bread Street) Ltd.* [1958] 3 All E.R. 621.
[16] *Theodorou* v. *Bloom* [1964] 3 All E.R. 399n., 400; and see *supra*, p. 207.
[17] See s.1 of the Landlord and Tenant Act 1988.
[18] Which term includes superior landlords: s.5(1) of the Landlord and Tenant
      Act 1988.

of his duties under the Landlord and Tenant Act 1988.[19] It is an action in tort and the tenant[20] would have to show that one of the statutory duties had been broken and that damage, of a type foreseeable at the time the tort was committed, resulted. The clearest case would be where as a consequence of an unreasonable delay in responding or unreasonable refusal of consent on the part of the landlord, the tenant has been unable to fulfil his contract with a third party disponee and has thus lost his bargain.

An action for damages for breach of statutory duty can be brought in the County Court so long as the claim does not exceed £5000, the current limit of its jurisdiction in tort,[21] otherwise the High Court must be used. The County Court can also grant an injunction, restraining a threatened breach of duty, where such injunction would be ancillary to a claim for money or other relief within its substantive jurisdiction.[22]

---

[19] See ss.1(3), 2 & 3 & Chap. 5 *supra*.
[20] Which term includes his mortgagee where the latter is proposing to exercise his express or statutory power of sale under the mortgage: s.5(1) of the Landlord and Tenant Act 1988.
[21] See County Court Practice 1989, p. 1517.
[22] s.35 of the County Courts Act 1984; County Court Practice 1989, p. 35.

APPENDIX 1

Landlord and Tenant Act 1988

1988 CHAPTER 26

An Act to make new provision for imposing statutory duties in connection with covenants in tenancies against assigning, underletting, charging or parting with the possession of premises without consent.   [29th July 1988]

Be it enacted by the Queen's most Excellent Majesty, by and with the advise and consent of the Lords Spiritual and Temporal, and Commons, in this present Parliament assembled, and by the authority of the same, as follows:

Qualified duty to consent to assigning, underletting etc. of premises

1.—(1) This section applies in any case where—

   (a) a tenancy includes a covenant on the part of the tenant not to enter into one or more of the following transactions, that is—

       (i) assigning,
      (ii) underletting,
     (iii) parting with the possession, of,

the premises comprised in the tenancy or any part of the premises without the consent of the landlord or some other person, but

   (b) the covenant is subject to the qualification that the consent is not to be unreasonably withheld (whether or not it is also subject to any other qualification).

(2) In this section and section 2 of this Act—

   (a) references to a proposed transaction are to any assignment, underletting, charging or parting with possession to which the covenant relates, and

   (b) references to the person who may consent to such a transaction are to the person who under the covenant may consent to the tenant entering into the proposed transaction.

(3) Where there is served on the person who may consent to a proposed transaction a written application by the tenant for consent to the transaction, he owes a duty to the tenant within a reasonable time—

   (a) to give consent, except in a case where it is reasonable not to give consent,

(b)   to serve on the tenant written notice of his decision whether or not to give consent specifying in addition—
  (i)   if the consent is given subject to conditions, the conditions,
  (ii)   if the consent is withheld, the reasons for withholding it.

(4) Giving consent subject to any condition that is not a reasonable condition does not satisfy the duty under subsection (3)(a) above.

(5) For the purposes of this Act it is reasonable for a person not to give consent to a proposed transaction only in a case where, if he withheld consent and the tenant completed the transaction, the tenant would be in breach of a covenant.

(6) It is for the person who owed any duty under subsection (3) above—

(a)   if he gave consent and the question arises whether he gave it within a reasonable time, to show that he did,
(b)   if he gave consent subject to any condition and the question arises whether the condition was a reasonable condition, to show that it was,
(c)   if he did not give consent and the question arises whether it was reasonable for him not to do so, to show that it was reasonable,

and, if the question arises whether he served notice under that subsection within a reasonable time, to show that he did.

Duty to pass on applications
2.—(1) If, in a case where section 1 of this Act applies, any person receives a written application by the tenant for consent to a proposed transaction and that person—

(a)   is a person who may consent to the transaction or (though not such a person) is the landlord, and
(b)   believes that another person, other than a person who he believes has received the application or a copy of it, is a person who may consent to the transaction,

he owes a duty to the tenant (whether or not he owes him any duty under section 1 of this Act) to take such steps as are reasonable to secure the receipt within a reasonable time by the other person of a copy of the application.

(2) The reference in section 1(3) of this Act to the service of an application on a person who may consent to a proposed transaction includes a reference to the receipt by him of an application or a copy of an application (whether it is for his consent or that of another).

Qualified duty to approve consent by another
3.—(1) This section applies in any case where—

(a)   a tenancy includes a covenant on the part of the tenant not without the approval of the landlord to consent to the sub-tenant—
  (i)   assigning,
  (ii)   underletting,
  (iii)   charging, or
  (iv)   parting with the possession, of,

the premises comprised in the sub-tenancy or any part of the premises, but

(b) the covenant is subject to the qualification that the approval is not to be unreasonably withheld (whether or not it is also subject to any other qualification).

(2) Where there is served on the landlord a written application by the tenant for approval or a copy of a written application to the tenant by the sub-tenant for consent to a transaction to which the covenant relates the landlord owes a duty to the sub-tenant within a reasonable time—

(a) to give approval, except in a case where it is reasonable not to give approval,

(b) to serve on the tenant and the sub-tenant written notice of his decision whether or not to give approval specifying in addition—

    (i) if approval is given subject to conditions, the conditions,

    (ii) if approval is withheld, the reasons for withholding it.

(3) Giving approval subject to any condition that is not a reasonable condition does not satisfy the duty under subsection (2)(a) above.

(4) For the purposes of this section it is reasonable for the landlord not to give approval only in a case where, if he withheld approval and the tenant gave his consent, the tenant would be in breach of covenant.

(5) It is for a landlord who owed any duty under subsection (2) above—

(a) if he gave approval and the question arises whether he gave it within a reasonable time, to show that he did,

(b) if he gave approval subject to any condition and the question arises whether the condition was a reasonable condition, to show that it was,

(c) if he did not give approval and the question arises whether it was reasonable for him not to do so, to show that it was reasonable,

and, if the question arises whether he served notice under that subsection within a reasonable time, to show that he did.

Breach of duty   4. A claim that a person has broken any duty under this Act may be made the subject of civil proceedings in like manner as any other claim in tort for breach of statutory duty.

Interpretation   5.—(1) In this Act—

"covenant" includes condition and agreement,

"consent" includes licence,

"landlord" includes any superior landlord from whom the tenant's immediate landlord directly or indirectly holds,

"tenancy", subject to subsection (3) below, means any lease or other tenancy (whether made before or after the coming into force of this Act) and includes—

(a) a sub-tenancy, and

(b) an agreement for a tenancy

and references in this Act to the landlord and to the tenant are to be interpreted accordingly, and

1925 c. 20   "tenant", where the tenancy is affected by a mortgage (within the meaning of the Law of Property Act 1925) and the mortgagee proposes to exercise his statutory or express power of sale, includes the mortgagee.

(2) An application or notice is to be treated as served for the purposes of this Act if—

(a) served in any manner provided in the tenancy, and

(b) in respect of any matter for which the tenancy makes no provision, served in any manner provided by

1927 c. 36   section 23 of the Landlord and Tenant Act 1927.

(3) This Act does not apply to a secure tenancy (defined in

1985 c. 68   section 79 of the Housing Act 1985).

(4) This Act applies only to applications for consent or approval served after its coming into force.

Application to   **6.** This Act binds the Crown; but as regards the Crown's
Crown   liability in tort shall not bind the Crown further than the
1947 c. 44   Crown is made liable in tort by the Crown Proceedings Act 1947.

Short title,   **7.**—(1) This Act may be cited as the Landlord and Tenant
commencement   Act 1988.
and extent

(2) This Act shall come into force at the end of the period of two months beginning with the day on which it is passed.

(3) This Act extends to England and Wales only.

APPENDIX 2

Operation of the Landlord and Tenant Act 1988

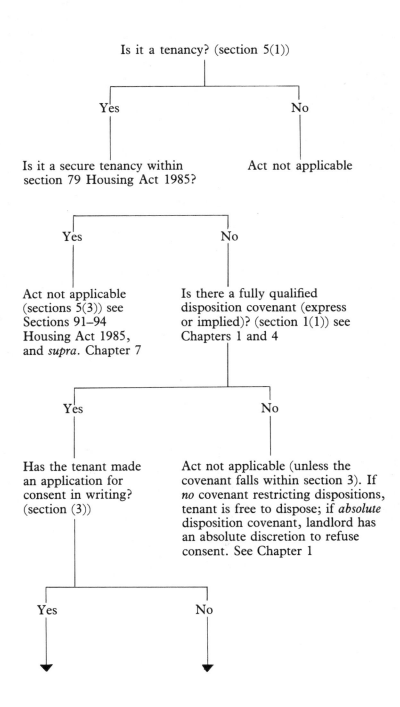

Is it a tenancy? (section 5(1))

Yes — Is it a secure tenancy within section 79 Housing Act 1985?

No — Act not applicable

Yes — Act not applicable (sections 5(3)) see Sections 91–94 Housing Act 1985, and *supra*. Chapter 7

No — Is there a fully qualified disposition covenant (express or implied)? (section 1(1)) see Chapters 1 and 4

Yes — Has the tenant made an application for consent in writing? (section (3))

No — Act not applicable (unless the covenant falls within section 3). If *no* covenant restricting dispositions, tenant is free to dispose; if *absolute* disposition covenant, landlord has an absolute discretion to refuse consent. See Chapter 1

Yes

No

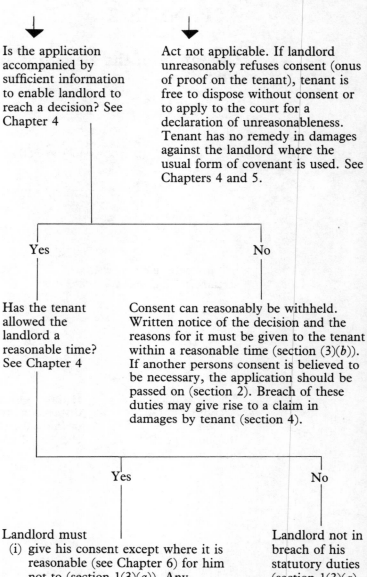

Is the application accompanied by sufficient information to enable landlord to reach a decision? See Chapter 4

Act not applicable. If landlord unreasonably refuses consent (onus of proof on the tenant), tenant is free to dispose without consent or to apply to the court for a declaration of unreasonableness. Tenant has no remedy in damages against the landlord where the usual form of covenant is used. See Chapters 4 and 5.

Yes   No

Has the tenant allowed the landlord a reasonable time? See Chapter 4

Consent can reasonably be withheld. Written notice of the decision and the reasons for it must be given to the tenant within a reasonable time (section (3)(*b*)). If another persons consent is believed to be necessary, the application should be passed on (section 2). Breach of these duties may give rise to a claim in damages by tenant (section 4).

Yes   No

Landlord must
(i) give his consent except where it is reasonable (see Chapter 6) for him not to (section 1(3)(*a*)). Any conditions attached to the consent must be reasonable (section 1(4)). Burden of proof on the landlord (section 1(6)).
(ii) notify the tenant of his decision. Notification to include any conditions attached to a consent and the reasons for any refusal (section 1(3)(*b*)).
(iii) pass the application on if another person's consent is believed to be required (section 2).

Landlord not in breach of his statutory duties (section 1(3)(*a*) and (*b*); section 2).

Breach of any of the above duties may give rise to a claim in damages by the tenant. Breach of (1) may additionally entitle the tenant to proceed with the transaction without consent or to apply to the court for a declaration that consent has been unreasonably withheld. See Chapter 11.

APPENDIX 3

International Drilling Ltd. v. Louisville Investments [1986] 1 Ch. 513 (C.A.) Balcombe L.J.:

From the authorities I deduce the following propositions of law.

H (1) The purpose of a covenant against assignment without the consent of the landlord, such consent not to be unreasonably withheld, is to protect the lessor from having his premises used or occupied in an undesirable way, or by an undesirable tenant or assignee: per A. L. Smith L.J. in *Bates v.*

A *Donaldson* [1896] 2 Q.B. 241, 247, approved by all the members of the Court of Appeal in *Houlder Brothers & Co. Ltd. v. Gibbs* [1925] Ch. 575.

(2) As a corollary to the first proposition, a landlord is not entitled to refuse his consent to an assignment on grounds which have nothing whatever to do with the relationship of landlord and tenant in regard to the subject matter of the lease: see *Houlder Brothers & Co. Ltd. v. Gibbs*, a decision which

B (despite some criticism) is binding on this court: *Bickel v. Duke of Westminster* [1977] Q.B. 517. A recent example of a case where the landlord's consent was unreasonably withheld because the refusal was designed to achieve a collateral purpose unconnected with the terms of the lease is *Bromley Park Garden Estates Ltd. v. Moss* [1982] 1 W.L.R. 1019.

C (3) The onus of proving that consent has been unreasonably withheld is on the tenant: see *Shanly v. Ward* (1913) 29 T.L.R. 714 and *Pimms Ltd. v. Tallow Chandlers Company* [1964] 2 Q.B. 547, 564.

(4) It is not necessary for the landlord to prove that the conclusions which led him to refuse consent were justified, if they were conclusions which might be reached by a reasonable man in the circumstances: *Pimms Ltd. v. Tallow Chandlers Company* [1964] 2 Q.B. 547, 564.

D (5) It may be reasonable for the landlord to refuse his consent to an assignment on the ground of the purpose for which the proposed assignee intends to use the premises, even though that purpose is not forbidden by the lease: see *Bates v. Donaldson* [1896] 2 Q.B. 241, 244.

(6) There is a divergence of authority on the question, in considering whether the landlord's refusal of consent is reasonable, whether it is permissible to have regard to the

E consequences to the tenant if consent to the proposed assignment is withheld. In an early case at first instance, *Sheppard v. Hongkong and Shanghae Banking Corporation* (1872) 20 W.R. 459, 460, Malins V.-C. said that by withholding their consent the lessors threw a very heavy burden on the lessees and they therefore ought to show good grounds for refusing it. In *Houlder Brothers & Co. Ltd. v. Gibbs* [1925] Ch. 575, 584, Warrington L.J. said:

F   "An act must be regarded as reasonable or unreasonable in reference to the circumstances under which it is committed, and when the question arises on the construction of a contract the outstanding circumstances to be considered are the nature of the contract to be construed, and the relations between the parties resulting from it."

G   In a recent decision of this court, *Leeward Securities Ltd. v. Lilyheath Properties Ltd.* (1983) 271 E.G. 279, concerning a sub-letting which would attract the protection of the Rent Act, both Oliver L.J. and O'Connor L.J. made it clear in their judgments that they could envisage circumstances in which it might be unreasonable to refuse consent to an underletting, if the result would be that there was no way in which the tenant H (the sub-landlord) could reasonably exploit the premises except by creating a tenancy to which the Rent Act protection would apply, and which inevitably would affect the value of the landlord's reversion. O'Connor L.J. said, at p. 283:

A   "It must not be thought that, because the introduction of a Rent Act tenant inevitably has an adverse effect upon the value of the reversion, that that is a sufficient ground for the landlords to say that they can withhold consent and that the court will hold that that is reasonable."

    To the opposite effect are the dicta, obiter but nevertheless B weighty, of Viscount Dunedin and Lord Phillimore in *Viscount Tredegar v. Harwood* [1929] A.C. 72, 78, 82. There are numerous other dicta to the effect that a landlord need consider only his own interests: see, e.g., *West Layton Ltd. v. Ford* [1979] Q.B. 593, 605, and *Bromley Park Garden Estates Ltd. v. Moss* [1982] 1 W.L.R. 1019, 1027. Those dicta must be qualified, since a landlord's interests, collateral to the purposes of the lease, are in any event ineligible for consideration: see C proposition (2) above. But in my judgment a proper reconciliation of those two streams of authority can be achieved by saying that while a landlord need usually only consider his own relevant interests, there may be cases where there is such a disproportion between the benefit to the landlord and the detriment to the tenant if the landlord withholds his consent to an assignment that it is unreasonable for the landlord to refuse consent.

D   (7) Subject to the propositions set out above, it is in each case a question of fact, depending upon all the circumstances, whether the landlord's consent to an assignment is being unreasonably withheld: see *Bickel v. Duke of Westminster* [1977] Q.B. 517, 524, and *West Layton Ltd. v. Ford* [1979] Q.B. 583, 604, 606–607.

APPENDIX 4

Miscellaneous Statutory Provisions

LAW OF PROPERTY ACT 1925

Power to discharge or modify restrictive covenants affecting land

84.—(1) the Lands Tribunal shall (without prejudice to any concurrent jurisdiction of the court) have power from time to time, on the application of any person interested in any freehold land affected by any restriction arising under covenant or otherwise as to the user thereof or the building thereon, by order wholly or partially to discharge or modify any such restriction on being satisfied—

(a) that by reason of changes in the character of the property or the neighbourhood or other circumstances of the case which the Lands Tribunal may deem material, the restriction ought to be deemed obsolete, or

(aa) that in a case falling within subsection (1A) below the continued existence thereof would impede some reasonable user of the land for public or private purposes or, as the case may be, would unless modified so impede such user; or

(b) that the persons of full age and capacity for the time being or from time to time entitled to the benefit of the restriction, whether in respect of estates in fee simple or any lesser estates or interests in the property to which the benefit of the restriction is annexed, have agreed, either expressly or by implication, by their acts or omissions, to the same being discharged or modified; or

(c) that the proposed discharge or modification will not injure the persons entitled to the benefit of the restriction:

and an order discharging or modifying a restriction under this subsection may direct the applicant to pay to any person entitled to the benefit of the restriction such sum by way of consideration as the Tribunal may think it just to award under one, but not both, of the following heads, that is to say, either—

(i) a sum to make up for any loss or disadvantage suffered by that person in consequence of the discharge or modification; or

    (ii) a sum to make up for any effect which the restriction had, at the time when it was imposed, in reducing the consideration then received for the land affected by it.

(1A) Subsection (1) (*aa*) above authorises the discharge or modification of a restriction by reference to its impeding some reasonable user of land in any case in which the Lands Tribunal is satisfied that the restriction, in impeding that user, either—

    (*a*) does not secure to persons entitled to the benefit of it any practical benefits of substantial value or advantage to them; or

    (*b*) is contrary to the public interest;

and that money will be an adequate compensation for the loss or disadvantage (if any) which any such person will suffer from the discharge or modification.

(1B) In determining whether a case is one falling within subsection (1A) above, and in determining whether (in any such case or otherwise) a restriction ought to be discharged or modified, the Lands Tribunal shall take into account the development plan and any declared or ascertainable pattern for the grant or refusal of planning permissions in the relevant areas, as well as the period at which and context in which the restriction was created or imposed and any other material circumstances.

(1C) It is hereby declared that the power conferred by this section to modify a restriction includes power to add such further provisions restricting the user of or the building on the land affected as appear to the Lands Tribunal to be reasonable in view of the relaxation of the existing provisions, and as may be accepted by the applicant; and the Lands Tribunal may accordingly refuse to modify a restriction without some such addition.

(2) The court shall have power on the application of any person interested—

    (*a*) To declare whether or not in any particular case any freehold land is or would in any given event be affected by a restriction imposed by any instrument; or

    (*b*) To declare what, upon the true construction of any instrument purporting to impose a restriction, is the nature and extent of the restriction thereby imposed and whether the same is or would in any given event be enforceable and if so by whom.

Neither subsections (7) and (11) of this section nor, unless the contrary is expressed, any later enactment providing for this section not to apply to any restrictions shall affect the operation of this subsection or the operation for purposes of this subsection of any other provisions of this section.

(3) The Lands Tribunal shall, before making any order under this section, direct such enquiries, if any, to be made of any government department or local authority, and such notices, if any, whether by way of advertisement or otherwise, to be given to such of the persons who appear to be entitled to

the benefit of the restriction intended to be discharged, modified, or dealt with as, having regard to any enquiries notices or other proceedings previously made, given or taken, the Lands Tribunal may think fit.

(3A) On an application to the Lands Tribunal under this section the Lands Tribunal shall give any necessary directions as to the persons who are or are not to be admitted (as appearing to be entitled to the benefit of the restriction) to oppose the application, and no appeal shall lie against any such direction; but rules under the Lands Tribunal Act 1949 shall make provision whereby, in cases in which there arises on such an application (whether or not in connection with the admission of persons to oppose) any such question as is referred to in subsection (2) (*a*) or (*b*) of this section, the proceedings on the application can and, if the rules so provide, shall be suspended to enable the decision of the court to be obtained on that question by an application under that subsection, or by means of a case stated by the Lands Tribunal, or otherwise, as may be provided by those rules or by rules of court.

1949 c. 42

(4) ....

(5) Any order made under this section shall be binding on all persons, whether ascertained or of full age or capacity or not, then entitled or thereafter capable of becoming entitled to the benefit of any restriction, which is thereby discharged, modified, or dealt with, and whether such persons are parties to the proceedings or have been served with notice or not ...

(6) An order may be made under this section notwithstanding that any instrument which is alleged to impose the restriction intended to be discharged, modified, or dealt with, may not have been produced to the court or the Lands Tribunal, and the court or the Lands Tribunal may act on such evidence of that instrument as it may think sufficient.

(7) This section applies to restrictions whether subsisting at the commencement of this Act or imposed thereafter, but this section does not apply where the restriction was imposed on the occasion of a disposition made gratuitously or for a nominal consideration for public purposes.

(8) This section applies whether the land affected by the restrictions is registered or not, but in the case of registered land, the Land Registrar shall give effect on the register to any order under this section in accordance with the Land Registration Act, 1925.

1925 c. 21

(9) Where any proceedings by action or otherwise are taken to enforce a restrictive covenant, any person against whom the proceedings are taken, may in such proceedings apply to the court for an order giving leave to apply to the Lands Tribunal under this section, and staying the proceedings in the meantime.

(10) ....

(11) This section does not apply to restrictions imposed by the Commissioners of Works under any statutory power for the protection of any Royal Park or Garden or to restrictions of a like character imposed upon the occasion of any enfranchisement effected before the commencement of this Act

in any manor vested in His Majesty in right of the Crown or the Duchy of Lancaster, nor subject to subsection (11A) below to restrictions created or imposed—

1920 c. 80

1949 c. 67

(a)   for Naval, Military or Air Force purposes,
(b)   for civil aviation purposes under the powers of the Air Navigation Act, 1920 or of section 19 or 23 of the Civil Aviation Act 1949.

(11A) Subsection (11) of this section—

(a)   shall exclude the application of this section to a restriction falling within subsection (11)(a), and not created or imposed in connection with the use of any land as an aerodrome, only so long as the restriction is enforceable by or on behalf of the Crown; and

(b)   shall exclude the application of this section to a restriction falling within subsection (11)(b), or created or imposed in connection with the use of any land as an aerodrome, only so long as the restriction is enforceable by or on behalf of the Crown or any public or international authority.

(12) Where a term of more than forty years is created in land (whether before or after the commencement of this Act) this section shall, after the expiration of twenty-five years of the term, apply to restrictions affecting such leasehold land in like manner as it would have applied had the land been freehold:
Provided that this subsection shall not apply to mining leases.
(13) ....

LANDLORD AND TENANT ACT 1927

Landlord's right to object

3.—(1) Where a tenant of a holding to which this Part of this Act applies proposes to make an improvement on his holding, he shall serve on his landlord notice of his intention to make such improvement, together with a specification and plan showing the proposed improvement and the part of the existing premises affected thereby, and if the landlord, within three months after the service of the notice, serves on the tenant notice of objection, the tenant may, in the prescribed manner, apply to the tribunal, and the tribunal may, after ascertaining that notice of such intention has been served upon any superior landlords interested and after giving such persons an opportunity of being heard, if satisfied that the improvement—

(a)   is of such a nature as to be calculated to add to the letting value of the holding at the termination of the tenancy; and

(b)   is reasonable and suitable to the character thereof; and

(c)   will not diminish the value of any other property belonging to the same landlord, or to any superior landlord from whom the immediate landlord of the tenant directly or indirectly holds;

and after making such modifications (if any) in the specification
or plan as the tribunal thinks fit, or imposing such other
conditions as the tribunal may think reasonable, certify in the
prescribed manner that the improvement is a proper
improvement:

Provided that, if the landlord proves that he has offered to
execute the improvement himself in consideration of a
reasonable increase of rent, or of such increase of rent as the
tribunal may determine, the tribunal shall not give a certificate
under this section unless it is subsequently shown to the
satisfaction of the tribunal that the landlord has failed to carry
out his undertaking.

(2) In considering whether the improvement is reasonable
and suitable to the character of the holding, the tribunal shall
have regard to any evidence brought before it by the landord or
any superior landlord (but not any other person) that the
improvement is calculated to injure the amenity or convenience
of the neighbourhood.

(3) The tenant shall, at the request of any superior landlord
or at the request of the tribunal, supply such copies of the
plans and specifications of the proposed improvement as may
be required.

(4) Where no such notice of objection as aforesaid to a
proposed improvement has been served within the time allowed
by this section, or where the tribunal has certified an
improvement to be a proper improvement, it shall be lawful for
the tenant as against the immediate and any superior landlord
to execute the improvement according to the plan and
specification served on the landlord, or according to such plan
and specification as modified by the tribunal or by agreement
between the tenant and the landlord or landlords affected,
anything in any lease of the premises to the contrary
notwithstanding:

Provided that nothing in this subsection shall authorise a
tenant to execute an improvement in contravention of any
restriction created or imposed—

(a) for naval, military or air force purposes;
(b) for civil aviation purposes under the powers of the Air
     Navigation Act, 1920;
(c) for securing any rights of the public over the foreshore
     or bed of the sea.

1920 c. 80

(5) A tenant shall not be entitled to claim compensation
under this Part of this Act in respect of any improvement
unless he has, or his predecessors in title have, served notice of
the proposal to make the improvement under this section, and
(in case the landlord has served notice of objection thereto) the
improvement has been certified by the tribunal to be a proper
improvement and the tenant has complied with the conditions,
if any, imposed by the tribunal, nor unless the improvement is
completed within such time after the service on the landlord of
the notice of the proposed improvement as may be agreed
between the tenant and the landlord or may be fixed by the
tribunal, and where proceedings have been taken before the
tribunal, the tribunal may defer making any order as to costs

until the expiration of the time so fixed for the completion of the improvement.

(6) Where a tenant has executed an improvement of which he has served notice in accordance with this section and with respect to which either no notice of objection has been served by the landlord or a certificate that it is a proper improvement has been obtained from the tribunal, the tenant may require the landlord to furnish to him a certificate that the improvement has been duly executed; and if the landlord refuses or fails within one month after the service of the requisition to do so, the tenant may apply to the tribunal who, if satisfied that the improvement has been duly executed, shall give a certificate to that effect.

Where the landlord furnishes such a certificate, the tenant shall be liable to pay any reasonable expenses incurred for the purposes by the landlord, and if any question arises as to the reasonableness of such expenses, it shall be determined by the tribunal.

Provisions as to covenants not to assign, &c. without licence or consent

19.—(1) In all leases whether made before or after the commencement of this Act containing a covenant condition or agreement against assigning, underletting, charging or parting with the possession of demised premises or any part thereof without licence or consent, such covenant condition or agreement shall, notwithstanding any express provision to the contrary, be deemed to be subject—

(a) to a proviso to the effect that such licence or consent is not to be unreasonably withheld, but this proviso does not preclude the right of the landlord to require payment of a reasonable sum in respect of any legal or other expenses incurred in connection with such licence or consent; and

(b) (if the lease is for more than forty years, and is made in consideration wholly or partially of the erection, or the substantial improvement, addition or alteration of buildings, and the lessor is not a Government department or local or public authority, or a statutory or public utility company) to a proviso to the effect that in the case of any assignment, under-letting, charging or parting with the possession (whether by the holders of the lease or any under-tenant whether immediate or not) effected more than seven years before the end of the term no consent or licence shall be required, if notice in writing of the transaction is given to the lessor within six months after the transaction is effected.

(2) In all leases whether made before or after the commencement of this Act containing a covenant condition or agreement against the making of improvements without a licence or consent, such covenant condition or agreement shall be deemed, notwithstanding any express provision to the contrary, to be subject to a proviso that such licence or consent is not to be unreasonably withheld; but this proviso does not preclude the right to require as a condition of such licence or consent the payment of a reasonable sum in respect of any

damage to or diminution in the value of the premises or any neighbouring premises belonging to the landlord, and of any legal or other expenses properly incurred in connection with such licence or consent nor, in the case of an improvement which does not add to the letting value of the holding, does it preclude the right to require as a condition of such licence or consent, where such a requirement would be reasonable, an undertaking on the part of the tenant to reinstate the premises in the condition in which they were before the improvement was executed.

(3) In all leases whether made before or after the commencement of this Act containing a covenant condition or agreement against the alteration of the user of the demised premises, without licence or consent, such covenant condition or agreement shall, if the alteration does not involve any structural alteration of the premises, be deemed, notwithstanding any express provision to the contrary, to be subject to a proviso that no fine or sum of money in the nature of a fine, whether by way of increase of rent or otherwise, shall be payable for or in respect of such licence or consent; but this proviso does not preclude the right of the landlord to require payment of a reasonable sum in respect of any damage to or diminution in the value of the premises or any neighbouring premises belonging to him and of any legal or other expenses incurred in connection with such licence or consent.

Where a dispute as to the reasonableness of any such sum has been determined by a court of competent jurisdiction, the landlord shall be bound to grant the licence or consent on payment of the sum so determined to be reasonable.

(4) This section shall not apply to leases of agricultural holdings within the meaning of the Agricultural Holdings Act, [1986], and paragraph (b) of subsection (1), subsection (2) and subsection (3) of this section shall not apply to mining leases.

HOUSING ACT 1980

81.—(1) The following provisions of this section have effect with respect to protected tenancies and statutory tenancies in place of section 19 (2) of the Landlord and Tenant Act 1927.

(2) It is by virtue of this section a term of every such tenancy that the tenant will not make any improvement without the written consent of the landlord.

(3) The consent required by virtue of subsection (2) above is not to be unreasonably withheld and, if unreasonably withheld, shall be treated as given.

(4) Subsections (1) to (3) above do not apply in any case where the tenant has been given a notice—

(a) of a kind mentioned in one of Cases 11 to 18 and 20 in Schedule 15 to the 1977 Act (notice that possession might be recovered under that Case); or

(b) under section 52 (1) (b) of this Act (notice that a tenancy is to be a protected shorthold tenancy);

unless the tenant proves that, at the time when the landlord gave the notice, it was unreasonable for the landlord to expect to be able in due course to recover possession of the dwelling-house under that Case or, as the case may be, Case 19 of Schedule 15 (added by section 55 of this Act).

(5) In Part I, and in this Part, of this Act "improvement" means any alteration in, or addition to, a dwelling-house and includes—

   (a)   any addition to, or alteration in, landlord's fixtures and fittings and any addition or alteration connected with the provision of any services to a dwelling-house;
   (b)   the erection of any wireless or television aerial; and
   (c)   the carrying out of external decoration;

but paragraph (c) above does not apply in relation to a protected or statutory tenancy if the landlord is under an obligation to carry out external decoration or to keep the exterior of the dwelling-house in repair.

82.—(1) If any question arises whether the withholding of a consent required by virtue of section 81 above was unreasonable it is for the landlord to show that it was not; and in determining that question the court shall, in particular, have regard to the extent to which the improvement would be likely—

   (a)   to make the dwelling-house, or any other premises, less safe for occupiers;
   (b)   to cause the landlord to incur expenditure which it would be unlikely to incur if the improvement were not made; or
   (c)   to reduce the price which the dwelling-house would fetch if sold on the open market or the rent which the landlord would be able to charge on letting the dwelling-house.

(2) A consent required by virtue of section 81 may be validly given notwithstanding that it follows, instead of preceding, the action requiring it and may be given subject to a condition.

(3) Where the tenant has applied in writing for a consent which is required by virtue of section 81 then—

   (a)   if the landlord refuses to give the consent it shall give to the tenant a written statement of the reasons why the consent was refused; and
   (b)   if the landlord neither gives nor refuses to give the consent within a reasonable time, the consent shall be taken to have been withheld, and if the landlord gives the consent but subject to an unreasonable condition, the consent shall be taken to have been unreasonably withheld.

(4) If any question arises whether a condition attached to a consent was reasonable, it is for the landlord to show that it was.

TELECOMMUNICATIONS ACT 1984

96.—(1) Subject to subsection (4) below, where any provision contained in a lease to which this section applies, or in any agreement made with respect to premises to which such a lease relates, has the effect of imposing on the lessee any prohibition or restriction with respect to any of the matters falling within subsection (3) below, that provision shall have effect in relation to things which are done—

(a) inside a building, or part of a building, occupied by the lessee under the lease; or

(b) for purposes connected with the provision to the lessee by any telecommunications operator of any telecommunication services,

as if the prohibition or restriction applied only where the lessor has not given his consent in relation to the matter in question and as if the lessor were required not to withhold that consent unreasonably.

(2) Where a provision of a lease or agreement imposes (whether by virtue of this section or otherwise) a requirement on the lessor under a lease not to withhold his consent unreasonably in relation to any matter falling within subsection (3) below, the question whether that consent is unreasonably withheld shall be determined having regard to all the circumstances and to the principle that no person should unreasonably be denied access to a telecommunication system.

(3) The matters falling within this subsection are—

(a) the running of relevant telecommunication systems;

(b) the connection of any telecommunication apparatus to a relevant telecommunication system or of relevant telecommunication systems to each other; and

(c) the installation, maintenance, adjustment, repair, alteration or use, for purposes connected with the running of a relevant telecommunication system, of any telecommunication apparatus.

(4) The Secretary of State may by order provide, in relation to such cases, prohibitions or restrictions as are specified in the order, or are of a description so specified, that subsection (1) above shall not apply.

(5) This section applies to any lease for a term of a year or more granted on or after the day on which this section comes into force; but the Secretary of State may by order provide that this section shall apply, subject to such transitional provisions as may be contained in the order, to leases granted before that day.

(6) This section is without prejudice to paragraph 2(3) of the telecommunications code.

(7) In this section—

"alteration" and "telecommunication apparatus" have the same meanings as in Schedule 2 to this Act;

"lease" includes any leasehold tenancy (whether in the nature of a head lease, sub-lease or under lease) and

any agreement to grant such a tenancy, and cognate
        expressions, and references to the grant of a lease,
        shall be construed accordingly;
"relevant telecommunication system" means a public
        telecommunication system or a telecommunication
        system specified for the purposes of this section in
        an order made by the Secretary of State, or a
        telecommunication system which is, or is to be,
        connected to a public telecommunication system or
        to a system so specified.

HOUSING ACT 1985

97.—(1) It is a term of every secure tenancy that the tenant
will not make any improvement without the written consent of
the landlord.

(2) In this Part "improvement" means any alteration in, or
addition to, a dwelling-house, and includes—

(a)   any addition to or alteration in landlord's fixtures and
       fittings,

(b)   any addition or alteration connected with the provision
       of services to the dwelling-house,

(c)   the erection of a wireless or television aerial, and

(d)   the carrying out of external decoration.

(3) The consent required by virtue of subsection (1) shall not
be unreasonably withheld, and if unreasonably withheld shall
be treated as given.

(4) The provisions of this section have effect, in relation to
secure tenancies, in place of section 19(2) of the Landlord and
Tenant Act 1927 (general provisions as to covenants, &c. not to
make improvements without consent).

98.—(1) If a question arises whether the withholding of a
consent required by virtue of section 97 (landlord's consent to
improvements) was unreasonable, it is for the landlord to show
that it was not.

(2) In determining that question the court shall, in
particular, have regard to the extent to which the improvement
would be likely—

(a)   to make the dwelling-house, or any other premises, less
       safe for occupiers,

(b)   to cause the landlord to incur expenditure which it
       would be unlikely to incur if the improvement were
       not made, or

(c)   to reduce the price which the dwelling-house would
       fetch if sold on the open market or the rent which the
       landlord would be able to charge on letting the
       dwelling-house.

(3) A consent required by virtue of section 97 may be validly
given notwithstanding that it follows, instead of preceding, the
action requiring it.

(4) Where a tenant has applied in writing for a consent which is required by virtue of section 97—

(a) the landlord shall if it refuses consent give the tenant a written statement of the reason why consent was refused, and

(b) if the landlord neither gives nor refuses to give consent within a reasonable time, consent shall be taken to have been withheld.

APPENDIX 5

Draft of a Bill appended to Law Com. No. 178, Landlord and Tenant Law, Compensation for Tenants' Improvements.

DRAFT OF A BILL TO

End the right to compensation under the Landlord and Tenant Act 1927; to provide for the authorisation under section 3 of that Act of tenants' improvements to any property held under a tenancy to which Part II of the Landlord and Tenant Act 1954 applies or would apply but for section 43(1)(d) of (3) of that Act; and to extend section 19 of the Landlord and Tenant Act 1927 to mining leases and leases of agricultural holdings.

BE IT ENACTED by the Queen's most Excellent Majesty, by and with the advice and consent of the Lords Spiritual and Temporal, and Commons, in this present Parliament assembled, and by the authority of the same, as follows:—

Limitation claims compensation 1927 c. 36

1. No claim for compensation under Part I of the Landlord and Tenant Act 1927 shall be effective unless—

   (a)   notice under section 3(1) of that Act is served before the date on which this section comes into force; and

   (b)   the claim is made before 1st January 2105.

Authorisation of improvements

2. For the purposes of service of a notice under section 3(1) of the Landlord and Tenant Act 1927 on or after the date on which this section comes into force and of proceedings under that Act consequent on such service, section 17 of that Act shall have effect as if the following definition of a holding to which Part I applies were substituted for the definition in subsections (1) to (3)—

   "(1)   References in this Part of this Act to holdings to which this Part of this Act applies are references to property subject to a tenancy to which Part II of the Landlord and Tenant Act 1954 applies or would apply but for section 43(1)(d) or (3) of that Act."

Application of provisions as to covenants against improvement to mining leases and leases of agricultural holdings, 1927 c. 36

3.—(1) Subsection (4) of section 19 of the Landlord and Tenant Act 1927 (which excludes the whole section from applying to lease of agricultural holdings and parts of it from applying to mining leases) shall be amended in relation to leases to which this section applies—

   (a)   by the insertion of the words "Subsections (1) and (3) of" at the beginning; and

   (b)   by the omission of the words "subsection (2)".

(2) This section applies to any lease granted on or after the date on which this section comes into force, other than—

(a)   a lease granted in pursuance of a contract entered into before that date; and

(b)   a lease granted in pursuance of an option created before that date.

Commencement   4. Sections 1 to 3 above shall come into force at the end of the period of six months beginning with the date on which this Act is passed.

Citation and extent   5. (1) This Act may be cited as the Landlord and Tenant (Tenant Improvements) Act 1989.

(2) This Act extends to England and Wales only.

INDEX